PENGUIN BOOKS

CLARKSON ON CARS

Jeremy Clarkson made his name presenting a poky motoring programme on BBC2 called *Top Gear*. He left to forge a career in other
directions but made a complete hash of everything and ended up back
on *Top Gear* again. He lives with his wife, Francie, and three children
in Oxfordshire. Despite this, he has a clean driving licence.

Clarkson on Cars

JEREMY CLARKSON

PENGUIN BOOKS

To Jesse Crosse –
who started the ball rolling

PENGUIN BOOKS

Published by the Penguin Group
Penguin Books Ltd, 80 Strand, London WC2R 0RL, England
Penguin Putnam Inc., 375 Hudson Street, New York, New York 10014, USA
Penguin Books Australia Ltd, 250 Camberwell Road, Camberwell, Victoria 3124, Australia
Penguin Books Canada Ltd, 10 Alcorn Avenue, Toronto, Ontario, Canada M4V 3B2
Penguin Books India (P) Ltd, 11 Community Centre, Panchsheel Park, New Delhi – 110 017, India
Penguin Group (NZ), Cnr Airborne and Rosedale Roads, Albany, Auckland 1310, New Zealand
Penguin Books (South Africa) (Pty) Ltd, 24 Sturdee Avenue, Rosebank 2196, South Africa

Penguin Books Ltd, Registered Offices: 80 Strand, London WC2R 0RL, England

www.penguin.com

All articles in Part 1 first appeared in *Performance Car* between 1985 and 1993
All articles in Part 2 first appeared in the *Sunday Times* between 1993 and 1995
This collection first published by Virgin Books 1996
Published in Penguin Books 2004

18

Copyright © Jeremy Clarkson, 1996
All rights reserved

The moral right of the author has been asserted

Contents

Part 2

Acknowledgements

As I have no ambition, I have to be spurred on by others. It was Jesse Crosse, the first editor of *Performance Car*, who said I should write a column, and I shall forever be in his debt. And it is my wife, Francie, who makes sure these days that I'm always in the right place at roughly the right time. I honestly don't know what I'd do without her.

There are people in the motor industry too who gave me a leg up in those early days: Barry Reynolds at Ford, Chris Willows at BMW, John Evans at Mercedes and Peter Frater at Chrysler are four notable examples.

And then there are friends like Jonathan Gill, Andy Wilman, Anthony ffrench Constant and Tom Stewart whose wit and wisdom I've plagiarised shamelessly for years.

Part 1

Dear Diary

I do not wish to regale you with tales of my movements towards the end of this month, for two reasons. Firstly, you would be unutterably bored; and secondly, I will miss most of the engagements involved anyway.

I will miss them because I have not written them down anywhere. People have rung to invite me for a weekend's skiing, for a two-day trip to Scandinavia, for dinner, for whatever.

Not being used to such popularity, I have said yes to everything, without really knowing whether anything clashes or, to be honest, when anything is.

It is a minor miracle if I ever manage to get anywhere in the right decade, let alone on the right day.

The reason for this shortfall is that I have never kept a diary. Oh to be sure, I've started many a year with every good intention, filling in my blood group in the personal section and entering things that happened a week ago so that if anyone peeps, they'll be gobsmacked at what appears to be a gay social life.

By February the entries are getting pretty sparse. By March I've lost it or Beloved, in a flurry of domesticity, has fed it, along with the odd airline ticket and several cufflinks, to the washing machine. You may be interested to hear that I have the cleanest cheque book in Christendom.

Most of my time on New Year's Eve was spent dreaming up all sorts of resolutions. This year, in among things like a four-weeks-and-already-broken ban on alcohol, and a fairytale promise to get fitter, I vowed to keep a diary.

The question was, which one? In the run up to Christmas, any number of motor manufacturers sent such things. And, as they say in Scunthorpe, very nice too.

Slimline and quite capable of fitting in a jacket pocket without making me look like an FBI agent, they do however face some stiff competition.

First, there's the Peugeot 405 Fil-o-fax-u-like. Now, these things are of enormous benefit to the likes of Beloved, who has simply millions of absolutely lovely friends and needs to remind herself when my Visa card needs a wash. But to unpopular people like my good self, they're rather less use than a trawlerman in Warwick.

With just five friends and, on average, two party invites a year, there's no real justification for me to be strolling around the place with something the size of a house brick under my arm.

Besides, it has a section for goals, which I presume refers to ambition rather than football. I have several ambitions but writing them down won't get me any nearer to achieving them. I want to be king, for instance, and being able to see tomorrow's racing results today would be pretty useful too.

Then there's my Psion Organiser. It's advertised on television as a sort of portable computer that fits neatly in a briefcase and acts out the role of diary, alarm clock, address book and calculator all rolled into one.

As far as I'm concerned, though, it is of no use whatsoever, because I can't be bothered to learn how it works. The instruction booklet is bigger and even more boring than the *Iliad* and anyway I think I've broken it by getting into edit mode and telling it to bugger off.

Casio do the Data Bank which is disguised as a calculator. It can even be used as one but beware, those who even think about entering an address or an appointment will screw up the innards good and proper. Well I did anyway.

These electronic gizmos are all very well but I want to know what is wrong with a good old pencil and a piece of paper?

I mean, if someone rings up (chance'd be a fine thing) and asks me to a party next week, I could have it written down in what; two, three seconds? I would need a team of advisers and a fortnight's free time even to turn the Psion on.

The advantage is that it does have an ability to remind me audibly when I'm supposed to be going somewhere. This is where Pepys's little tool falls falt on its face.

It's all very well remembering to write something down but this is about as much good as cleaning your shoes with manure if you don't look at the diary on the day in question.

Even so, I'm a man of my word and, consequently, I'm keeping a diary like a good little boy.

Choosing which book to use was not easy. I have the sex maniac's diary, which tells me where in the world I can have safe sex, how to apply a condom and on what day of the week I can indulge in what they call the Strathclyde muff dive.

I also have the Guild of Motoring Writers' Who's Who diary but it is full to bursting with bad photographs of people in brown suits.

The International Motors' diary – they're the people who import Subarus, Isuzus and High and Dries – is a convenient size and has all the usual Letts schoolboy stuff in it about temperature and time zones and Intercity services.

But I do not urgently need to know when the main Jewish festivals are. Nor, frankly, am I terribly bothered about when Ramadan begins.

Toyota's diary begins with a lovely shot of their Carina car in front of the Pont du Gard in the Ardèche, skips blissfully over the Letts schoolboy behaviour and gets straight on to page after page of slots for the parties.

But far and away the most tasteful offering for 1989 comes from those Italian chappies at Fiat. Largely, the editorial section at the front of their book is taken up with a list of decent restaurants.

It doesn't *say* they're decent though, which should make for some fireworks when a trainee Fiat mechanic from a dealer in

Bolton comes to the capital on an Awayday and gets presented with a £60 bill at Poons.

You can tell Fiat have aimed their diary at men near the top. But this one is no good to me either, because the allergies section on the personal page is far too small. I am allergic to cats, penicillin, pollen, house dust, nylon, trade union leaders and that man with the Tefal forehead who masquerades as Labour's health spokesman.

Ford's gives no space at all to allergies and is full of all sorts of stuff I never knew I didn't need to know – but this is the one I've selected. Instead of giving each week a page of its own, Ford have crammed an entire month on one double-page spread.

This means I can do my shoelaces up on 4 April and feed the hamster on 16 May, and those who peek into the book will think I'm as busy as hell.

Golf GTi Loses Its Crown

At this rate, the weightlifting gold at the 1992 Olympics will be won by a paperboy from Basildon. And apart from having arms like the hind legs of a rhino, he will believe the world is full of cars that can go faster than 300 mph.

Since the advent of what the publishing industry calls new technology, it has become a great deal cheaper to produce the printed word. This is why one now needs the anatomical properties of Kali to read the *Sunday Times*, and why the shelves at your local newsagent's are groaning under the weight of perfect-bound, laminated forestry.

You may have wondered how the producers of *Successful Cauliflower* magazine make any money. The answer is, they don't, but seeing as it costs naff all to make it in the first place, nobody's complaining!

Not so long ago, people bought their favourite magazine for a decent read on the bus. It would be stitched together from shoddy paper and when it was finished, it could be hung on a clip by the lavatory. Not any more.

Take *Country Life*. Full of ads for houses that no one can afford and no one wants; you don't read it, you arrange it on the coffee table as you would arrange a bunch of flowers. You may even feel the need to iron it occasionally.

It is not a magazine. It is a statement. It says that while you may live in a neo-Georgian semi with a purple up 'n' over garage door, you are fully conversant with the delights of hopelessly expensive manor houses in Oxfordshire.

Or *Horse and Hound*, with its nonsensical line, 'I freely admit that the best of my fun, I owe it to *Horse and Hound*.'

Nowadays, there are a million country-house and interior-design glossies full of curtains which cost £8000 and would look stupid anywhere but Castle Howard.

Two luminaries in this domain are *Tatler* and *Harpers and Queen*, which *are* read a *bit*, but only by the middle classes scouring 'Bystander' or 'Jennifer's Diary' for photographs of their horrid, frilly-dress-shirted friends.

But the best of all are the car magazines.

There was a time when they treated the car for what it was – a device which used a series of small explosions to move people around. But now, it is an artform. The days when you could get away with a front three-quarters shot taken in the office car park are gone.

Then there are the front covers. How many times has the Golf GTi lost its crown? To my certain knowledge, the Escort XR3 was the first to steal it, yet when the Peugeot 205 GTI came along a couple of years later, somehow, the Golf had got it back again.

And therefore we read in 72-point bold that the Golf GTi had lost its crown *again*, this time to the 205 GTI.

So the Vauxhall Astra, you might imagine, would have to pinch it from the 205; but no, at some point Peugeot had given it back to VW – who reluctantly had to hand it over again, this time to Vauxhall.

Then in no particular order it has been worn by the Peugeot 309 GTI, the Astra GTE 16v, the Escort RS Turbo, the Delta Integrale and the Corolla GTi. But for some extraordinary reason, the prized headgear never gets handed directly from one winner to the next. It always goes back to VW in between times.

For now, it is being worn by the 16-valve Astra but you can bet your bottom dollar that VW will have it back in time to lose it to the new 16-valve Integrale.

The Quattro has been through a similar series of machinations. The Delta Integrale pinched its number one slot but had to give the crown back to Audi shortly afterwards because it was wearing the Golf's at the time.

Audi held on to it for a bit but only a couple of months ago, relinquished it to Porsche's 911 Carrera 4.

And aside from dispensing crowns on a weekly basis, headline writers have become obsessed with speed.

'WE DRIVE THE 220-MPH JAG THEY DARE NOT BUILD' is the latest game. Not to be outdone, a rival publication, you can be assured, will drive a 230-mph Jag that can't be built the very next week. And so on towards infinity perhaps.

We smirk when we read that Freddie Starr ate someone's hamster, yet we are expected to believe that some scribbler has driven a Jaguar that no one has built at a speed that current tyre technology won't allow anyway.

I have driven a BMW 750iL at an indicated 156 mph on the *autobahn* and believe me, it is a bowel-loosening experience I do not wish to relive. Sure, I enjoy going quickly, but the notion of driving something like a Porsche 911, which has been tuned by a foreign grease monkey, at the speed of sound in a Welsh valley, appals as much as it amuses.

The thing is that if you have a magazine on your coffee table that talks on its front cover about a car that hasn't been built doing 300 mph on the Milton Keynes ring road, visitors to your home will be impressed.

If you leave motoring publications lying around which talk about how seatbelts save lives, those same visitors will drink their coffee very quickly and leave.

Business-speak impresses too. Honda have smashed Porsche 48 times and Toyota have bludgeoned BMW to death on a weekly basis for two years. And all this smashing and bludgeoning has resulted in every move a manufacturer makes being seen as utterly crucial.

As in, 'ON THE LIMIT IN ROVER'S LIFE-OR-DEATH MAESTRO'; or how about this recent gem: 'LOTUS'S MAKE-OR-BREAK ELAN.'

Lotus are owned by General Motors, who are one of the world's biggest companies. Their R&D department is universally revered, with lucrative contracts from such financially secure outfits as the MoD.

The Elan, successful or otherwise, will neither make nor break the company. It might on the other hand pinch the Golf GTi's crown. Clarkson Decides.

Dishing It Out

It ought to be safe to assume, I thought, that if 60,000 Brits go to France and sit in a field all weekend, BBC news editors would be intrigued. They would, I was sure, despatch their best available crew to find out just what had driven so many people to do such a thing.

After all, when twelve women with short hair and dubious sexual preferences camped outside an Oxfordshire air base for a few days, they were besieged by TV reporters.

When a couple of hundred Kentish ruralites wandered down to the village hall to hear a man from British Rail explain why their houses must be pulled down, they emerged two hours later, blinded by camera arc lights.

When one man set up shop on Rockall, both the BBC and ITV hired helicopters at God-knows-how-much-a-minute to film the weird beard's flag-waving antics.

And the South Ken embassy zone is permanently full of film crews, furiously rushing between the two people who have turned up to protest about the treatment of badgers in North Yemen and the half dozen who think the Chilean milk marketing board is overcharging.

So, how come when 60,000 Brits formed part of the 200,000-strong crowd at the 24 hours of Le Mans, it didn't even get a mention on the *BBC News*?

Rather than turn up for work on the Monday morning and face ridicule for not knowing who had won, I set aside twenty minutes on Sunday evening to find out.

I noticed with glee that the newsreader chappie hurried through the usual bits on China and the Maggon's opposition to European monetary union and I fully expected the saved time would be used to show us how bronzed men and true had thrilled the crowds in what is easily the world's most famous motor race.

But no. We had an interview with a cricketer who had hurt his cheek and couldn't play. Lots of people hurt their cheeks and can't do what they want as a result. I rubbed a chilli in my eye last night and they didn't send Michael Buerk round to find out how much it hurt. When they beamed us back to the studio, there was the presenter with the Refuge Assurance Sunday League cricket results.

We heard how Mohammed from Leicester had scored 72, how Gary from Essex had bowled out six people and how Yorkshire were top of something or other.

I kid you not. They devoted more time to cricket than they did to the slaughter of 2600 people in China. And, of course, there was not one word about Le Mans. In the next day's newspapers, it was the same story, with page after page about cricket followed by a brief paragraph that said, 'Merc won Le Mans and Jag didn't.'

Now, the argument that cricket fans trot out at times like this, and we can safely assume that the BBC's news editors *are* fans, is that cricket has a bigger following in Britain than motor racing.

Bull. The Test and County Cricket Board tell me that in 1988, 137,583 people turned up to watch Sunday league cricket. That means the seventeen teams each have an average weekly gate of 1074. They get five to ten times that to watch a Formula Three race at Donington.

A Test match at Lord's can pull in about 80,000; the British Grand Prix manages almost exactly double that number of spectators.

The *Cricketer* magazine has a circulation of 35,000 a month. *Motoring News* sells 78,000 copies *every week*. And then there's *Motor Sport* and *Autosport*.

Those who claim cricket has a bigger following than motor racing are the sort of people who claim that fish are insects and that the Pope is a water buffalo; they should be made to live in rooms with rubber walls, and to wear suits with the arms sewn on sideways.

You will never convince the old boy network that runs things round here that cricket should be banished from television and replaced with motor sport; but you *could* buy a HAL 9000 satellite dish. Mine is sculpted into a two-fingered salute and pointed at Broadcasting House. The reception is awful, actually, but it amuses all the neighbours.

Quite apart from the fact that Sky is prepared to show us breasts and bottoms on a regular basis, it has two sport channels which devote a proper amount of time to the world of motor cars.

Now, you know about how the satellite dish and the scrambler and the installation will cost you £350, and you probably know that Rupert Murdoch runs the whole show, but you probably *don't* know that, at any particular time of day, there will be some sort of motor sport being broadcast on the box. So when you're bored with Mickey Rourke and Kim Basinger sweating their way through another game of tonsil hockey, simply hit the force and watch Al Ulcer and Mario Androcles Jr slogging it out Stateside.

Tonight, you will go home for a diet of cricket, interrupted briefly at 7.00 p.m. for *Terry and June* and again at 10.30 p.m. for *Little and Large*. After *The Terminator*, I will watch some Indycar racing followed by a bit of in-car action from the CRX Challenge.

If you want to protest about the Beeb's apathy on the motor-sport front, then for heaven's sake, do absolutely nothing. Stay at home. Tidy your sock drawer out. Grade your grass clippings according to length. Do *anything*, but certainly do not form yourselves into a chanting, 60,000-strong mob or else the news crews will choose to ignore you.

Fear not though because I know exactly how to get coverage. Tomorrow, the six of us who have been converted to *USS Enterprise* space television will become homosexuals and make camp outside Broadcasting House. We will have our heads shaved and refuse to eat anything except almonds and watercress.

The day after, if the TV crews start to look bored, we will set fire to David Gatting.

Cars in Review

Vauxhall Belmont SRi

On the basis that children should neither be seen nor heard, it seems absurd that airlines and other people movers do not provide soundproof boxes into which they can be inserted.

There are even people out there who, when buying a car, actually consider the well-being of their offspring. Manufacturers like Mitsubishi and Volvo use them as active selling aids even.

But why on earth should you worry about the comfort and safety of something that will do nothing on the entire journey other than fight with its sister, vomit and make loud noises?

When I produce children, I shall buy a Vauxhall Belmont. In order to fit in the back even half properly they will have to screw themselves up like one of those magician's foam balls. Even then, they will not be able to see where they're going because the Vauxhall has headrests like blackboards.

There are more comfortable fairground rides than the Belmont.

Eventually, they'll beg to be put in the really rather commodious boot. Which is where they should have been in the first place.

Toyota Camry V6

This time next year, if someone were to ask if I've ever driven a Toyota Camry V6, I will look gormless for a minute or two. Then I will say no.

This will be wrong because I have driven a Toyota Camry V6 – the Bob Harris of motordom.

Turn on the engine, there is no sound; press the accelerator and still the only noise you can hear is a chaffinch, 50 yards away, rummaging through some discarded fish-and-chip papers.

In a temper, you engage D on the purrundah gearbox and bury the throttle in the pleblon carpet. The chaffinch looks over to see what the chirp was and goes back to his rummaging.

You could drive this car round a library and no one would look up. I live twelve miles from Heathrow, yet the sound of jets on their final approach is enough to warrant the evening TV being turned up. When Concorde is bringing Joan Collins's hairstyle over again, a full-scale Judas Priest concert is unable to compete.

What I want and want now is for Toyota to buy Rolls-Royce, Pratt and Whitney and that French outfit that doesn't know its left from its right.

I want them to show Europe and America that it is entirely possible to build an engine that doesn't make any noise at all.

Volkswagen Passat 1.9 Diesel

If you need to get from A to B in a hurry and the only car at your disposal is a Passat 1.9 diesel, then might I suggest you try jogging.

We are talking here about a very slow car indeed. 0 to 60 is possible, but only just.

At its launch VW talked at some length about how clean the new engine is. They used graphs to show what they were on about but these looked only like Luftwaffe air traffic in the 1940s.

They were at pains to point out that the new engine has not been designed with speed in mind but glossed over the fact that it's barely capable of independent movement.

And to cope with the power it gets two first gears, a third and two very high fifths.

Mark my words, the trees'll love it.

Proton Saga 1.5 SLX

This is how the steering in a Proton works. You twirl the wheel as quickly as possible and two whisks attached to the end of the column stir up a sort of box full of yoghurt. When the yoghurt is spinning fast enough, centrifugal force rotates the box and the wheels turn.

Volkswagen Corrado

The brown-suited wise men of the motoring world have been saying that the new Corrado should have the 200SX's chassis, the Celica's equipment, the Piazza's price, the Prelude's engine and the 480 turbo's computer.

But their opinions go for nought because in the coupe market, it is style that counts.

Which of the following answers would you like to give if an impressionable young lady were to ask what sort of car you drove? a) a Nissan b) a Toyota c) a Volkswagen d) an Isuzu e) a Honda f) a Volvo?

She equates VWs with Paula Hamilton and Nissans with zero per cent finance; thus the Corrado is bound to be more sought after than any Japanese competitor, no matter how many horsepower are entrusted to their rear wheels.

Big Boys' Toys

It seems to me, Sir Isaac Newton could have been more gainfully employed. Any man who has the time to sit around in an autumnal orchard wondering why apples don't float around in space once they part company with the parental bough, ought to be out looking for a proper job.

Maybe it was in the hobbies section of his c.v. or maybe employers in the seventeenth century were a trifle anti-Semitic, but either way, Isaac never did get a proper job and went on instead to design what was marketed ten years ago as the Ballrace, or Newton's Cradle.

It set the scene for a host of so-called executive toys and relied for sales on the premise that the average high flyer doesn't have anything better to do while at his desk than sit watching a load of chrome balls bash the hell out of each other until it's coffee time or the phone shrills a cheery message that his wife's burnt supper again.

Newton's thingumijig is, however, confined to page seven of yesterday's news now – its headline grabbing antics of yesteryear fulfilled, in these days of war, hunger and crisp packets without little blue salt sachets in them, by a veritable myriad of toys all of which are jostling for pole position by the blotter.

My rare sorties to the world of big business and, rarer still, my visits to the offices of those that control it, have revealed a constant.

Whether the executive has plumped for red walls, white shag pile and chairs shaped like mattress springs or traditional oak panelling, leather seating and standard-lamp lighting, the centre-piece of his room is always an absolutely massive desk . . . a desk that's as uncluttered as a hermit's address book.

To the right, there's the telephone; to the left, an intercom. Dead ahead, beyond the equally uncluttered blotter there are dog-eared photographs of his wife, taken in those salad days when she didn't burn supper, and his children, taken when they were angelic rather than punk.

Somewhere, though, there will also be a toy – not an Action Man or a Care Bear. An executive toy has to be more than just fun to play with. It must also be an attractive, decorative item which doesn't look out of place in a professional setting.

You have to understand that the *street cred* of a top businessman would be seriously impaired should anyone bodyswerve his personal secretary, make it into the inner sanctum and catch him playing with a Scalextric set.

But if you broke in and found him struggling with a Puzzleplex jigsaw, all would be well. These jigsaws are extraordinarily beautiful *objets d'art* which, almost incidentally, happen to be infernally difficult puzzles.

Each one of these three-dimensional, wooden jigsaws is hand-made, each is completely different from anything that has gone before and, best of all, the manufacturer, an eccentric called Peter Stocken, will create your puzzle in any shape you like – a car, a Welsh dragon, an artificial lung, anything.

You need an afternoon to complete a simple one and about £50 to buy it. For the more difficult variety, extend the time allowed to a day and start adding the noughts.

I must confess I was hugely tempted to invest but had I succumbed, I fear you would not be reading this and that my superhuman, week-long struggle to give up smoking would have been thwarted.

Another great puzzle is the much cheaper Philosopher's Knot, the idea being that you have to extricate a larger glass ball from a surrounding web of knotted string. It looks even trickier than that Hungarian cube thingy from last year.

But the interesting thing about it is that were the ball made from shoddy plastic and the string from something of inferior quality, sales to businessmen would be sluggish. It looks good in between the telephone and the blotter on an executive's desk.

Similarly, I noticed Fortnum and Mason are selling a twisted length of black and white plastic tubing for £35 in their gift department. I spent many minutes poring over this most unusual creation hoping an assistant would overcome any prejudices my tatty jeans were instilling in him and volunteer an explanation.

None was forthcoming and because I always feel so foolish when asking such people what various things do, I kept my mouth shut. If I were in their shoes and such a question were fired at me, I should want to know why someone would be considering the purchase of an item without knowing what it was or did.

Thus, I reserve behaviour of this kind until about 5.25 p.m. on Christmas Eve when, in desperation, I have been known to spend a week's wages on a device for melting the teeth of dead okapis merely because 'it looks nice'.

The upshot of all this nonsense is that my notebook says 'funny plastic tubing. Fortnum's. £35'. If it is merely decorative, then it works well but costs rather a lot. If it has a function, then I should enjoy being enlightened.

I'd actually gone to Fortnum's in search of a truly great executive toy – an 18-inch-high suede rat in a blue leather coat and a felt hat. It is supposed to be Reckless from the Captain Beaky gang but he seems to have died now the hype has all quietened down as no one seemed to remember the item in question or from whence it came.

I recall it cost close on £40 but, believe me, as a desk centre-piece, it had no peers.

Unless, of course, you're a gadget kinda guy in which case 1986 holds much more in the way of excitement than dear old suede Reckless ever could.

Take telephones. Quite why an executive needs the 15-memory variety with built-in answerphone, hands-off dial facility, digital read-out, supersonic turbo recall, optic fibre laser and lcd handset, I know not.

Especially when I consider all he ever does is pick the damn thing up and say to his secretary, 'Get me whatsisname of doodah limited.'

Hands up all those who are familiar with the wide-open secretary who's all set to transfer you to her boss until she finds out you've got something to do with his work when all of a sudden she will announce, 'He's in a meeting.'

Is he hell. He's playing with his Philosopher's Knot and wanting to know why his wife has burnt supper for the eighth successive night.

Or else he's sitting back, eyes half closed and fingers steepled enjoying the strains of Beethoven on the mini compact disc system with twin cassette auto play reverse and solar powered volume knob. Oh, and it can play music too.

This is usually located in the bottom drawer – a space which, in that bygone age before floppy discs (which I will not spell with a 'k') and cursors, was taken up with things called files.

These stereos fascinate me. The smaller they are, the more expensive they are to buy. I don't see what's wrong with my simply enormous Rotel, Pioneer, Akai circa 1976 set up but evidently, it is miles too big – and judging by some of the prices these days, it didn't cost enough either.

Having said that though, I was staggered to see a Sinclair flat screen telly in a dusty corner of the Design Centre selling for just £99.95. As is the current vogue, the screen was the same size as your average sultana but the wiry bit round the back was encased in a washing machine-sized shell. No wonder old Clive had to sell out.

Doubtless, he'll soon come up with a television so small that you won't be able to see it at all.

When the days of invisible gadgetry are upon us, I may well take my place on the bandwagon and reap the benefits of being able to cover my desk with everything from a sunbed to a nuclear power station without my work space being pinched.

At present though I have just three executive toys, not counting my telephone which is a straightforward British Telecom Ambassador and therefore doesn't count.

Behind the Citroen press release to my left is the Waterford Crystal aeroplane I was given for Christmas by someone I didn't like very much until I found out it cost more than £50.

Lost in the vicinity of a half-eaten packet of McVities dark chocolate biscuits – remember, I'm trying to give up smoking – and the designer-label notebook is a half-inch-high, hand-painted pig. Always have loved that.

And occupying pride of place is my helicopter – a stunningly good toy made by Mattell in the 1970s and foolishly dropped from the line-up a couple of years back. Tough luck you can't buy one these days.

The machine, which is genuinely powered by its blades, is connected to a central command post by a wire and flies round in circles with a hook dangling underneath poised to pick up empty matchboxes and old Coke cans.

Such precision flying requires 100 per cent Chuck Yeagerish concentration so, when I'm airborne, little thought is given to burnt suppers or indeed any of the rigours encountered in daily life.

What lunchtime? What meeting? What Citroen press release?

Mobile Phones

'Yes darling. I'll pick you up at eight . . . No this time I promise
. . . Well, I know, but last night was different . . . Yes, well the
night before was different too . . . No, standing around on
Fulham Broadway isn't much fun . . . OK listen, if I'm late
tonight, I'll buy you dinner at San Lorenzo. Bye.'

Gulp. I've got an appointment in Twickenham at six.

San Lorenzo costs twenty quid a head and that's without going
bonkers on the port and brandy. Then there's the taxi and they
don't take credit cards so I'll have to get some money out and
the banks are closed.

Now, my autobank's a dodgy little blighter. Sometimes it
enjoys Gettyish generosity and will plunge wads of Harold
Melvins into the recipient maulers but on other days, for no
apparent reason, it's tighter than a Scotsman on holiday in
Yorkshire and won't hand over so much as a damn penny.

I wouldn't mind if the green screen was polite and said something like, 'Sorry old chap but your overdraft's a little excessive
and it'd be more than my job's worth to hand over the cash at
the moment.'

But 'insufficient funds available' is so terse; so final. And the
queue behind, already exasperated by my inability to remember
my code number on the first attempt, is reduced to a giggling
mess as I shrug nonchalantly and, fighting back the tears of
humiliation, stroll away as if it doesn't matter.

But with the threat of an £80 experience among the stars at San
Lorenzo hanging wearily about my person, there is no alternative
and I find myself approaching the damn thing, dripping like ageing
cheese in an old sock.

Inevitably there's a queue. Inevitably a gang of screeching

Hoorays fall in line astern of me. Inevitably I programme in the wrong number twice and inevitably I'm told, to the accompaniment of a crescendo of shrieks from the Ruperts, that I'm a miserable pauper.

Boarding the tube at Sloane Square, I consider my predicament and weigh up the consequences of a late arrival at Fulham Broadway. They are too dire to contemplate. Eighty quid is a lot of money for a pauper. Oh God, please help.

Now I bet you didn't know that God works in Volkswagen's press office. Because after my return to the den of iniquity that afternoon, Charles, who is VW's effervescent delivery driver, wandered in brandishing the keys to a 16-valve Scirocco I was due to test that week.

And joy of joys, nestling in that sombre but tasteful interior was nigh on two grand's worth of Panasonic Vodaphone. Better still, VW would pick up the tab for any calls I made.

If the meeting in Twickenham dragged on and I found myself in the kind of snarl-up only the A316 can muster, it was a simple question of ringing the beloved and thus avoiding an £80 outlay that would mean I'd have to live on a diet of small Macs and stickleback and chips for the forthcoming decade.

Sure enough, the meeting did go on and on, despite endless tutting and continual references to Omega's finest. And sure enough every Cherry this side of Chernobyl was on the 316, misjudging approach speeds and getting confused by roundabouts.

At ten to eight I realised there wasn't a hope in hell of getting to the Broadway on time and resorted to the Vodaphone. 'Hello sweetheart . . . no, don't shout at me . . . no, listen . . . I wa . . . Becau . . . No, I'm using a car phone and if this Nissan gets out of my way I'll be with you in about twenty minutes.'

That simple message cost VW 10p and saved me eighty quid.

This phone-in-the-car business was definitely worth looking into. I had at my disposal a Panasonic EBC1044 with hands-free facility which retails for £1774 excluding VAT. On top of this outlay you are faced with a £50 connection charge and a monthly fee of £25.

Calls made between 7.30 a.m. and 7.30 p.m. from Monday to Friday cost 25p per minute but at all other times the cost is a mere 10p per minute.

Any one of VW's 350 dealers can fit the hardware, which is broken down thus: £1375 for the handset and a complicated-looking box which was in the boot, £290 for the hands-free facility, £28.95 for the mounting kit and a whopping £79.95 for an aerial which would have to be replaced every time Chelsea played at home.

Hands free, for those of you who've just returned from a sightseeing trip on Voyager Two, is a wonderful innovation which allows a driver to hold a conversation without taking his paws from the wheel.

You simply dial up the number you wish or, if it's logged in the set's memory, press the appropriate code number, and hey presto, the job's done. A couple of seconds later you'll hear the ringing tone from a speaker located near your right ankle. The microphone into which you speak is attached to the sun visor.

Trouble is, those without cars are unwise in the ways of modern automotive technology and, on one occasion, I noticed a few raised eyebrows from the incumbents of a bus queue as I sat in a traffic jam shouting at my sun visor.

Because the Scirocco GTX 16v is a left hooker, they were that much closer and consequently their surprise turned into uncontrollable mirth as I went on to tell the visor I would meet it in the pub in ten minutes.

Then there was the instance when I called a friend to ask about the availability of tickets for a ball I was due to attend.

He said that I could bring along anyone I liked except 'that balding so-and-so' – a mutual friend.

Unfortunately, the gentleman in question was in the car at the time and heard every word.

I did notice that the unit's performance is impaired to a notable degree when the hands-free facility is employed, so that the vocal chords of both conversationalists have to be strained to be audible.

It's actually worse for the driver because whenever I used the device, I was invariably alongside a 3,000,000-hp Volvo tractor unit.

And drivers of 3,000,000-hp tractor units don't like squirts in bright-red Sciroccos with telephones, so they rev their engine up to a point where the pistons are moving faster than a Beirut window shopper and it's making more noise than Pete Townsend on a Gibson pile driver.

This effectively blots out conversation to the point that on many occasions I had to resort to the dangerous and potentially illegal practice of using the handset like a normal phone.

Anyway, after saving the day with regards to dinner at San Lorenzo, I figured a call to dear old mother, who's utterly bemused by anything electronic, would be in order.

I did, however, make the mistake of giving her the unit's number, which meant she rang at all the wrong times to find out a) where I was and b) how fast I was going.

Three days later I found myself using every reserve of concentration as I tried to overtake a speedily driven 200 Turbo Quattro on a delightful stretch of A road in Hampshire – a manoeuvre made even more difficult by my seating position and the Scirocco's 139 bhp against his 182.

Quite the last thing I needed was a telephone call from the dear old soul up North and the resultant lecture on the dangers of driving too fast. I still think she believes I was doing 100 mph with one hand on a phone. Hands free is a difficult facility to explain when the Quattro up front is gaining ground and the sun roof's open.

Besides, the Audi had a £79.95 aerial poking through the rear windscreen and I was busy plotting a means of finding out his number so I could call him up to say something dastardly like 'Your rear tyres are on fire'.

When I finally lost him I let my mind drift into scenes where the car phone could be even more useful than for warning womenfolk you're going to be late. Like if I saw a bank robbery and gave chase to the villains. I could call up the police and tell them what they were up to. I could be a hero. I'd be on the front page of the *Sun*.

I know the manufacturers of these phones harp on about lost business and sales reps and traffic jams, but half the value is encased in their fun and snob value. Otherwise why is it everyone begins their conversation by saying, 'I'm on the car phone'?

And why is it everyone who rode shotgun in the Scirocco that week ignored the technical sophistication of its 16-valve engine, ignored the fact it was left-hand drive, ignored the admiring glances from GTi pilots and said 'Ooh, it's got a phone'?

I could have picked them up in Thrust Two or the space shuttle. They wouldn't have been bothered so long as they could play with a device that when placed on a hall windowsill is readily available courtesy of the DHSS.

Two grand is a lot of dosh for someone whose autobank regularly says 'insufficient funds available', but if I spent a great deal of my time in one car rather than a very little of it in several, I'd be hugely tempted to invest.

Last Year's Model

Yesterday, a great many things went wrong. The girl at Suzuki said I couldn't drive a new Swift until next year and she'd call back when she knew precisely when.

This, past experience has taught me, actually means get lost toerag.

Moments later, I had the most awful row with two security guards at Earls Court because they wouldn't let me back a BMW twenty yards down a ramp. Sadly, the issue became personal as I enquired of them why it is that small people in peaked caps are always so damned intransigent and they, of me, why BMW drivers are always so ??$*!ing pushy.

Eventually a bossy woman with a loud and hectoring demeanour came but I couldn't understand what she was saying to me because she was holding one of those walkie-talkie affairs that seem to emit nothing but white noise punctuated with people saying 'Roger' a lot.

I finally managed to squeeze past the music teacher lookalike and her SS sidekicks when a charming man stepped from his Volvo Estate to ask them why it is that the working class always vote Labour. I didn't actually see what bearing his line of questioning had on the issue but his suicide antics diverted the heat for just long enough for me to win my battle.

Sadly though, my war with the day was far from over. My Fiat test car ignited warning light after warning light until its interior began to resemble a Jean Michel Jarre concert, my doctor warned once again that if I didn't have a week off, my eczema would envelop the last vestiges of skin and Barry Reynolds rang up from Ford to say the Cosworth I was due to get next week would, in fact, be an XR2.

Now, I have many weak spots – my face is perhaps the most apparent – but I do pride myself on an ability to maintain an even strain when the adversity is piling up.

Some people, I know, reach for the paraquat if the sponge cake doesn't rise correctly. Others weep for weeks upon finding out their son's motorcycle isn't taxed. But I do none of these things, not least because I don't know how to make a sponge cake and don't have a son.

What I do in times of crisis is try to put my predicament in perspective. As I sat on the phone listening to Mr Reynolds explaining why the Cosworth would not be winging its way to Fulham, I merely thought about that time when my sister ripped the last page from the Famous Five book I was reading and I was smacked for beating her up. And those dreadful tea-time visits to Aunt May's – a sizeable woman who always sat with her bandaged legs wide apart and began all her toothless monologues with 'Do you remember when . . .'

I even summoned up from the memory bank's deepest recess that incident when a load of town boys stole my school cap and put something a dog had done in my satchel.

Still though, the pain of not getting a Cosworth hurt – it hurt in the same way a Sherman tank would hurt if it ran over your legs. What I needed was to recall something so terrible, a moment that produced so much anguish, that not having a Cosworth would become joyous in comparison. I thought about the red mullet I'd eaten on the BMW 7-Series launch and how sad it was that I'd never again enjoy this, the best piece of food created by any chef anywhere, ever before.

But the pain didn't go away until I remembered that moment on 10 October 1969 when I crashed my brand-new Buick Riviera into the coffee table and one of its four gleaming headlights dropped from the grille.

This was the pride of my Dinky/Corgi fleet because it sported mirrors in the front and rear windows which, when covered up, dimmed the head and tail lamps.

It cost 5/6d and was the envy of everyone at school. Once, Gary Needham offered to swap his Mercedes Pullman with the dirty front windscreen for it, but I refused. He even offered to throw in his Batmobile but I already had one of those even though Robin's window was broken after my sister trod on it. I beat her up for that too.

She also lost the little yellow pellets you could fire from the boot-mounted mortars and I was the school laughing stock because I had to resort to matchsticks instead.

I've still got my entire collection and am told the earlier variety with detachable rubber wheels will one day be worth a few bob.

But I somehow doubt the ones I Humbrolised with all the finesse of a charging rhino will ever be worth more than the 5/6d I paid for them. The paint seemed to go everywhere except on the bodywork and because I usually did the red stripe down the side before the green job was dry, it all ran. If anyone out there will offer me 30p for a sludge-coloured Citroen DS Safari with a fingerprint on the bonnet I'd be willing to consider a trade.

The best Citroen I ever had was a Citroen Pallas coupe finished in a metallic cherry red. That is still in perfect condition as are all the models I bought when rubber wheels were being phased out to be replaced by the plastic variety. There's an Alfa Pininfarina and another white Alfa with a gold spoiler and no roof. Looks like something from Thunderbirds but at least it enables me to trace the roots of my current love affair with the GTV6.

I suppose my trips to Youngsters in the high street every Saturday ceased in the 1970s when die cast went out of fashion and Dinky died. An Esso oil tanker was, I believe, my last purchase.

I was once given a plastic kit of the MR2 by Toyota which I tried fashioning into something resembling a car but the disaster which ensued convinced me that model-making is an avenue I should not pursue. The finished article is a bloodstained mess that visitors to my house think is an aubergine.

In recent years my preoccupation with cars has centred around the variety that are too big for my sister to tread on.

However, as she is now a solicitor and presumably responsible enough not to smash up her brother's belongings, I have recently begun wondering whether a foray into the world of toy cars might be a good plan.

On a recent trip to Sicily I noticed every shop window was full of die-cast toy cars made by Burago. They're a good deal bigger than my Dinky and Corgi collection and, even allowing for inflation, they're a good deal more expensive too but I swear on my Buick's lost headlight, they really are superb. And you can buy them here.

Foolishly, I went all the way to Hamleys to check on prices only to discover that my local filling station sells them. In case you're interested, set aside around a tenner for the best examples.

There's a massive range encompassing all kinds of models and all kinds of sizes but having scrutinized the line-up, considered my age and the use to which I would put them, I reckon those which are produced to a scale of 1/18 are best.

For sure, an eleven-year-old who has a penchant for Humbrolising his toy prior to racing it through a sandpit would be better off with the tinier, and therefore cheaper variety but the bigger ones are so beautifully crafted, they don't look out of place among the Lladro and leather-bound Britannicas on your bookcase.

Without question, the best of them all is the Testarossa which is mounted on a lovely piece of wood. Now, I don't like the look of full-size Testarossas with their Vauxhall Astra front ends, their silly door mirrors and boot scrapers down the side but in model form, they look superb.

The bonnet, boot and doors open to reveal faithfully scaled-down copies of the car's innards – even the tyre treads are accurate. Another masterpiece is the 250GTO which comes with chromed bonnet catches and the E-type – a proper one from 1961 – can't be ignored either. Others are the Mercedes

SSKL, the Bugatti Type 59, the Jaguar SS100, the 250 Testarossa, the Alfa Romeo 2300 Spider, the Mercedes SSK, the Lancia Aurelia Spyder, the Bugatti Grand Prix, the Mercedes 300SL and the Alfa Romeo 8C 2300 Monza, drool drool drool.

There's also a model of the Rolls-Royce Camargue though I swear that if you painted it pink, it would look just the same as the car Parker used to chauffeur for Lady Penelope. Also, the windscreen wipers look like a pair of silver telegraph poles sprouting from the bonnet.

Burago's best sellers are now sitting in moist soil at home receiving a daily dosage of Fison's Make It Grow fertiliser.

Watch It

I suppose if one were to weigh up all the pros and cons, one would probably decide that it is a good idea to wear trousers while out shopping on a Saturday morning.

If one were to peruse the pots, pans and Pyrex in Boots, for instance, wearing nothing below the belt except socks, shoes and underpants, one would feel silly and, well, really rather naked.

Builders spend six months of the year with no shirts on and people from Islington wander around in bare feet, but no one aside from pupils at a strange public school in North Yorkshire, women, and Scotsmen would dream of venturing from the confines of a homestead without strides.

Bearing this argument in mind, it would be all too easy to assume that trousers are the most important item in my wardrobe but believe me, they're not.

I would rather go to a Buckingham Palace garden party clad only in a pair of day-glo 'Willie Hamilton for Prime Minister' Y-fronts than spend so much as ten seconds of my day without a watch.

With nothing around the left wrist, my whole arm feels like one of those Birds Angel Cream Delight blancmange thingies you see floating around in telly ads.

Take my watch off and I begin to get some idea of what Alan Shepard must have felt like when he became the first American to do something the English hadn't done before.

Not knowing what the time is makes me more miserable than missing a premium-bond jackpot by one digit. More angry than I was the other night when I discovered the reason why I'd been stationary on the M1 for three hours was because some buffoon with his bottom hanging out had dumped a pile of gravel in the outside lane and gone home.

And right now, I am miserable because the watch I was given on my first day away at school has developed a tendency to stop every few minutes and my replacement, a twenty-first birthday present, is so exquisite I daren't wear it for the everyday hustle and bustle one encounters when waging war with a wayward word processor.

And anyway, its strap's broken.

This has therefore meant that as I sit here writing, I do not know what time it is. It's dark so that means it's way past six o'clock. If it's later than eight, it means I've missed my weekly game of snooker. If it's later than ten, I'm not being paid enough.

Today, I've been out and about trying to find a stand-in timepiece.

The local watch emporium does some very natty lines but somehow, I don't see myself in a pink see-through number. Nor am I particularly interested in those chromium washing machine sized things that tell you what the chairman of Suzuki had for breakfast that morning.

Being of a weedy disposition, I would imagine I'd be allergic to metal straps so the watch of my dreams has to have a hide strap – none of this namby-pamby plastic for me. I like people who disembowel lizards.

I want a circular face with two hands, numbers and the date. That's it. No alarm bells if you forget to wake up. No Mickey Mouse noises. No colour-coded laser-optic workings.

Everything in the shop either fitted the bill perfectly but was far, far too expensive, or was correctly priced but made by somebody called Swatch or Crutch or something.

There was even one horrid white thing with the legend 'TURBO' writ large all over it. To call an aftershave 'TURBO' is fair enough. To call a vacuum cleaner 'TURBO' is fairer enough still, but a TURBO watch is plain ridiculous.

Turbo in my book means nasty lag and torque steer, which

are unwelcome in a car let alone a watch. I mean how useful is a timepiece if the hands dawdle their way past midday with all the alacrity of a damp log and then explode through the afternoon like an F-14 on combat power with excess torque making the minute hand go backwards?

If I were going to write something about cars on a watch, I'd be inclined to go for the economy angle. Surely no one buys a watch because it goes fast, but there must be people around who would like the idea of one that needs winding infrequently on account of its aerodynamic cogs or whatever.

Yes, when Omega come to me for the name of a new watch, I shall suggest 'spoiler' or 'thin tyres' or maybe 'fuel cut off on the overrun'.

After a good deal of huffing and puffing I stormed out of the shop. It's not that I object to having things written on the strap or face but I can't abide some of the words dreamed up by blue-spectacled berks in marketing departments.

One of the finest watches I have ever clapped eyes on was designed to commemorate the launch of the Mark Two Golf and given by Volkswagen to every journalist in Britain from the newest trainee on the *Rotherham Advertiser* to Ian Hislop.

Sadly, at the time, my worth in the eyes of the powers that be at VAG amounted to little more than it would if I were a scuba diver for the Galapagos Islands Turtle Preservation Society, so I did without. Which a) was a shame and b) explains why I called them VAG and not Volkswagen Audi as they now prefer.

Thinking that the same designer who came up with the GTi timepiece might still hold sway in VW's good offices, I made enquiries about other watches they market.

Evidently there's just one, for those who have a Quattro or those who want us to think they have a Quattro, but it's awful. The sort of thing a second-division footballer would covert. You can't see the watch for all the dials and I'd like to bet its weight is somewhere in the region of eight tons. Besides, it costs £345 plus VAT.

Equally exorbitant is the Ferrari Formula collection which is made up of a wide and delightful selection. Leaving aside those with allergenic straps, you're left with the Marine Collection with their racy two-tone straps or the City Collection with an ease of style that reminds me of Anthony Hopkins's performance in *Pravda*.

They're perfect in every respect except one. I can't abide Ferraris. I don't like the way they look, the noise they make, or the people who drive them. What I'd like to know is how on earth can the same people who sanctioned the aesthetic abortion called the Testarossa possibly be responsible for a collection of watches that are an equal of Kim Basinger in the beauty stakes.

It all came to nought though because they had Ferrari written on them and things with Ferrari written on them are pricey.

Things, at this stage, were beginning to get desperate. BMW don't do watches at all and I didn't dare ring Jaguar because they were too busy being smug about their new XJ6 – even though the one I drove was of marginal merit. The boot clanged. The steering was too light. The glovebox didn't fit properly and I didn't like the dashboard. Here speaks the only man in Britain who prefers, by a mile, the new 7-Series BMW.

I know it's possible to buy Aston Martin or Lamborghini or Rolls-Royce watches but quite frankly it's also possible to go bankrupt. And wearing one of those is just another way of saying in the most ostentatious way possible, 'Hey everyone, I'm very rich.'

Which I'm not.

And this is why the watch I have finally decided to buy only costs £30.

It doesn't meet one single criterion I'd laid down except price, but I was so taken with the idea, I don't care that it's plastic or that its face looks like Joseph's dreamcoat or that it is made by the Swatch empire.

Marketed by Alfa Romeo and sold through their dealer network – all seven of them – it has a navy-blue plastic strap, a navy-blue surround and a great big Alfa Romeo cross and serpent on the face.

It doesn't sport any numbers and in the words of the girl at Alfa, the winder is gold but it isn't gold.

It's got a date hole, it's got heaps of character and because it bears the Alfa badge, it says to those who see it, 'I'm someone who appreciates Italian style but not to the extent that I'm going to pay £4 billion for it.'

Those prepared to read even further between the lines will notice that it tells people I'm also the kinda guy who hasn't lost sight of his youth, who has a devil may care attitude to institutionalisation. Well that's what some idiot with blue spectacles told me last night. I reckon the most important things it tells people are the time and that I like Alfa Romeos.

The chairman of Suzuki can have black pudding and treacle in the morning, the Dow-Jones index can collapse and the sugar-beet price in Albania can go through the roof but I will have no way of knowing.

And I will not care.

The bungalow itself warranted little merit. The bay windows played host to a selection of bull's-eye glass, carriage lamps illuminated the neo-Georgian front door and gnomes with fishing rods frolicked among the horribly organised front garden.

There is little doubt that I would not enjoy the company of whoever had chosen this mish-mash of tasteless addenda. People with carriage lamps are people who have children called Janet. And children called Janet aren't allowed to eat sweets between meals or wear jeans.

Ordinarily, I would not concern myself with this sort of house or the people who occupy it, but in this instance I am sorely tempted to write them a letter explaining why they are the most ghastly individuals this side of anyone who indulges in tactical voting to oust the Conservatives.

You see, nailed to their teak gatepost is one of those polished tree-trunk slices with the legend 'Olcote' picked out in Olde Worlde York Tea Shoppe script.

That's bad enough but to make matters much, much worse, I have learned that this quaint mnemonic stands for Our Little Corner Of The Earth.

Point one: if your house is numbered, don't mess up the postman's schedule by giving it a name. And point two: if you insist on making everyone wait two weeks for their letters, at least give it a name with some credibility.

If you have an awful bungalow with a ning-nong illuminated doorbell, you should call it 'The Foul Little Bungalow That's Equipped With Every Nasty Piece Of DIY Kit I Could Find At Alabama Homecare'.

You should never call it 'Olcote'. I can think of some pretty unsavoury corners of the Earth to which I would despatch people who do: Beirut for those who do it by accident, West Thurrock for persistent offenders and Basrah for those who see nothing wrong with it.

Out there it would be a case of calling your AK47-pock-marked shack 'Olcote Babama'. This, for the uninitiated, stands for Our Little Corner Of The Earth's Been Annihilated By A Mig Again. And given half a chance, I'd be the pilot.

It's all to do with taking the art of personalisation to extremes. You can make your house more comfortable by fitting central heating and thick carpets or you can distinguish it from those up the road by painting it day-glo lime green. These moves are fine; they make life more comfortable, more aesthetically pleasing. More of a statement.

But do tell, what are the advantages of changing your address from 22 Laburnum Drive to Sunny View, Laburnum Drive? Do you really think you should command any more respect from people who are writing to you simply because Sunny View might conjure up the mental picture of a Baronial Hall perched atop a cowslip-thronged hillside meadow, whereas number 22 sounds like it's just part of a vast neo-Georgian estate?

It's the same with motor cars. Speaking personally, I don't much care for after market add-ons like spoilers and floodlights and rear speakers the size of Wales but if such paraphernalia are your bag, then go ahead.

Similarly, if it riles you to spy 2000 other guys driving around in identical Ford Sapphires every day, go on, get the spray can out and give it one of those paint jobs which hippies lavish on their ageing Bedford vans.

But, for heaven's sake, stop there. Do not invest in a personalised number plate or else the next fully operational jet fighter that whistles toward your frolicking gnomes will have me at the helm and my fingers on the Sidewinder release mechanism.

I do not understand what appeal a cherished registration plate has unless it says something funny like DEV1L, or ORG45M, or PEN15.

I have spent, oh, it must be close on fifteen minutes now, desperately trying to think of one reason why I should spend many hundreds, if not thousands, of pounds just so those within the vicinity of my battered CRX would know my initials are shared with Mr Christ.

If I were so intent on relaying this information to all and sundry, why couldn't I simply put up big notices in the windows? Or buy one of those electioneering loud hailers?

I was once forced to spend a week behind the wheel of an FSO which sported a registration plate that said FSO5. This was more embarrassing than the time when I spent an hour damning the dreadful Shake 'n' Vac advert on television only to discover I was sitting opposite the copywriter who'd written it.

You see, FSO5 is probably worth well into four-figure territory and I could see the drivers of neighbouring cars howling with Pythonesque laughter at me, the buffoon they thought had spent so much on a number plate, he couldn't afford anything better than a Polonez.

Worse are the idiots who spend a fortune on numbers like 316BMW for their BMW316s.

We all know it's a 316 because the badge says so and anyway, had the buffoon not bought the number plate, he could probably have afforded a 325i.

While I object in the strongest possible sense to those who simply buy their initials or those of their car and to hell with what number comes in tandem, I have been amused in the past by various stories and sightings.

There's the tale of a chap who lost a retina in World War II and now drives round in a car which bears the registration number, 1 EYE.

Then there's a friend of Beloved, called Tammy, who has TAM1 69. I've been dying to meet her but, so far, various endeavours have ended with stern words and threats of no morning coffee for six weeks.

According to the autonumerologist's bible, called *Car Numbers*, Jimmy Tarbuck owns COM1C but unless he drives a black Mini which is parked in a very seedy part of Fulham every night, I suspect an error has been made.

Other celebrities to own cherished plates are Max Bygraves who, it is said, turned down a £30,000 offer from Mercedes Benz for MB1, Kevin Keegan with KK A1, Jimmy White with 1 CUE, Bernard Manning with BJM 1 and Petula Clarke with PET 1.

Notice any similarity between these characters? Well I'll tell you. They are the staple diet of *TV Times* profiles and ITV quiz shows which have purple and orange backdrops, question masters in brown suits and lots of inane innuendo about bottoms.

In short, they are working-class heroes, the televisual *nouveau riche*, beloved by the kind who live in gaudy bungalows called Olcote.

And don't think I've been through the book looking for people of this ilk. I searched in vain for mention of gentlemen like David Attenborough and Michael Palin but I fear they are not the sort to advertise their arrival.

They are the sort who would invest in a cherished plate only if it were likely to shock or amuse. And there's plenty of scope. Michael Palin would, I'm sure, shy away from PAL 1N but if you offered him TAX1 or TUR8O, I'm sure he'd take the plunge. I know I would.

The thing is that when the registration system changed from suffixes to prefixes in 1983, the chances of any more cherished plates emerging from the DVLC evaporated.

In a bid to cut the pressure on staff who were forever being pestered by dealers for decent combinations, they no longer issue plates bearing any number less than 21. So it's tough luck to all you Dianas and Nigels out there who were waiting with bated breath.

However, it is still possible to buy numbers that were issued when civil servants didn't mind spending a few minutes each day acting the role of their job title.

If you wish to buy a registration number, it must be from a vehicle that is currently taxed or has been taxed within the past six months.

No longer is it any good to find some old wreck in a farmyard with the plate you've always wanted. And anyway, in 1983, the Swansea computer erased all knowledge of any car which hadn't been taxed within the previous two years.

Providing, however, the donor and recipient vehicles meet with the approval of those inscrutable chappies at your local vehicle-licensing office, all you have to do is obtain a V317 form from your LVLO, fill it in, hand it, along with the two requisite tax discs and registration documents to the inscrutable chappie, give him £80 and head off back to your little corner of the earth.

Alternatively, you can ring up one of the endless cherished-number-plate dealers in the *Sunday Times'* Look Business Personal Finance News, section 24, and tell him what you're after.

They keep details of what's on offer and who wants what and are normally able to help, providing your request isn't too parochial.

However, if you wish to take the plunge, I should do so in a hurry because when I win the football pools, I shall buy up every number I consider tasteless and throw them into the Marianas Trench.

Then, I shall bomb all numbered houses with names and if there's anything left in the kitty, I will erect kart tracks on every cricket pitch in Christendom.

Big Bikes

I do not hold with the decision to hold Britain's première motor race at Silverstone for five years on the trot, because it is a very boring circuit indeed, but at least if you're important, like me, you can camp out in the middle and run into nice people who say even nicer things, like why don't you come and have a spot of lunch?

The big hassle is that if you wish to run into a lot of these people you must be in several places all at the same time.

Which in turn means you have to forge expeditions that make Ranulph Fiennes's Transglobe jaunt look like a Saturday cycle ride to the shops.

The last time I spent a few days at Silverstone I had a motor-cycle at my disposal which, in theory, is the ideal tool for the job but (and this may come as a surprise to those of you who know me as a devil-may-care kinda guy who thinks nothing of hanging upside down in stunt planes) I do not know how to ride things with two wheels.

I had a go but after I'd engaged the clutch and applied full throttle, I found myself spinning round in a rather noisy circle.

This, I learned later, was because I'd forgotten to release the front brake. I also learned that the onlookers would have been immensely impressed with the stunt had they not caught a glimpse of my countenance, which, instead of bearing a proud and cocky grin, registered only abject terror.

And that was the end of my brief encounter with motorcycles, which, I have decided, should be left to those with acne, no imagination and a penchant for wearing rubber clothes.

Not being someone who readily goes back on his word, I found myself facing something of a dilemma as the Grand Prix weekend loomed ever nearer. Was I, a) to forget my vow and get a motorcycle; b) get a push bike and risk a cardiac arrest; or c) should I rely on shoe leather, which would mean a range limitation of no more than one or two feet in any direction as a result of acute, inherent and irreversible laziness?

The answer, as is always the case in such cheap games, was in fact, d) none of these.

Suzuki and Honda came to the rescue with a brace of four-wheeled motorbikes which seemed to offer the perfect blend of nippiness (sorry), fresh-air thrills and car-like safety.

In fact, they didn't. The Honda fell short of the mark by some considerable margin because it is, without a shadow of doubt, the most frightening thing yet created by man. Which is saying something.

The Suzuki failed to live up to my expectations because it is runner-up to the Honda in the sheer terror stakes.

Richard Branson has driven a powerboat across the Atlantic in seven minutes; he has flown a hot-air balloon the size of Birmingham over the same distance in nine and a half seconds but he knows nothing of real danger because, as far as I know, he has never tried to go anywhere on a quad bike.

You see, it's no good just sitting on these four-wheeled motor-cycles and hoping you can get to where you want to go, because, depending on which machine you choose to use, you will either end up at your destination covered in bruises or you will end up at completely the wrong place.

The £2495 Honda TRX 250 fourtrax is an out-and-out racer, with extrovert styling and a two-stroke 250-cc motor which will propel it to 100 mph having dispensed with the 0 to 60 increment in about five seconds.

Although it could be used in farms or forests, because nature has yet to invent an obstacle to stop these buzz bombs, the TRX is bought in small numbers only by people who wish to win various off-road races.

The controls are familiar to any motorcyclist, the only fundamental difference being the throttle, which is not activated by a twist grip. Instead, there's a little thumb-operated lever which stands no chance of jamming open should the infernal thing fall on its side.

Which it does. Often.

While it is akin to a Group B evolution car, the £2999 Suzuki LT4WD is sort of Range Roverish. Like the Honda, it gets mostly motorcycle controls but it has no clutch, a reverse gear, three ranges, a locking differential and switchable two- or four-wheel drive.

We are forever being told how clever the Japanese are becoming in the art of miniaturisation, but to have crammed this little lot into a machine the size of a salted peanut is nothing short of remarkable.

It's powered by a four-stroke 250-cc engine which develops 20 bhp and has five forward gears which can be shifted even with the throttle wide open. Every other lever on it, and there are 37, is a brake.

The Honda's main failing is a simple one. With 45 bhp on tap, it is too bloody fast for appalling weeds like me.

When it's off the cam, everything is fine and it potters round at a leisurely pace, popping and spluttering a bit but getting by all right.

However, if you inadvertently get the motor in its thankfully narrow power band, then the front wheels leave the ground and you must sit there and do nothing until you hit something. Well that's what I did anyway.

If you remove your thumb from the accelerator, the engine braking is sufficient to hurl you over the handlebars. If you steer, the back slews round and you roll, and if you keep the power on, you just end up going faster and faster, until you're scared rigid and incapable of taking any preventative action at all. You are, not to put too fine a point on it, stuck in a no-win situation from which there is only one escape: an accident.

The Suzuki has a less serious problem but it's one that warrants a mention none the less. In essence, the rider has no say in which direction it goes.

You can do what you will with the handlebars but you will continue to make straight line forward progress until a) you stop by applying one of the 37 brakes or b) you run into something.

Now, if you stop, you will have to dismount, lift up the front, take a theodolite bearing on where you want to go, drop the front down so it points in the proper direction and set off again towards the next accident.

I found the best way to alter course was to strike things a glancing blow. With practice, it's possible to bash into the selected target at exactly the correct speed and angle so you emerge from the confrontation pointing at your destination. A bit like snooker on wheels.

The best targets for such assaults are people, as they're mushy and don't harm the bike's bodywork or tracking. Car doors are good too because they buckle and bend long before anything on the super sturdy Suzi gives up the ghost.

So, after a brief flirtation on the Honda, I gave it to a colleague for the duration and I later saw him fairly regularly, on each occasion wearing a frightened look on his face and heading off towards whatever horizon was currently nearest.

I stuck with the Suzuki, and, after a while, became quite accustomed to ricocheting my way from baby to grannie to car door to helicopter landing gear in a sort of large-scale demonstration of Brownian motion.

Only once did I hurt myself on it. Because of its huge, underinflated tyres and plethora of gear ratio and drive selection levers, I figured it would be as adept at traversing rough ground as those hamster lookalike thingummys which live in the Andes.

So, bearing this in mind, I tried to scale a 45-degree slope which felt, as I reached halfway house, like I'd overdone things. Doubtless the bike was sailing through the test without even gently perspiring, but from where I sat, it felt like there was no way we'd reach the crest.

The foot I put down to act as a sort of stabiliser was promptly run over by the back wheel which, thankfully, wasn't as painful as you might imagine. This though is because my left foot is used to being squashed. In the past year, it's been run over four times, once by myself in an XJS and three times by other people. And I'm not joking either.

Happily, on rough ground, the front tyres do enjoy a modicum of grip so I was able to turn round and head back to *terra firma* where they became as sticky as sheet ice again.

All the while, I kept being overtaken by this maniac on the out-of-control Honda who kept squeaking about how he'd just overtaken Gordon Murray and run Nigel Mansell off his moped. Poor chap spent the entire evening muttering about power to weight ratios and how slow Thrust Two is.

As I loaded my Suzuki on the back of a Mitsubishi pickup truck for the homeward voyage on Sunday evening, I was quite sad. There's a challenge in mastering a four-wheeled bike that one simply does not encounter in the everyday world of electric-windowed cars.

I should like to be able to buy such a beast for everyday use but unfortunately, because they have no indicators or tax discs, they cannot be taken on public highways and byways, which is a shame. It should be much easier to drive on a road than in a field, there's so much more to hit.

I don't understand how F. Giles Esq can be allowed to pedal his pre-Boer War tractor up the A1 at 2 mph when the lord of the manor isn't even able to dart across the Nether Middlecombe to Lower Peasepottage back road on a Suzi Q to see how his sheep are doing.

Unless this silly law is repealed immediately, I shall become an anarchist.

Invaders from Cars

Now let me make one thing perfectly clear. If I say I will be in the pub at 8 o'clock, I will be in the pub at 8 o'clock.

I will not arrive, breathless, at a quarter past blaming the traffic or an unlikely encounter with a crazed Bengal tiger.

Punctuality is a fine art and I have mastered it to such a degree that as the second hand of my unusually accurate Tissot rock watch – the one that's as individual as my own signature – sweeps round to herald the appointed hour, I will be just about to enter the pre-arranged venue. My expected companion, however, is rarely, if ever, in evidence. This makes me mad.

What I can't understand is how on earth other people aren't able to manage the business of being on time quite as well as I do. Some do the breathless bit, some try to claim that they've been in a meeting which went on a bit but these people are usually estate agents and thus not worth talking to anyway. Then there are those who saunter in an hour late with nary an apology.

No matter. The thing is that if you arrive before the people you're supposed to be meeting, you must find something to do.

Something that lets other people in the bar know that you haven't been stood up. You can always hear them muttering about how 'she isn't coming' and sometimes how they're 'not in the least bit surprised with a face like that'.

You try desperately not to look at your watch every four seconds until eventually you are forced to cast aside all thoughts of giving the person just another five minutes. When you leave without speaking to anyone, it lets those who have been laughing at you know they were right all along.

Thus, if you're ever in a Fulham pub and someone greets you

like he's your best friend, it'll probably be me, so don't worry about it.

Far and away the best way of passing the time on such occasions is to insert various coinage into a space invader machine thingy. I do this a lot.

In fact, I've just worked out that I spend more time playing computer games than I spend on the loo. This makes me an addict. I need help. These machines have become my confidants. I talk to them, thank them when they're kind, swear at them when they're not.

And I've become rather good at them, which is a shame. Of all the things I could have been good at, it would have to be computer games, wouldn't it? What about raising money for the deaf? Or organising RNLI balls? Or being able to drive round the Nurburgring with gusto?

Some of the more modern games are a bit baffling; you know, the ones where you insert 20p in exchange for six seconds of bangs and explosions, none of which have anything whatsoever to do with the buttons you're hitting, before a terse message explains that the game is over.

Worse than my autobank, some of them.

Asteroids will always hold a special place in my heart along with Scramble and Pole Position but recently I've discovered that one can buy similar games for use on home computers like the one I'm using to write this story now.

The best I've found to date is called Grand Prix Simulator which costs a meagre £1.99. Such is its popularity that it is currently topping the little known Gallup charts for home computer games. How long will it be before someone commissions a bunch of pollsters to find out which flower shop is selling the most hyacinths?

Anyway, you control a little car which beetles round a track trying to beat either the bogey car or an opponent or both. Complete the first course successfully and you get to reach stage two, where the track becomes trickier and the bogey car driver more competent.

Happily the programmers at Codemasters who make Grand Prix Simulator have resisted the temptation to use complicated graphics such as one finds on modern-day arcade machines. I always find that home computer games programmed by clever dicks are harder to play than a game of archery in a foggy beehive, don't you?

Thus, the cars are simple squares and you, the player, look down on the circuit rather than along the bonnet of your steed.

Funniest of all, though, is the fact that leering from the promotional material that accompanies this game is the dreadfully ugly face of my old mate Johnnie Dumfries, the man who lost his job at Lotus when Camel insisted that at least one of their Grand Prix drivers had a face to match their new yellow paintwork.

Johnnie, says the Codemasters' press release, reckons the game is every bit as exciting as the real thing – a comment which should, I feel, be taken with liberal helpings of salt.

How, pray, can sitting in your living room steering some electrons round a TV screen be as exciting as travelling at 200 mph behind a crazy Italian who, on balance, would rather you didn't overtake him?

As it turned out, Johnnie was more than willing to take me on in a do-or-die battle to the death . . . er, I mean flag.

Needless to say, I thrashed him and like a true cynic did not accept any of his feeble excuses. I know his wife was in hospital at the time and I know the burden of having accepted a Jaguar drive was hanging heavily on his shoulders but I have problems too, you know. I mean, the shoe-lace in my left brogue is getting awfully thin and, not being the sort of person who ever sets foot in a shop, I have no idea where one sets about borrowing a replacement. Do Russell and Bromley, for instance, have a press test fleet I wondered as I lapped the Scottish Earl before he'd even left the grid.

Time and time again I explained that in order to go forward, you simply press the letter 'F'. But he just couldn't grasp it.

I wonder if the bosses at Codemaster realise this. These two younglings, six-year-old David Darling and his four-year-old brother, Richard, expect to sell well over 200,000 copies of their latest offering – and that will mean a substantial injection to their £2 million turnover.

Fair enough, they have become very rich because they exploit the weaknesses of people like me. But is their life really complete?

Have they ever seen a ptarmigan in its full winter plumage? Do they know where Siena is? Is it possible they've never ridden on the back of a dolphin? These are the things that matter in life. Playing with computers just fills in the gaps.

2001 isn't that far away any more you know.

The Revenger

I was never allowed to play with guns when I was a child. While various friends were able to scamper around the local woods with their Johnny Sevens, I had to make do with an old twig. And convincing an eight-year-old he was dead simply because I'd pointed a piece of larch his way was not quite as easy as you might imagine.

Twenty years on and the ban still exists. However, this is probably just as well because if the law did permit me to bear arms, then this week alone two people at least would have died horrible, bloody deaths.

First to receive a neat 9 mm hole in the side of his face would have been the service manager at a large London Fiat dealer who tried to charge Beloved a staggering £418 for some minor work on her Panda.

Second would have been the driver of a Citroen CX estate who, in a display of intransigence to rival Mrs Thatcher at an EEC farm subsidy committee meeting, brought Fulham Road to a grinding standstill.

The plethora of smashed computer keyboards and broken telephones that litter the office are testimony to the fact that not so very far below my veneer of calm lies a rampant beast with foam round its mouth and a bright-red countenance.

This aspect of my make-up was, I think, inherited from my grandfather who regularly threw his shoes through the television screen whenever Harold Wilson's face appeared on it.

Now, as things stand, the situation is not too complicated. After I've dialled directory enquiries for the ninth time and it's still engaged, I will hurl my telephone at the wall. It's my plaster. It's my phone. I can thus do as I like with them.

Similarly, when I've spent two days working on a story and my computer announces that it's made a syntax error and, as a result, the fruit of my labours has vanished into a silicon no man's land from which there is no escape, the keyboard and sometimes its accompanying screen often learn what it's like to collide with a sledgehammer.

Again, the consequences, as far as others are concerned, amount to a big fat zero. The world continues to revolve, various whales still get regular supplies of plankton and biscuit-and-raisin Yorkies don't seem to get any cheaper.

Now, when stuck behind some moron in a Nissan who is driving with all the alacrity and the verve of a koala bear on Valium, just what options are open to the unarmed Britisher?

One can shout a little but she will not hear. One can, one probably does, salivate to some extent – but she will not notice – or one can resort to the horn and lights, but she will not care.

As a result, one is forced to let one's pacemaker take the strain while dreaming of thumbscrews and racks and vats of boiling oil into which all Nissan drivers should be immersed.

Sticks and stones may break her bones but words etc, etc.

I'd like to think that if an Uzi machine pistol was lying on the seat beside me, I'd only use it to shoot holes in the culprit's tyres – but this is a bit like thinking I could sit here at 11 in the morning with a biscuit-and-raisin Yorkie and not eat it.

In America, of course, one is allowed to go about one's business carrying an entire armoury in one's flak jacket, and this explains why we are forever being regaled with tales of cabbies in New York who shoot people whose cars have stalled at the lights. I don't blame them. I know I would.

A country where one is given the wherewithal to rid the roads of awful drivers seems like one helluva place to live and I'd be off like a shot if I thought I wouldn't have to adopt a silly accent, wear daft clothes and drive around in a soggy car with chrome all over it.

These drawbacks have always been enough to make staying

in Britain worthwhile . . . just. Now, though, thanks to my 'Revenger', the land of hope and glory is a much more satisfactory place in which to lay my hat.

This £9.95 toy, according to its Taiwanese manufacturers, is the ultimate weapon in the fight against frustration. It can, they say, reduce tension and hostility in almost any circumstances. And they speak the truth.

It is a small black box with high-tech knobs and BMW-style service indicator flashing lights all over it, which one attaches to one's dashboard with the provided Velcro strips.

What it does is make a selection of noises. Press button A and the speaker emits a death ray sound similar to the awful cacophony space invader machines make in pubs when you're trying to speak with someone you haven't seen for ages.

Button B is labelled 'front machine gun', and this predictably makes sort of Bren noises, while button C reproduces the sound of a high-velocity shell: wheeeeeeeeeeeeekaprunch!

Apparently, Bloomingdales in New York sell one of these things every four minutes and Selfridges on Oxford Street report a similar level of interest.

However, my example has been somewhat modified to make it even better. The trouble is that the standard kit deafens only those who are sharing a vehicle with it. You can stab all three buttons at once but Mrs Nissan-Driver, in blissful ignorance, will continue to stall in that yellow box every time those infernal traffic lights indulge in a spot of metamorphosis.

As I've said before in this column, I am to engineering what parsley sauce is to Bosch fuel injection but when it comes to electronic whizzkiddery, I'm a match for that bald chappie who made a million electric slippers that no one wanted to buy.

Thus, I have been able to run a wire from my Revenger to a much more powerful speaker which is located just behind the radiator grille of my CRX.

Its inventor, 29-year-old David McMahan, says: 'The

Revenger is as harmless as jingle bells but has a tremendous therapeutic effect.' Not any more it ain't me old mate.

Such is the authenticity and volume of my machine-gun sound that I have actually seen people duck when my finger hits the 'trigger'. One day, one of the Nissan-clad berks will have a heart attack when they hear the 84,000 decibel rendition of a shell heading their way. This will be a good thing. I see myself as a RoSPA pioneer.

Time and time again, blithering idiots have given me palpitations with their unbelievable antics on the road. Well, no longer am I going to get mad. I'm going to get even.

Unfortunately, a group calling themselves the moral majority – actually, they're surprisingly few in number and live in socially aware places like Hampstead and Barnes – will undoubtedly kick up the most godawful fuss when my modified Revenger gets its first victim.

But these people must stick with their muesli and their lentils. I'm on a mission.

Charades

His slippers were slightly at odds with the neat brown suit, pristine white shirt and silk tie but, nevertheless, he was the managing director of a major Japanese corporation. Clad in a pair of Chinos and an open-neck shirt, it didn't tax anyone's powers of perception to ascertain that in the world of motoring journalism, I rank well down with the chaps who rewrite press releases for papers like the *Bengal Bugle*.

Yet the man in the brown suit was indulging in a bow which took his face so close to the ground that just for a moment, I figured he was smelling the gravel.

He wasn't the only one either. Everyone with whom I came into contact on my two-day, whistlestop tour of Japan spent the entire duration of our conversation rubbing their noses in the dirt. It takes some getting used to.

But I managed it and now I am fast losing friends by insisting that if they wish to speak to me, they avert their eyes.

I read somewhere the other day that nearly 80 per cent of Britishers had never been in an aeroplane. Taking that quite remarkable fact a stage further, it would be sensible to assume that the vast majority of the 20 per cent who have flown some-where have flown within Europe be it southern Spain, a Greek island or Majorca.

Among those who have ventured futher afield, I would hazard a guess that America is usually the most popular destination.

In essence, Japan is still an unknown quantity in terms of per-sonal experience. Sure, we all are fully aware that it's a paid-up member of the capitalist Western world but because it's on the other side of the globe and doesn't have holiday-isle status, it isn't all that popular with foreigners from the English-speaking world.

Generally speaking, I've always had the world divided into four categories and largely, these views are echoed by those with whom I've conversed on the subject.

We have countries behind the Iron Curtain where we expect to find downtrodden people in brown coats shuffling from one decaying tower block to the next in search of a lettuce or a Beatles album.

Then we have the third world where lots of people in loin cloths sit around wondering why there are no more lettuces.

Third comes the West, with billions of lettuces that everyone can afford to buy whenever they want.

And finally there's the Far East – Thailand, Burma etc – where everyone sits in the lotus position with their hands on their heads wondering what on earth a lettuce is.

Go to any of these places and you know what to expect. You know America is full of people in checked trousers who say 'gee' a lot. You know people in Australia go to work in shorts and call one another mate. You know the French will be rude, that the Burmese will be polite, that Hong Kong's full of skyscrapers and imitation Rolexes and that Antarctica is bloody cold.

Since all those spoilsport explorers wandered round the world last century discovering places and writing about them, there are no surprises left. And it's still going on today. Between them, Wilbur Smith and Bob Geldof have given me a razor-sharp, Kodacolor Gold image of exactly what Africa is like. And I've never even been there.

Japan, though, was a shock. Because they build television sets that look like European television sets, gramophones that look like European gramophones and motor cars that look like European motor cars, it's easy to believe that they're as Westernised as a plate of McDonald's fries or the Queen.

But this, I can assure you, is not the case. They may have all the exterior trappings of what you and I would call Western civilisation but they are fundamentally different both deep down and on the surface.

My two-day visit to the Daihatsu factory provided a fascinating insight into just what makes these chaps tick and more importantly, whether I was wrong in a *Performance Car* story twelve months or so ago to argue that they would never be able to destroy the European car industry with the same consummate ease they crushed various local motorbike businesses.

Obviously, in two days, you cannot glean all that you could in a lifetime but I've heard politicians spout wildly on subjects about which they know absolutely nothing. And people listen to them.

The first thing that will strike you as odd in Japan is how polite everyone is. Quite apart from the neverending bowing, they have obsequiousness down to an art that even the Chinese haven't mastered.

The Daihatsu PR man who sat in the back of my car to explain how I should get about in what is the world's worst-signposted country epitomised this. Whereas in England, you or I would shout, 'Take the next left', he would lean forward, apologise for blocking the view in my rear-view mirror and say, 'Excuse me, Mr Crarkson, would you mind taking the next turning you find to the reft.' By which time I'd gone past it.

The Daihatsu factories and offices were bedecked with Union Jacks to mark our visit, receptionists bowed so low that they disappeared behind their desks and everywhere there were signs saying things like 'Welcome respectful journalists from UK'. I am not respectful. I have a criminal record in France and I pick my nose.

Whereas at European press functions, a PR person and a couple of directors will play host to upwards of 50 journalists, Daihatsu wheeled out their president, Mr Tomonaru Eguchi, and enough hierarchy to make up six rugby teams. The result was that I felt sorry for them if something went wrong with their arrangements.

At an Audi press launch recently, one errant driver finished the slalom by smashing his Quattro into the electronic timing gear. It was hugely funny to watch the stony faced Germans trying to cope with this unexpected hiccough.

In Japan, the test route Daihatsu had chosen for us to evaluate their new four-wheel-drive Charade was plagued with an eight-mile traffic jam which wrecked their schedule. I nearly cried. If this had happened in Germany where they tried just as hard to be organised, you'd have heard me laughing in Aberdeen.

Similarly, when a lift at the company headquarters refused to leave the basement, thus forcing some of my colleagues to use the stairs, you could see they were close to tears. Some had to be helped from the building when they heard the lift operator plunge a sword into her belly.

I think we ate her that night for supper. And the liftmaker. And his wife.

Not only are they more polite than any Westerner I've ever met, they're also more weird. Their tables and chairs don't have legs which, if you ask me, is a bit silly.

Also, one of the things that didn't feature in my hotel room was a bed. Some of the things it did feature were five pairs of slippers, one for the hallway, one for the bedroom, one for the loo, one for the washroom, and one for the bathroom.

I just wore my brogues all the time.

This though was not allowed at supper time when a geisha girl spent the entire meal cooking each mouthful of lift operator individually and dropping it between my ever-ready lips. She even dabbed my battered, time-worn face with a warm flannel in between chews.

Now, you might imagine that I've returned from my visit a fully converted Japophile but I haven't, because I simply can't work out what makes them tick. Trying to fathom them out is like trying to contemplate the infinity of space or how Seat sell any cars. It just can't be done.

I've had business dealings with Japan in the past and have emerged from every meeting staggered at their intransigence. They simply will not take no for an answer and will, if needs be, scheme and connive way into the night until their opponent is a pulsating wreck beyond argument.

This feature was evident in various conversations I had with Daihatsu's engineers. 'Why don't you buy SCS brakes from Lucas?' 'Because we're making our own.' 'Wouldn't it be cheaper to buy them now?' 'We'd rather develop our own.' 'Don't you think it would help create a favourable impression of Daihatsu in Europe if you bought some European equipment?' 'We've got some Pirelli tyres and anyway we can do better than SCS.' End of story.

Language was always a stumbling block but the stock answer to everything was always, 'We're working on it' and they probably are.

It's easy to be working on lots of things when 1500 members of your 11,000 strong workforce are in the R&D department.

I suspect there are two reasons why they are working on everything. One is because of that indigenous Japanese trait called nationalism and the other is because that was the only phrase these guys have licked. Even the translators were about as good at English as I am at French.

I know things like '*Et maintenant, comme le chien*' and '*Vous avez des idées au dessus de votre gare*'. But a full-scale technical press conference would, I fear, leave me floundering.

It seems strange that having gone to what were obviously enormous lengths to make sure our stay was totally trouble free, they didn't find bilingual chappies who know how to say 'three-speed automatic gearbox' in Japanese and English.

Maybe they could and weren't letting on. Maybe I'm a cynical old sod.

Certainly, it seems at first that they're being more open than any industry chappy you've ever encountered; not once, for instance, did anyone say 'no comment' or 'I can't tell you that' and they did show us a top secret prototype, but I do get the impression that half the time they don't understand your question and the other half, they just tell you what they think you want to hear. Maybe again.

While touring their Shiga factory, I was desperate to see what measures were incorporated to make their damned cars so reliable. There were none. The plant was no more automated than European equivalents, quality control no more strident.

There were just a few guys working on machines the size of Coventry that churn out a completed 1.3-litre engine every 28 seconds. There were big digital scoreboards announcing how close to target they were and there was an air of cleanliness. In short, the only thing that stood out as being special were the workers, who behave rather differently from those I've encountered in Europe. They didn't flick V signs at us. Perhaps it's because they were too busy bowing.

Then there was the rendition of Johnny Mathis's 'When A Child Is Born' which was playing over the loudspeaker system to commemorate our visit.

We were shown every engine being tested to 4500 rpm, and we were shown the camshaft machine which must have breathed a sigh of relief when the engineers announced the new 16-valve engine wouldn't be a twin-cam and we were shown the tropical fish aquarium. No, I don't know why either.

We also saw an MR2 being tested and Bertone's name in a visitors' book but still they maintained a sports car is not in the offing. 'We're working on the idea,' said one of the translators.

Maybe the reliability just comes because of the workers' devotion to duty. My personal guide hasn't taken a holiday in ten years and is currently owed 130 days off. 'I'm just too busy to go away but I'm working on it,' he says.

Maybe it is as a result of there being no women on the factory floor. I dunno but I do know there is no obvious reason why the average Daihatsu is a whole lot more reliable than the average Eurobox.

'We don't have hooligans,' suggested one hopeful individual

who helps make the cars, but I hardly think that all Rover SDIs broke down because they were vandalised on the production line.

After the factory tour it was back onto the bus for a lesson in why Japanese interiors are so universally awful – have you seen the interior of the new Toyota Landcruiser? It's disgusting.

But it's nothing when stacked up against that bus, which in turn was positively tasteful compared with the innards of a Japanese taxi – I've been in a Nissan Cedric and let me tell you that if it were fitted with a tachograph, the damned thing would blow up.

They actually *like* crushed velour seats, antimacassars with scenes of Japan on them, swinging things on the rear-view mirror and gaudy striping to go with the fake stitching. And chrome. Oh boy, they can't get enough of it.

To complicate matters, they simply couldn't understand why we all clutched our mouths and went green when presented with this sort of addenda.

A problem here is that while they realise the British and the Japanese have different tastes, they seem to think we are like the Americans. I haven't heard such a loud chorus of 'Oh no we're not' since I was at a pantomime back in 1968.

Funnily enough, Daihatsu are one of the better interior stylists. God knows how they do it.

It's hard, as I said earlier, to form cast-iron opinions after two days of fact finding, but certainly, the Japanese cannot be underestimated.

We already know that a great many Japanese cars are equal, if not superior, to their European equivalents but this is not the issue here for a couple of reasons. Firstly, such discussions are getting boring now and secondly, Britain, at least, is protected by import quotas.

It's the latter point which is what I'm most concerned about and not just because every Japanese company, including relative minnows like Daihatsu, have either established some kind of assembly base in Europe or are about to do so.

No, come 1992 when internal borders between member states of the EEC are broken down, the gentlemen's agreement that currently limits Japanese imports to 11 per cent of the UK market will be worth less than a Lira.

Daihatsu admit they expect to sell more cars in Britain after 1992.

One day, someone is going to have to get round a table with the Japanese manufacturers to see what can be done; and I don't envy whoever gets this job.

He'll feel honoured with all the bowing, he'll be overawed at the politeness, particularly if he's French, he might even feel sorry for them. Certainly, long periods of sitting on the floor will make him uncomfortable and, thus, he might concede more than he might otherwise.

One thing, though: he must never be rude. I learned this by telling the driver of a Toyota Crown Royale that his car was very nasty. Luckily, we moved off before his verbal abuse turned into a full-scale kung fu demonstration.

We must face facts. In ten years' time, I shall be driving a Daihatsu Charade.

If it's the GTti, I won't mind an iota.

Pedal Pusher

If the Queen were to have a sex change, one of your eyebrows might shift inadvertently upwards an inch or two. If Mike Tyson were to be exposed as a closet ballet dancer, the other would surely join it.

If I announced I had bought myself a bicycle you would faint and probably die.

The bicycle was not invented for people with beer bellies like barrage balloons and lungs like Swiss cheese. People like me in other words.

Nevertheless, two weeks ago, in a moment of unparalleled rashness, I decided to invest in a three-speed Raleigh Wayfarer.

This is why.

Platform boots may come and lamps with oily bubbles in them may go, but the White Horse is here to stay.

This drinking establishment situated in the heart of Sloane-dom, on Parsons Green in south-west London, regularly takes in excess of £4000 a day. And much of this income is my personal responsibility.

Since it became fashionable to drink there some six or seven years ago, a host of competitors have opened up, ranging from champagne bars to riverside inns to spit and sawdust pubs resonating with some of that renowned London character.

But they've failed and you still can't get a drink in the White Horse without queuing up for hours. Days even.

Since I moved to Fulham back in 1984 I have lived within an easy stroll of this cultural oasis, this spiritual haven. And it has therefore been no hardship to drive home from work, abandon the wheels, and sally forth on foot for an evening spent expanding the girth. I do it a lot.

The trouble is, though, that I recently moved to a new flat which is simply too far away. I once tried walking but ended up in an oxygen tent. I've tried driving, but tomato juice gets to be as dull as wallpaper paste after 23 pints of the stuff – no matter how much Tabasco they put in it. I've even tried finding a new pub but there isn't one.

So I bought the Wayfarer.

There is a veritable and unplumbed ocean of reasons why no one should ever use one of these antiquated deathtraps for getting around, but the fact remains that, when you're blind drunk, they make a deal of sense. For a kick off, you can't lose your driving licence; but, more importantly, you can't do much damage when you accidentally run into something.

In fact, for drunkards, the bicycle is bettered by only two other forms of transport: the pram and the sedan chair.

Sure, I considered both these, but was forced to discount the pram idea when I couldn't find one seven feet long, and the sedan chair when my staff inexplicably declined to carry me around in it.

So I went into a second-hand shop with £30 and emerged a few minutes later with the Wayfarer in tow.

Now before you dismiss me as a damned traitor to the cause of performance motoring, I must stress that I will continue to drive as I always have done: in other words, with no regard whatsoever for those who use the roads without paying tax.

I am fully aware every time I mount the mighty Raleigh that I am a guest in the motor vehicle's territory and must learn to get out of its way.

So do not expect a barrage of whinges and moans about how the Mamito Honi lot in their rusty Jap boxes couldn't judge the width of their cars if you gave them a theodolite, a computer, a tape measure and six weeks.

Nor should you think that this is to be a stream of abuse directed in the general direction of lightly warmed hatchback scramblers, who seem to think that they're going backwards unless movement is accompanied by large quantities of wailing rubber.

And I am not about to criticise the Archies and the Sids in their Maggie-wagon taxis who are too busy haranguing their fares about how 'there are too many A-rabs in the country' and how 'Mrs Thatcher – Gawd bless 'er – has set the country on its feet again' to notice cyclists – even when they're 200 feet tall and 60 feet wide like me.

I was going to lambast London Regional Transport for their inability to make a bus work without it leaving the sort of smoke screen the navy use in the heat of battle, but what the hell, they've got a job to do. And, like I said, the road is for motor vehicles, not for cyclists on an Alpen trip.

I'm not all that bothered, either, about the drivers of artics who need an area the size of Wales to turn left. No, the breed I hate most while astride the Wayfarer are the breed I hate most when I'm driving my car. People in vans.

There are always three of them in the front, and while I am an active campaigner for the abolition of all speed limits, I really do have to concede that they travel far too quickly.

It seems sensible to make them forfeit one limb for every wing mirror they smash. The fifth offence should lead them straight to the guillotine. I mean, if they can't steer their van through a gap without removing the mirrors from whatever it is they're going between then they should either slow down or get spectacles.

Do they not realise that little old me on the Wayfarer is a good deal less stable than a nuclear power station with Ray Charles at the controls? Can they not see that my centre of gravity is higher up than the tip of the CB aerial on their Transit and that, as a result, a sudden breeze or a momentary lapse in concentration could have me veering wildly from side to side like an SDP MP or, as has happened on six occasions to date, falling off?

What I've learned to do when I hear the unmistakable sounds that herald the imminent arrival of a Garymobile – megabel stereo, graunching gears and 94-zillion-rpm engine – is to dismount and walk along the pavement for a while.

Trouble is, if I encounter six vans in my mile-long journey, then I may as well not bother taking the Wayfarer out in the first place because I'll spend most of the time pushing it.

Anyway, all this is of no moment now because, last week, I came out from the pub and found two padlocks securing my steed to the railings. Since I'd put just the one on, it means that someone out there has a finely honed sense of humour.

It took two hours and some seriously sophisticated cutting gear to free the beast, but the effort was to no avail. Last night it was stolen, so now I'm going back to walking.

Unless someone steals my shoes in the meantime.

Girls and Rubber

The Kings Road, as usual, was at a standstill. There was a garden-ing programme, as usual, on Radio Four, and Capital, as usual, was playing the latest splurge from Kylie Astley.

But things could have been a whole lot worse. It was a sunnyish sort of day, and the Kings Road shopperettes were out and about, competing with one another to see who could get away with wearing the least amount of cloth around their person.

I just sort of fiddled with the door mirror to get a better view of the one in the suede mini skirt who'd gone into Fiorucci, and then slumped down in the seat so that I could see the one in the convertible Golf without her noticing the leer that was parked on my countenance.

I even beckoned one over and reminded her that five years earlier we'd had a few dances together at a hunt ball. She wasn't all that bothered.

Neither was another one impressed when I told her that we'd once shared a table in Puccis.

Now, this is one day in the life of the Kings Road. Go down there right now and you will see attractive women, hundreds of them, deliberately being pretty.

So, what I want to know is why on earth those who choose models for calendars don't use the location as a hunting ground.

Let's face it; a lot of real models are simply not pretty. Worse, a lot of real models look as though they may have spent the last eighteen years head butting bulldozers; yet if you turn to any page in some of the glossier mags you will see them, half dressed in some bizarre fashion undergarment, half not dressed at all.

Some of the fat slobs who man the ironmongery stalls in

provincial market towns would make better subject matter. For heaven's sake, I could do a superior job with those things you see on the Readers' Wives pages in Paul Raymond's *Menshouse Clubnational Only Boy*.

Only last week, I was in Honfleur in Northern France where they were shooting the sort of picture you'll find in a subsequent issue of *Harpers and She*.

The photographic equipment, all three lorry-loads of it, was set up in a smashing little bar and on a table by the window they'd carefully placed a crushed Disque Bleu packet, a half-eaten croissant, a half-cup of French coffee and a model.

Wearing the sort of coat you would more normally associate with a cartoon char lady, she had the figure of a garden hoe and the face of a long-dead turbot.

And the problem was compounded because she was wearing bright scarlet lipstick and a layer of mascara so heavy her eyelids kept closing under the strain. Finally, she had a facial complexion and colour that reminded me of unbaked pastry.

Thumb through any women's magazine and occasionally you come across the sort of person you'd eat dung for, but mostly they're the sort that would have you leaving with sonic booms.

Never has this phenomenon been more keenly obvious than in the 1989 Pirelli calendar.

While Unipart and a host of other component manufacturers do their level best to make their calendars sell in the face of fierce competition from the *Sun* and *Penthouse*, Pirelli claim to be in a class of their own.

Now 25 years old, this titillatory publication was a British invention and, even now, is orchestrated from London. Top models have appeared in it, big-name photographers have been selected to shoot it.

And each year since the whole caboodle began, the makers have kept the contents of the calendar a closely guarded secret until publication – though from whom, God only knows, so few copies are ever produced.

Few, in 1988, means 40,000 — which, say Pirelli, is way, way down on demand.

Oh yeah? Apparently, liberated 1960s parents are now writing to Pirelli for copies of the earlier efforts to give as presents to 'maturing offspring'.

Of course, all this is pure hype, designed to generate mystique and consequently foster a desire to own something which is actually no more out of the ordinary than salt water.

Certainly, it isn't 'acknowledged as the most potent status symbol in the world'.

I can hear Richard Branson now: 'Oh yes, I own several jetliners, an island in the Caribbean, a collection of beautiful hotels, a couple of boats, a number of fine cars, a hot air balloon and more houses than Barratt have ever built — *but most of all, I treasure my Pirelli calendar.*'

And even if he really *does* get off on past efforts from the eyetie rubber boys, I doubt whether he'll think too much of *Possessions* — which is what they've called the 1989 edition.

Firstly, it's shot by a woman. Now, women are forever telling me that I do not understand the bond of motherhood and appeal of babies, so let me tell *them* something for a change: they do not understand what men want from pictures of naked ladies.

We want heaving chests, white beaches, glistening coconut oil and as much subtlety as you get at a Guns 'N' Roses concert.

We do not want to spend fifteen minutes searching for a nipple that might or might not be in shot. And we don't get turned on by buttocks, because *we* have them as well. Well I do anyway.

And great store has been made this year of the photographer's decision to use Polaroid film.

I cannot tell the difference. You will not be able to tell the difference either.

Anyway, what's so great about using a film that always fades to nothing four seconds after you pull it out of the camera and is about as accurate at reproducing living colour as the male half of Peters and Lee.

And instead of using months of the year like every other diary and calendar ever made, Pirelli have used astrological signs instead. I do not know when these are. Next year, I will go everywhere either a month early or seven months late.

On the 3rd of Capricorn next year, for instance, I am going to a party. When should I go?

Finally, there's the women. They're all ugly to varying degrees and one or two don't even have nice figures. One's got nipples like dinner plates.

And another has a bottom so baggy it looks just like two sacks of King Edwards.

I suppose though that, for the first time, Pirelli cannot be accused of exploiting women. They cannot be accused either of sexism or of favouring those born to stroll the Kings Road.

But for heaven's sake chaps, if Beloved can waltz in and order me to pay for two skirts, a packet of stockings and a bedside table, why can't *I* spend even a few minutes staring wistfully at a decent pair of greased bosoms?

Rat Boy

There are mutants in the sewers. Each night as darkness falls and a clinging fog descends to envelop the city in an eerie and impenetrable blanket, you can hear, if you listen carefully, the manhole covers sliding back.

From deep beneath the streets, the hordes, horribly disfigured by exposure to state education, emerge into the silence. Clad in tattered rags, their eyes glint in the oddly transfused glow as they drift into the sodium lighting.

Stealthily, they move unseen from street to street in a hunt for the currency of that mutant world beneath the catseyes.

Down there, order has broken down and decency has become anarchy. There is no social structure as we know it; everyone is awful. The mutants only trade in two commodities. Ecstasy and car stereos.

In order to get the drug, you need the music machines. And in order to get the music machines, you need to emerge into the old world where greed is good, where people wear double-breasted suits they bought in Next and talk into cellphones about how they've moved their wedge from copper to sugar.

They watch items on the television called *Hot Property* and *The City Programme*. Their success is measured by the initials on the back of their cars.

The mutants understand this grading system too. The wise elders say they know it because in the past, they too lived among us in the real world.

They know that they will get more ecstasy from The Man if they break into the cars with an 'i' on the back.

This is why, in the past two weeks, I have woken up on successive Sunday mornings to find one of my car windows completely reshaped. Go to bed and it's a flat piece of green tinted glass. Wake up and it's many immensely tiny pieces of glass spread over a huge area. Most of them, though, are in the heater vents where they can rattle.

Trouble is, I am the sort of person who enjoys confusing the mutants. They break into my car because it looks as though it will sport the sort of stereo that can be exchanged for six or seven tabs. In fact, it is worth, in earth money, about £3.25.

Nowadays, they break into my car to laugh at it.

The mutants have left me alone for two years but with the emergence of Acid House music, their need for spiritual enlightenment is ever greater. Make no mistake, no one can be safe until the council weld up the manhole covers and pump cyanide gas into the web of tunnels beneath.

You might imagine as you sit there in your Next suit that even if your car is broken into, so long as nothing is stolen – all is well: if that's the case, you obviously don't drive a Honda.

If you *don't* drive a Honda, you will be able to telephone one of the mobile glass repair outfits that fill 85 per cent of the *Yellow Pages* and a cheery man in an overall and an Escort van will come and kiss it better.

Some say these men are mutant spies who are cashing in on the antics of their blood brothers in the sewers but this is only conjecture. Probably.

If you *do* drive a Honda, you will spend Sunday ringing these people and becoming increasingly fed up with them calling you guv and saying they can do nothing until Monday.

You just *know* they're the sort of people who hold their cigarettes between thumb and forefinger with the hot bit pointing inwards. You *know* they spent every minute of their state education dreaming of being a taxi driver. They have the banter.

Why, you enquire, can they not send round one of their men? Because, they say, Honda will not let them carry original equipment stock.

Later, their bosses are more precise. Er, it's not that they won't let us actually. We just don't because the Japanese change their models every six minutes and glass manufacturers in Europe can't keep up.

This means those of you who drive a Honda that's been subjected to the attention of a mutant on Saturday night cannot get it mended until Monday morning. And this in turn means you must hope the cardboard you insert in the hole is a sufficient barrier to another mutant attack on the Sunday night.

When you do get to a dealer, he will lighten your wallet to the tune of 90 quid. And break your door. Well, he broke mine.

So I reckon a two-pronged attack is in order and I am volunteering to the last vestiges of law enforcement in this country as a back-room boffin.

First we must look at the root cause of the problem. That leads inexorably to the conclusion that all state schools must be closed down. Never mind opting out of local authority guidance. Close them. All of them. Now.

While the teachers with their beards and corduroy jackets are trying to teach the urchins how to do binary numbers and where Africa is, the kids at the back are thumbing through Vauxhall manuals to see how best to get round a dead lock.

Then we must attack those who have already moved underground. That means posting teams of heavily armed ex-boxers outside manhole covers, with Uzis, flamethrowers and some of those guns Christopher Walken used in *Dogs of War*.

You probably think all this is a load of rubbish, but before you reach for the headed notepaper, consider two things. Firstly, who are the people that break into cars? Do you know one?

No, of course you don't. No one does, so they must come from *somewhere else*.

Secondly, who the hell is buying all the stereos they steal? Where are all the shops that sell them? And if what they're selling is obviously stolen and on offer in such mind-boggling numbers, why on earth can't someone with a firearms licence pay the vendor a call?

You can't pay them a call because it isn't a them. It's a he, a sort of Thatcherday Fagin who lives underground, distributing ecstasy tabs with gay abandon.

I promise that if I actually catch someone in my car, I will not stop hitting them over the head with something blunt until they are in as many pieces as the glass they broke to get in.

In a Flap

Imagine, for a moment, the face of an opera aficionado if, halfway through a performance of *Don Giovanni* at Covent Garden, Bruce Springsteen bounded on stage and began a 120 decibel rendition of 'Born To Run'.

Or picture, if you will, the depths to which a prison warder's jaw would drop if Ronnie Biggs appeared at the door of Wandsworth jail asking if his bedroom was still free.

Presumably neither Ronnie nor Bruce could be persuaded to stage these feats but if you, like me, enjoy watching innocent strangers in a flap, all is not lost – just try letting someone out of a side road in London.

It's a relatively simple procedure. Let's say you're in a slow-moving queue of traffic on Baker Street and you see a BMW driver who has quite obviously been waiting for some time to pull out (easy: he'll look like a non-opera buff at a performance of *Don Giovanni*). Simply stop and with a huge smile on your face, flash your lights, indicating that he may emerge into the traffic stream.

After he's looked gormlessly around to make sure you're not waving at a friend, and then peered into your eyes to ascertain there isn't a hint of lunacy hidden within their depths, the flap begins.

Once he has assured himself your intentions are genuine, his left hand will dart for the gear lever – put in neutral ten minutes earlier because the clutch leg was getting tired. Not only will the hapless hand in consequence drop the cigarette entrusted to it moments before but it will miss first gear anyway, and more often than not hit reverse. Happily, the tired clutch leg will have been slower on the uptake so passers-by will only be treated to an earful of crunching cogs rather than the sight of a BMW lurching unceremoniously backwards into the window of Mr Patel's sandwich bar.

Wait a little longer and the kangaroo petrol-powered BMW will be in front of you, complete with a driver equipped for the next month with the best 'guess what happened to me' story any Londoner could wish to relate.

Strangers to the city (yes, they exist) will be baffled by this scenario, but it isn't as crazy as it sounds. In London you do not let people in, make no allowances for the elderly or infirm, treat red traffic lights as no more than advisory stop signals and, if you plan to survive with your wings intact, you become bloody arrogant.

London is, of course, an exception: to some, horribly frightening; to others, a challenge that needs mastering. There are those who will drive miles to avoid any contact with its streets and yet also those who regard the new traffic lights at Hyde Park Corner as the brainchild of a spoilsport.

It is not, of course, only London that offers the motorist an insight into its inhabitants. It works on a worldwide scale. If one encounters a crashed or broken down vehicle in Pakistan, one simply makes a new road round it. In America, one wonders how on earth drivers can direct their huge automobiles through the haze of cigar smoke and the glare from oncoming sports jackets. In France, they haven't yet learned that you no longer yield to the right, and in Italy no one yields to anyone.

Nor is the phenomenon peculiar to capital cities. Ignoring London for the time being – have you ever been to Reigate? During the day, when husbands are away trying to save the Pound, their wives populate the town centre with VW Sciroccos and massive hairstyles. Their boutiques, bought to discourage them from seeking affairs, occupy their minds to a certain extent but meeting Sally Ann at the Bacchus Wine Bar for lunch is far more important.

For these women, the car is no more than a vanity mirror on

wheels. If ever you're driving down Reigate's main street and see a car that's about to pull out, for heaven's sake, beware. Although the Laura-Ashley-clad incumbent may appear to be checking her mirror for approaching cars, nothing is further from her mind. In reality, when she glances into a mirror, all she sees is a lovely made-up face, and it probably won't be yours.

This is why the Reigate wife likes Sciroccos. Not only is there a very local dealer to be summoned for help whenever she forgets to put that smelly stuff in the tank, but the vanity mirror (rear-view mirror to you and I) isn't ridiculously convex. Such mirrors may improve peripheral vision but they show up every skin blemish and wrinkle.

So be very careful in Reigate. Chances are, the car in front has no idea you're there and if its driver suddenly sees someone she hasn't seen 'for absolutely ages' – last night – coming out of Diana's dress shop, she will, without warning, pull up for a chat.

Further up the road in Woking, it's an entirely different story. Here, you'll find old couples lamenting the day when the town they had come to know and love was shaken up by developers to become Britain's biggest eyesore. The poor old dears in their pristine Marinas cannot work out for the life of them what a one-way system is and, while going the wrong way round it, can be seen pointing at concrete monstrosities saying, 'Do you remember when the police station was there?'

These people, like the womenfolk of Reigate, do not understand the motor car, or indeed any laws pertaining to it. To them, the road is a grey strip and grey strips can be driven on at as leisurely a pace as may be and in whatever direction the driver chooses.

Move up to Doncaster and a whole new world opens up. Here, in the heartland of mining, pigeon fanciers and Reliant Robins, driving is an art not yet mastered by the majority of the populace. Ineptitude reigns. It's a town where people take fifteen minutes to park in a space three times the length of their three-wheeler, where they don't pull out onto a roundabout until absolutely nothing is in sight, where you have to look out for apprentice dole queue jumpers in maroon pullovers, desperately trying to woo Dolcis shoe-shop salesgirls by spinning the wheels of their 1972 Capris – complete with dice, stripes and two dozen fog lamps.

The local police are too busy tracing whippet thieves to concentrate on these young blades with barely detectable moustaches and receding acne, so St Sepulchre Gate – closed to those who can read the signs – is jammed on a Saturday with a battery of primer splattered Sharon-loves-Garymobiles chewing up the Acrilan-smothered tarmac.

Eighty miles further north, amid Britain's most breathtakingly beautiful scenery, the Yorkshire Dales, lethargy abounds and in spite of the availability of some magnificent driving roads, 7 mph is the average speed. Two groups are largely responsible for this pace: the locals who crawl around in corrugated-iron Subarus collecting wayward sheep and mending walls, and the gongoozlers who flood up there in the summer to break them and scatter them again.

Ethel and Albert, too old by about fifty summers for Club 18–30 holidays in Benidorm, flock to the Dales to remind themselves of a lifestyle and pace not seen since 1473. Their spotless Maxi – ten years old with 900 miles on the clock – dithers around on the Askrigg pass with Ethel wondering whether her pallid demeanour is a result of Albert's driving or the dizzy heights, while Albert spends his time worrying about the stopping distance from 6 mph should a sheep wander into view on the horizon.

His mental meanderings are inevitably brought to an abrupt halt by either clouds of steam belching from his much-loved engine or a head-on collision with a corrugated-iron Subaru whose driver has been looking at broken walls and not the road. Either way, it's a relief for the incumbents of Albert's eight-mile tailback who are desperately trying to reach the Farmers Arms in Muker before it closes.

Birmingham you might liken to one of those 'power' houses

that used to be an expensive but essential extra with a Hot Wheels set. You remember, the little toy car could be pushed into the 'house' where two rapidly spinning rubber wheels would shoot the projectile out of the other side. Theoretically, the car would be given enough oomph to complete a circuit of the track and reach the spinning wheels for a second boost before its momentum ran out. Perpetual motion, until the batteries gave up.

In reality, the poor car shot out at such a rate it could never negotiate the first corner and would leap off the track to an expensive collision with the coffee table.

So, you want to go to the centre of Birmingham do you? Like scores of others, you will leave the M6 where a bold sign says 'City Centre' and you will find yourself on the grand-sounding 'Expressway' thundering towards the skyscrapers under the ever watchful eyes of a succession of video cameras. Presumably, the tapes from these cameras can subsequently be watched by the traffic police amid great hilarity as they're bound to depict scenes of strangers trying desperately to work out which lanes of the 'Expressway' are for northbound traffic and which are for those going south.

Anyway, after negotiating a couple of tunnels, you'll find yourself in Kidderminster.

So you do a U-turn and head back towards the skyscrapers again, but your perseverance will simply put you back on the M6 again and if you're dreadfully unlucky that could spell an encounter with the infamous Gravelly Hill interchange – Spaghetti Junction. Once here, no matter which way you try to enter Birmingham, you will be ejected out of the other side puzzled at how you managed to miss all of Britain's second-biggest city completely.

But don't worry, it's not just you. Glance into any other car as it shoots through the tunnels and over the overpasses and you'll see the occupants are unshaven creatures, gaunt and undernourished through lack of sleep and food.

If Ranulph Fiennes is looking for another challenge after his dangerous Transglobe Expedition, he could do worse than set out to find Birmingham's city centre without leaving the road system . . .

Where is New Street? What about the Bullring? What kind of people are stuck in this once great city: indeed, is there anyone in there at all? Come on Ranulph, these questions need answering.

Why can't Birmingham Council's Highway Department pay a visit to their counterparts in Bournemouth – surely the best-signposted town anywhere – and while they're at it, could they take along the idiots who dreamed up Oxford's one-way system as well? Whereas with Birmingham, no one can get in, quite the reverse applies in Oxford. Approach it from the east and you'll find yourself at a crossroads where you have to turn left. Do so and you're on the inner ring road with no exits. You're on it till you run out of petrol or sanity.

This is presumably why Oxford is a city of cyclists. The crazy one-way system, the labyrinth of bus lanes, and the traffic wardens who, with their little moustaches and greased-down forelocks (even the women) all resemble a famous German leader, combine to make the motor car in Oxford as welcome as Marlboro sponsorship at an ASH convention.

Perhaps the powers that be believe, and they have a point, that very pretty girls who have a penchant for wearing very short skirts and riding bicycles could raise accident statistics among male drivers to unacceptable levels.

Not too far away, in Cirencester, the danger looms in another form – swarms of tweed-clad hooray Henries in Lhasa green Golf GTis who, if asked, say they're students at the agricultural college, though their lecturers wouldn't know them from Adam.

Drink-driving laws do not seem to have a bearing in Ciren-cester, where these students spend 85 per cent of their time with Moët in hand, 14 per cent playing silly buggers in their Lhasa green GTis and 1 per cent at college. Thus the local residents must approach each bend with extreme caution because there's no way of knowing which side of the road Henry will choose to occupy as his blurred vision tells him the strip of tarmac is no longer quite so straight.

Happily, much of the sillier stunt work like trying to get the GTi up the college steps is executed away from the public highway but there's always a chance of the brogue-wearing masses being equally daft in the High Street so you can never be too careful.

Henry chooses his particular shade of GTi so that when he careers off the road – and he does, frequently – he can abandon the wreck without fear of its colour spoiling the countryside, particularly once the rust gets hold. He'll get hold of another GTi from surely the richest VAG dealer in Britain the next day.

Henry's elder brother, a stockbroker in the City, also drives a Lhasa green GTi but when he comes off the road, just as frequently as his sibling, it isn't a field of wheat that breaks his fall. It's usually a lamp-post in Parsons Green, London SW6.

Here, he has to mix it with Camilla taking the children to school, Reg, Ron and Arthur in the builders' truck, Ahmed in his Porsche Turbo and a whole host of Surrey-based commuters as well. All of these people are far too busy with their own hassles and Mach-4 lifestyles to be bothered with the finer points of driving technique so every street corner in Parsons Green is littered with broken glass – a sure sign that Camilla hit Ron and in the ensuing argument, Henry ran into the back of Ahmed.

The Parsons Green recipe, however, is nowhere near as dangerous as the concoction to be found on Britain's motorway network. Here, every weekend the whole lot, from Ethel and Albert to Henry, from Sally Ann to Gary, are thrown together in a massive uncertain bond. Suddenly everyone is taken from his or her own particular niche, where everybody behaves in the same way, and is thrown into a six-lane high-speed highway with thousands of others who are used to behaving quite differently.

Statistics show motorways to be the safest roads on which to travel. This must be because Sally Ann is unlikely to see a friend with whom she must have a chat, the old dears from Woking can't get unduly confused, Gary has no one to impress, there are no broken walls to be mended or lost sheep to be rounded up, Ethel and Albert are still waiting for the RAC in the Dales, the good folk of Birmingham haven't been seen for years so they can't mess things up and neither can people from Oxford who are still stuck on the infernal inner ring road. Henry is probably sober after a spell on the motorway and surprise, surprise, he's quite a good driver; his brother, Camilla, Ron and Ahmed are exchanging insurance particulars in Parsons Green and very pretty girls, on bicycles, in very short skirts, are a very rare sight indeed.

Sweet White Wine

On 15 October this year, wine connoisseurs the world over will focus their attention on a small, riverside village a few miles south-east of Bordeaux.

They will hope to hear that the day dawned to a blanket of fog which, during the morning, gave way to gorgeous autumnal sunshine.

Each subsequent day for the next few weeks, they will expect to receive reports that such weather conditions are persisting and that not one drop of rain has fallen on the plethora of precious vineyards.

If these conditions are met, there's a better than evens chance that we will be treated to a vintage crop of Barsac.

Barsac, evidently, is the world's greatest sweet wine. It is produced in comparatively minute quantities and an average bottle currently costs the off-licence punter here in Britain around £8 – double or treble that for a vintage Château Climens.

Now, I must be honest, I don't much care for white wine unless I'm drunk, in which case I don't care at all. Particularly though, I don't like sweet white wines. And Barsac is the sweetest of them all.

To the uninitiated (me), it looks like the kind of sample policemen take if you're frightened of needles, and tastes like a pound of diluted Silver Spoon.

However, if the figures are anything to go by, my views on the subject are not universally shared. In 1984, Barsac wine producers exported 4263 hectolitres of their 'deep golden nectar', nearly half of which reached the UK. America took a miserable 339 hectolitres which, in a funny sort of way, has to be a feather in Barsac's cork.

Generally speaking, if the Americans like something, I don't, and vice versa, but in this instance, grudgingly, I support their apathy.

What's more, the British are apparently buying the stuff more and more. According to Catherine Manac'h, PR person to Foods and Wines from France Ltd – an organisation set up twenty years ago to promote edible French produce on these shores – the average Briton is becoming more sophisticated. Has she seen how many Nissan Micras roam our roads I wonder?

She takes her argument a stage further by suggesting that, 'Before the war, sweet wines were very popular but ten years ago, Barsac and indeed its near neighbour, Sauternes, were rejected or, at best, merely served as dessert wines.

'One only has to talk to people in the trade and read about the trends with Barsac to realise that it is finding favour once more,' she added.

Her views are echoed by Cyril Ray in his *Book of Wine* where he says, 'There used to be a silly, snobbish prejudice against sweet wines but people who know and make them, know better.'

He then goes into a state of virtual apoplexy while describing how delicious a glass of Barsac is when served with a bowl of raspberries. Other books on the subject accuse you and I of being 'silly snobs' and cite Barsac as an ideal wine to serve, not only with fresh raspberries, but also as an aperitif, as a cocktail base, with cheese and with fish but only, for some reason, if it's in sauce.

In furtherance of this article, you understand, I tried Barsac with a boil-in-the-bag halibut and parsley sauce the other day and it still tasted nasty. It was marginally better with my Dairylea but I wasn't prepared to use my £8 bottle as a cocktail base to experiment in that direction and I shall reserve judgement on the raspberry combination until such fruit is in season.

Experts also claim the wine is particularly outstanding when drunk alongside *pâté de foie gras*. It isn't.

In fairness though, I tend to get very cross with people when

I tell them how marvellous the Peugeot 205 GTi is and they disagree, saying its wing mirrors are the wrong shape.

Doubtless, a wine connoisseur would stick his nose in the air just as though he'd encountered a bottle of 'Château Sans Jambes' if I fatuously declared that Barsac is awful because it's sweet.

Perhaps it's the Bristol of the wine world. Expensive, odd, rare and appreciated only by a few weirdos — sorry, enthusiasts. I needed to find out — hence my expert knowledge on this 15 October business.

You see, Barsac isn't your average wine that just happens to find favour among those blessed with noses and palates more sensitive than Ian Botham on the cocaine issue.

Over half the grapes are discarded if they do not meet the standards laid down by their almost ridiculously picky château *propriétaires* who zealously guard their reputations and, to a lesser extent, their status as second-, or in some cases, first-growth vineyards.

In the Barsac region, the grapes have to be more than just ripe in order to meet these standards. One has to wait for them to have reached an advanced stage of maturity and for them to have been attacked by a minute fungoid growth with a complicated Latin name that has, thankfully, become known as Noble Rot.

Unique in the world to the Sauterne/Barsac region, this mushroom-like fungus would normally be considered a pest, but it is essential in the production of great sweet wine.

As this murdering mushroom wreaks havoc on the poor defenceless fruit, the grape begins to shrivel, thus losing in volume but gaining all the while in sugar content.

But, the plot thickens. The maniacal mushroom will only flourish if, at harvest time (15 October), there is a soupçon of moisture and plenty of sunshine. It seems to like climatic changes — so why on earth does it choose to live in Bordeaux and not Rochdale?

Back to the plot: if it rains at all during harvesting and the warring grape and mushroom are subject to heavy moisture rather than just the right amounts contained in fog, the dreaded and utterly invincible Vulgar Rot moves in and any aspirations for a vintage Barsac are lost.

Evidently, the noble mushroom is a choosy little blighter which won't do as it's supposed to on every piece of fruit. This accounts for the huge wastage a Barsac winegrower has to endure. Such high standards are simply not found anywhere else but they've helped Barsac to a reputation as a region where quality is paramount and quantity is a dirtier word than Frascati.

In pursuance of this quality tag, the Barsac boys widen their individualistic streak still further when it comes to harvesting. Most vineyards send out waves of *camionettes* during October to round up the great unwashed who are then drafted in for picking.

But in Barsac such blanket measures are avoided. Eager children are told exactly what a grape suffering from Noble Rot looks like before they are sent among the vines.

If there are insufficient children around, help is sought from the more intelligent Spaniards who flock across the Pyrenees to help out.

Whereas an average vineyard probably gets its harvesting over and done with in one fell swoop, the eager children and intelligent Spaniards are sent out day after day looking for precisely the right quality of grape which must be picked at exactly the right time. It sounds like a dodgy business to me.

In 1971, it seems the château *propriétaires* were blessed with the right combination of fog, sun and Spanish MENSA candidates because experts claim that was Barsac's best ever year.

However, it isn't just the Noble Rot, the climate and the correct time of picking that count toward perfection. As any local down there will tell you, the soil upon which the vineyards rest is paramount too. Any deeper and apparently the wine would be too vigorous. Any more clay and it would presumably taste like a potter's wheel.

When the harvest is gathered in, the wine undergoes a procedure familiar to any amateur enthusiast. The grapes are crushed very slowly a few times and the resultant slush is allowed to ferment for three or so weeks in barrels made from new oak. Flavour from the wood seeps into the wine and compensates for the lack of tannin given out by the skins which are removed in the production of white wine. After this period is over, locals claim they can tell whether they have a vintage on their hands or not.

When the wine's alcohol content reaches 14.5 per cent, the wine makers decide if fermentation should be stopped and small quantities of sulphur dioxide are added to stop the yeast's activity on the wine – whatever it may be.

Bottling takes place when the wine has been in the casket for three years but in order that it should reach its peak of fitness, you should wait until its tenth birthday before imbibing.

An interesting(?) little booklet called *The Sweet Wines of Bordeaux* says that by this time, its 'oily characteristics, breeding and body should be most evident'. But, it goes on to add that if you decide to hang on, it is vital to check the cork every 20 years. Quite frankly, I have more important things on my mind than remembering to check my corks.

And where pray, in the middle of London, am I to find a place that meets the apparently critical storage conditions set out by the booklet: a cool dark place away from noise, vibration and smell where the bottles can be laid horizontally?

So there you have it. Barsac. A fussy little wine made from grapes, a fungoid growth, sulphur dioxide and essence of oak tree.

No wonder it's supposed to taste so good alongside a pâté that is produced by corking a goose's bottom and force feeding it with grain until its liver is about to explode.

Auto Football

Until a couple of weeks ago, I did not understand what it is about a ball that people find so fascinating.

Every Saturday in the winter, thousands and thousands of people turn out to watch men in little shorts playing football, a game that is not exciting. In the summer, many tens of people watch cricket, which is not only unexciting but terribly confusing as well.

I have never played cricket; at school, however, I spent two afternoons every week playing football because it was the law. Only once did I manage to score a goal and that was only because their goalkeeper, a chap after my own heart, had wandered off to talk to his girlfriend.

I have spent ten years trying to fathom out the reason why people watch sport and I think I now have the answer. They would like to be doing what the people they're watching are doing. People who go to football matches would like to think they could have been good enough to play professionally.

The reason I won't go is because I know for a fact that I could never have done it, even on an amateur basis. Octopi and football do not happy bedfellows make.

At last however, I have found a derivation of football that I do want to play and that I therefore would go and watch regularly if it were played here.

It's called *autofussball* and it's a cross between figure-of-eight stock-car racing, football and Thai boxing. The first thing you need is a pitch which can be of any size and of any surface. Any old car park will do. A stubble field would be even better.

The second thing you need are some old cars. My recommendation is to go for something large with a small engine mounted some considerable distance from the inner wings. A Ford Zephyr? The third thing you need is a 3-foot-diameter, fluorescent ball. And the fourth thing you need is some team-mates, who can come from any walk of life, though I would recommend you find people who walk up and down Oxford Street wearing a sandwich board, talking at length about how they've made a spaceship out of lavatory paper.

There are only two complicated rules. If you touch the ball with your hand, your opponents are allowed to take a penalty which they will miss because it is damnably hard.

The ball is placed 20 feet in front of the goal and the car must be raced at it backwards. Just before impact, the car must execute a J-turn, swiping the ball with its front wing as it spins and, hopefully, getting it in between the posts.

It never happens like that, so touching the ball with your hand is just fine.

The other rule is that defence of the goal-mouth is only permitted if an attacker is within 20 feet and in possession of the ball. If you use your car to block the goal when the attacker is outside the 20-foot marker, he is entitled to take a penalty which he will miss. Blocking the goal, therefore, is always worthwhile.

The only other thing to remember is that you will not be driving home in the car you use to play.

Now, this game is not some kind of fanciful figment of my imagination. I saw it being played in Stuttgart and I have never enjoyed being a spectator so much.

To prepare the cars, steel plates are welded to the bumpers and the windows are kicked out. The drivers do not wear crash helmets or seatbelts. When asked why, they spoke in German about their Andrex Apollos.

At face value, it looked like the red team, with their brace of Opel Asconas and a VW Beetle complete with a stoved-in bonnet for carrying the ball, had to be deemed hot favourites. The white team, believing nimbleness counted for more than strength, had rolled up with an Audi 50, a Renault 5 that wouldn't start and a Nova.

Things looked even more gloomy after five minutes when one of the red Asconas expired and was replaced by a massive Granada estate.

And I must confess that I felt the white team had had it when the Renault, having been bumped into life, coughed up blood the first time it went near the ball and retired.

But I was reckoning without the genius of the Audi driver who, single-handedly, scored sixteen goals before the Granada completely removed just about all its vital organs, by which I mean its engine, transmission and both front wheels.

The Granada, after this savagery, was then accidentally rammed and destroyed by the Beetle which suffered almost no damage whatsoever. Indeed, some fifteen minutes before the final whistle was due, it was the only car left running. That made life really rather easy for its driver who drifted back and forth scoring a goal every 30 seconds or so.

Now remember, this is the Germans I'm talking about here, a race that has almost no sense of humour, a race I can best sum up by the response of a girl in the Avis hire-car centre who was trying to sell me the idea of an Audi 80.

'Look,' I said, 'my briefcase has more space in it than an Audi 80.'

She studied my briefcase for a while before saying, 'No. It hasn't.'

Imagine, therefore, what could become of *autofussball* if it could be developed by the race that brought you the hovercraft and afternoon tea. Imagine, too, if Murray Walker were allowed to commentate.

The Best Man

I am having to practise the art of being boring. I have not been in the pub for a week, I care more for the well-being of my Royal Worcester collection than I do my Alfa and I am now an expert on the subject of vacuum cleaners.

Four inches have been hacked from my hair and when I went shopping for clothes the other day, it was to Hacketts and not Jean Machine.

Good Lord, as I write it is 2 p.m. on a Sunday, a time when normally I'd be in the White Horse, discussing the week's deals and conquests.

But no more. In exactly thirteen days' time, I will be standing at the top of an aisle promising all sorts of things to Beloved and listening to a man with his shirt on back to front talking about how marriage is an honourable institution.

From that moment on, I will be dull. I may even grow a beard.

The last few months have been hell on earth. Family feuds have been commonplace, the caterer said she wouldn't do asparagus rolls, the vicar said his church wouldn't accommodate the 230 people we invited, folk who hadn't been asked but thought they should have been are now ignoring me, and the whole engagement foundered on rocky ground when Beloved said she wanted the wedding list to be at GTC and I wanted it at HR Owen.

Then there was the marquee which was initially ordered with a brown lining, and the honeymoon which couldn't be spent in Thailand because of the weather, the Maldives because of political unrest, Tahiti because it's too far away, Africa because it's full of creepie-crawlies, Europe because it's awash with journalists on car launches or America because it's full of Americans.

But the worst bit of it all was getting the right cars for the right bits in the wedding ceremony.

This little job was entrusted to me. Any car in the world is just a phone call away, they said.

Wrong. The man at Bentley trotted out a ridiculous excuse which, when decoded, spelt out a message indicating that I should go forth and do what I will be spending my honeymoon doing anyway.

The small but perfectly formed chap at BMW was offering a 750, but as he'd be there on the day I figured it prudent to turn him down.

Jaguar, then. Oh yes, they'd be delighted to help with whatever I wanted but Beloved stamped her size seven down – she's tall you see – saying she'd rather roll up at church in a Nissan. It was starting to look like she might have to.

I liked the idea of a Countach, especially as it would mean leaving father-in-law at home, but protocol put the mockers on this brainwave.

I also toyed with the notion of asking to borrow Mitsubishi's hot-air balloon in the hope that the wind was blowing the wrong way and he'd end up in Tunisia. Only joking.

Finally came Range Rover. Yes, Beloved agreed this was a good idea. Yes, said Land Rover, they would be delighted to help.

'Would a black one do?'

'No.'

'How about green?'

'Yes, that would be super.'

'It's an SE.'

'Ooh good.'

Then Beloved entered the equation again, arguing that green was unlucky.

'What other colours have you got?'

'Er . . . brown.'

'Nope.'

'Silver?'

'Yes, yes, silver would be fine.'

'It's not an SE.'

By this stage, I didn't give a toss so long as it was capable of moving an 18-foot father-in-law, a chauffeur and Beloved in a big dress 200 yards from the house to the church.

Then father-in-law found out and said he wouldn't go in a Range Rover and why couldn't we use his Volvo? Using the technique I'd learned from the man at Bentley, I managed to swing him round.

This left me with the problem of finding something to 'go away in'.

I didn't particularly want people to smear lipsticked profanities all over the Alfa, even if it does play second fiddle to the porcelain. Nor did I relish making it work with an exhaust full of shaving foam and a kipper on the manifold.

Just in case I had to use it, and it decided to play silly sods at the critical moment, I took the precaution of booking a 75 V6. Just in case.

So, reserves in place, the hard work began.

Various circuses said they were a little reticent about lending me an elephant. And I failed to find anyone who owns a camel, let alone someone who would let my friends tie some balloons to its testicles.

Someone suggested a horse and cart would be a good wheeze, but he is the sort of person who has a velour, button-backed sofa which he calls a settee. So I ignored him. And his advice.

A tractor? What if it's raining? A steam engine? How does it get there? A good old vintage Rolls-Royce? Naff, very naff.

Then the best man stepped into the fray. He absolutely refuses to tell me what he has fixed up, saying only that it will make everyone laugh.

I am therefore frightened. I just know that it will be a Nissan Sunny ZX with side stripes. If so, his colleagues will wonder why he's turned up at work with his head on back to front.

Racing Jaguars

The pundits are predicting doom 'n' gloom time in Coventry. There is to be an XR3i Sovereign and a Daimler Granada. There will be a medium-sized Jaguar with Ford running gear and a Scorpio chassis. John Egan will be replaced by Donald E. Dieselburger junior, and the XJ-S will get tartan seats.

Quite aside from product juggling and the Americanisation of Jaguar's board, the economic ramifications must be taken into account as well. Unemployment is to double. Sterling will crash, the stock market will take on bearish dimensions and the government will fall.

I, however, know how to prevent all this. If Ford would appoint me as chairman of Jaguar, I would put Mercedes and BMW out of business in ten minutes. A quarter of an hour after that, Toyota would pull the plug on Lexus and Nissan would scrap Infiniti.

Let's just say you're a Gieves-and-Hawkes-suited BZW banker. You live in Barnes, are 40 and have a wife and two children aged six and four. Horrid huh? Anyway, protocol dictates that you must have a sober saloon, though the years haven't advanced so much that it has to be a Volvo. Of course, you have a BMW.

But it's time for a change. You've heard about Jaguar's sometimes successful efforts in Group C racing. You know there is a JaguarSport division and you keep reading in financial pages about D- and E-types selling for millions.

Yes, you reckon, Jaguar are making sporty cars once more. So you tool down to Follets in your 735i and you take a test drive. And you are horrified because Jaguar don't make sporty cars at all. Jaguar are to motordom what Dunlopillo are to bedding. You make a mental note that, when you are 50, you will come back to Jaguar. But for now, those Teuton Futon people at BMW will do just fine.

The first new car to emerge from Coventry under my dictator-ship will be a standard, manual, 4-litre XJ6 but it will have big BBS wheels, firmed up and lowered suspension, toughened up and speed-related power steering, sports seats, and ever so slightly flared wheel arches. And all its chrome will be flushed down the lavatory.

It will sell for exactly the same price as the standard 4-litre saloon and it will have an appeal among 40-year-old BZW bankers from Barnes.

The JaguarSport idea is very clever but not clever enough. They should be a wholly owned Jaguar thing. They should not allow automatic cars out of their gates. *And they should not make cars that have cream steering wheels.* Cream steering wheels, like white socks and beards, are for riff-raff. BZW bankers do not wear white socks. BZW bankers do not like cream steering wheels.

And if an American wants a car with a cream steering wheel, he can buy a Lincoln.

BMW obviously don't know that I am to be chairman of Jaguar because they recently took me around their Motorsport division, and now I have seen their mistakes.

I will not build my JaguarSport factory on an industrial estate next door to an odour-eater factory. And I will not be so stupid as to build it in Daimlerstrasse either. When I am looking for people to work in it, I will not insist they all look exactly like Ian Botham. And I will allow them to spill oil on the floor.

I will also make sure that every car which wears a JaguarSport motif is a proper JaguarSport car. Only the M5 and the M3 convertible are 'handmade' in Daimlerstrasse. The M3 saloon and the M635 coupe are 'line' cars.

In addition, I will not allow Jaguars to wear JaguarSport

badging just because they have a spoiler designed by a JaguarSport tea-boy.

Most importantly of all, anyone caught driving around with the equivalent of an 'M' badge on the back of their automatic XJ6 2.9 will be visited in the night by my secret service department who will wear leather coats and tall boots.

Believe you me, these rules will ensure that JaguarSport cars are very exclusive indeed.

The tricky bit is making them better than the astonishingly good M5 with which they would have to compete. Even on this point though, I have an answer. You don't get the best out of a workforce if you promise them sweeties when they get things right. You get the best out of a workforce if you promise to beat them up when they get things wrong. Having Dachau eleven kilometres down the road helps.

When all is said and done, I will have the current range of cars selling to the pensioners for whom they were designed. In addition, I will have a range that appeals to everyone else.

They will make money too; lots of it. Enough to pay for the racing programme, anyway. And they will help back up the pictures being painted by the Group C cars, the current XJ-Rs and the D-Types that are dominating all Jaguar stories in the newspapers.

If Jaguar can stand on their own two (or four) feet, shrugging off competition from Japan, Germany and America like you or I would shrug off a mild itch, Ford will not feel the need to start meddling. If, however, Jaguar plunge along their current course, being so vulnerable that a 0.5 cent shift in the dollar/pound exchange rate can screw the whole thing up, then expect to see Ford Fiesta XJ6s in your local showrooms soon.

If that is too awful to bear, simply buy a share or two and vote for me when the time comes.

Non-Sleeker Celica

Any chance of staying awake evaporated when the man said what sounded like, 'We have used organic rice to create neutral sexiness.' Until that point, I had been grappling with waves of boredom, pulling faces like rock guitarists do when they hit the highest note possible on a Gibson Les Paul.

But it was hopeless. I wouldn't have been all that interested even if it had been presented in a recognisable language. In a version of Engrish where all the 'l's are pronounced 'r's, sleep was a merciful relief.

This was the pan–European press raunch of the new Toyota Celica, a car I had already decided I was going to hate because of its extreme ugliness.

Toyota had taken over Cannes for the purposes of introducing it to the press. Here, the massed ranks of Britain's motor scribblers were confronted by several serious-looking German equivalents and a bevy of Danes who seemed to be much, much more concerned with the whereabouts of the nearest bar. Up front there were a bunch of Japanese chappies and an American called Reich. It was his job to act as translator. We shall call him Third.

After a great deal of sycophantic bowing and some blather about how hugely grateful they were to us for sparing some time to spend a couple of days in the south of France at their expense, the slide show began. So too did my war with the land of nod.

There were the usual charts showing how exhaust interference has been reduced, but stuck in the middle of them was a picture of a naked woman. This, Third claimed, is what the new Celica looks like.

No it doesn't. No one will ever mistake it for a naked woman.

And nor, despite Toyota's protestations, will it be mistaken for a pouncing cheetah either.

The British at this point began to snigger, some at the absurdity of it all, others at the Germans who were still furiously taking notes, and one or two at the Danes who were trying to catch the eye of a barman.

Finally, it was a time for questions and answers. Now, I've never understood the point of such an exercise because, if as a journalist you have something you wish to find out, it is always better to do it when no one else is in earshot.

This, however, was different. This was an excuse for some serious smartarsery. I asked what evidence there was that people want to buy cars that look like naked ladies.

Pleased with my eloquence, I turned to lap up the 'go get 'em boy' looks from various colleagues. But after much debate in Japanese, the panel crushed my ardour with their answer: 'It is a rounded car.'

Now, I suppose it would have been sensible to persist, arguing that if they spoke Engrish well enough to deliver a technical press conference like this one, then they should damn well stop pretending they didn't understand a straightforward question. But the Japanese have perfected the art of humility to such an extent that compassion simply bubbles to the surface in even the most arrogant of cynics.

The next day I was determined to tell whoever was interested that I didn't like the car one bit; that there are two ways of inducing a bout of vomiting. You can stick a couple of fingers down your throat or you can look at a Celica.

Instead, when confronted by an eager-looking Toyota minion who was keen to hear my thoughts, I said, 'Oh, it's quite nice.'

When the Germans or the British, or even the French, ask you what you think of their cars, you tell them straight. When it's a Japanese man, he manages to park an expression on his face that's doe-eyed, hangdog and sweet all at once.

Last year, I went to upwards of 60 beautifully organised, well-presented press introductions and I came home, aware that I could hit the word processor afterwards and say what I wanted.

There's the nagging doubt with the Celica that if I say it's not very good, and it isn't, several engineers on the project may be ordered to fall on their pencils. Or more likely, they will scurry around and have a replacement lined up in the time it takes people at Austin Rover to scratch their backsides and organise a meeting to discuss things.

I have a plan, and judging by what the man from the *Daily Mail* said about the Celica, he has it too. This plan will redress the balance of payments, bring down interest rates and ensure that Mr Kinnock is kept out of Number 10 for another five years.

We scribblers must say the Celica is an excellent car and that you should all go out and buy one tomorrow, or even this afternoon if you have time. This will lull the Japanese into a false sense of security and they will not start work on a replacement, thinking all is well.

You, in the meantime, will believe everything we've written and will take a test drive. But you won't buy the car because it is ugly, there is no space inside and you can't see out of it properly.

It will take months for sales figures to show the Celica has fallen on stony ground, precious months that the Europeans can use to finish scratching their backsides and get on with things.

The Japanese will learn, hopefully when it is too late, that the Dunkirk spirit is alive and well and living in Fulham.

Green Machine

The woman in the hotel was most insistent that the coastal path from Wadebridge to Padstow was absolutely level.

It mattered. It mattered because she had suggested we hire bicycles and go for a ride. She talked about how we'd enjoy the fresh air and how we'd be ready for a pint at the other end. She talked about the herons that we'd see and how the countryside was some of the most beautiful in Britain. And, she maintained, it was as flat as a pancake, as level as a crossing.

She was half right too. We paid our four pounds each for the 18-speed Dirt Fox 'hogs' and, after a five-mile ride, arrived in Padstow, surprised at the ease of the journey.

Sure, we all wanted pints badly and sure, I was grateful for the company of the O'Tine family and their son, Nic.

Over a game of dominoes in the London Inn near Padstow's harbour, we talked in a New Year's resolution sort of way about how it might be a good idea to have bicycles in London, how they would keep the dreaded DR code from our driving licences and how we could get fit at the same time . . . fresh air . . . bulging muscles . . . reduced congestion . . . blah . . . blah.

As we spoke though, some idiot was moving the countryside around. Basically, he tilted it so that the aforementioned completely level path became something not that far removed from Porlock Hill. After half a mile on the way back my legs hurt like hell. Not long after that, the hips started asking the head what the hell was going on and then the lungs just stopped.

In a futile bid to pacify these striking bits, the brain started to think a little more seriously about the bike's eighteen gears. But it was hopeless. In first my legs spun round like a washing machine on its final rinse cycle and, in everything from second to eighteenth, it felt like I was towing a 16-ton weight.

I swore, right there and then, that I would never ride a bicycle again. It is my New Year's resolution. Last year, my New Year's resolution was never to set foot in Spain again and, accordingly, I have just turned down Ford's invitation to the launch of the four-wheel-drive Sierra Cosworth in Barcelona.

Riding a bicycle can't possibly do any good whatsoever. Had I not dismounted and walked the last two miles, I would now be dead – the most unhealthy thing I can think of.

The bit of London where I live is pretty flat but getting to my favourite watering hole in Wandsworth involves a bridge. That means an incline must be tackled and that, in turn, means a heart attack. Plus, I have been reading recently that cycling in London now does you more harm than good because you are in among the traffic, breathing in the resultant fumes more deeply than ordinarily might be the case because it's all so damnably strenuous.

Now, I'm as green as a screen and will willingly drive to the bottle bank, resplendent in my ozone-friendly armpit spray and recycled jumper. As I struggled up that Cornish mountain, I was scarcely able to believe that I had actually considered only a moment or two earlier the notion of buying the ridiculous two-wheeled contraption that I was now having to push.

My mind was consumed with hatred. Hatred for the man who'd made me pay for the privilege of hiring his horrid bike. Hatred for the woman who said the path was flat. Hatred for the meddler who moved Porlock Hill. Hatred for Walter Raleigh, and his silly tobacco plant.

Darkness had almost fallen by the time I arrived back in Wadebridge. And it was almost morning before ACAS had sorted out some kind of settlement with the striking legs, hips and lungs. No one has ever been able to talk about how it feels to be that ill because anyone who has been that ill is now dead as a result.

I was brought back to life on the way home with a thought

that should come as a crumb of comfort to all those who like their motoring more than their bicycling. Sane people in other words. I was driving, at the time, an Audi 90 Quattro 20V which, like all Audis, has a catalytic converter shoved up its jaxi. And I know enough about cats to know that they make cars very nearly as clean as bicycles. Cleaner, in fact.

Sure the Audi still produces a teeny bit of nitrogen oxide, a little carbon monoxide and some carbon dioxide which would be turned into oxygen by the trees if only cyclist types would stop chopping down forests to fuel their environmentally friendly wood-burning stoves.

But now look at the bicycle which, unlike the galvanised Audi, will one day rust away and be discarded to mess up the countryside.

I don't know for certain but I'd make a big bet that there are more old bicycles on the bed of the sea than there are old Audis.

If you cycle from Wadebridge to Padstow, you will pollute the air with obscenities as you go, you will arrive dead and your bicycle will be tossed into the estuary where it will pollute the river and very probably snare one of the herons. If you drive an Audi from Wadebridge to Padstow, especially if you drive it with the windows down, the herons will wave cheerily.

You might not want a pint quite so badly when you get there but if you have to drive back again you couldn't have had one anyway.

Reasons for buying a car   8
Reasons for buying a bicycle   0

Democratic Party

It's funny, but for ages I've been under the misapprehension that Britain is a democracy. I suppose I concluded this from our electoral system. Two parties present their manifestos to the nation and after we've studied these and compared Thatcher to the Welshman, we vote. The party with the most seats is judged to be victorious. It all seems very fair to me.

Democracy works in all sorts of other ways too. As a shareholder in many companies, I am forever being asked to vote on takeover bids. If 55 per cent of Ford workers want to go on strike, they will be called out on strike. If six in a group of eleven want a burger and five want a pizza, everyone goes to a local McDonald's and not into one of those Pizza Huts.

I do not want a Labour government to achieve power, but if a majority of voters goes completely bonkers and allows that Welshman into the hot seat, I will accept the decision, albeit with bad grace, and move to a country with some common sense. Democracy works. Majority rule works. So how come we in Britain are obsessed with the interests of minorities?

If I were to approach my local council for funds to start a theatre group, they would turn me away, arguing that I was too middle class and far too apathetic about Mike Gatting's rebel cricket tour. The money would go instead to someone who has a predilection for members of the same genital group and a definite intention to employ at least three whales.

Now, if the majority isn't affected by a minority's aspirations, then it doesn't really matter all that much. It must be part of living in a caring society, I suppose. But when a minority wants something that is deeply offensive to a majority, then it must be told to bugger off. This is why every one of London's 5000 buses should be burned and their drivers put to death.

Each weekday, 9.3 million people move about the capital in cars or taxis, but there are just 3.3 million 'bus users'. For sure, this is a big majority but it's bigger still when you remember that if you take a bus to work, you sure as hell have to use it to get home again. That means the 3.3 million 'bus users' becomes 1.7 million. Then there are those who commute on the bus *and* use it at lunchtime.

Even London Regional Transport admit that only about 1 million people use a bus each day. This means that there are nine people in cars for every one on a bus. On that basis, it should be nine times harder for a bus to get around on our roads than it is for a car.

However, this is not so. There are 45 miles of bus lanes in London which, at certain times, cannot legally be used by cars. A majority, therefore, is squeezed into the resultant traffic jams and has to watch a minority whizz by in acrylic coats and plastic shoes.

To hammer the point home, buses are now to be seen carrying advertisements on their rumps telling car drivers that the bus lanes are London's arteries. 'If you drive your car in one, you're a clot' proclaims the tag line.

So, I pay £100 a year for the privilege of sitting in a jam, caused by a bus lane which is being used by people who pay a few pence. That is certainly not democratic.

Even when the buses aren't working, you aren't allowed to use these lanes, and the police, displaying their usual common sense, emerge in force to hammer this point home.

And who the hell do bus drivers think they are? As soon as the last pensioner is aboard, they pull out into the traffic stream, oblivious to the fact that I might be alongside at the time.

Only the other day, the avoiding action I was forced to take nearly resulted in that silly stolen baby being taken off the front pages. And in the ensuing discussion, the driver had the audacity to use the f word while explaining there was a poster on the back of his bus telling me to give way whenever he wants to set off. Why should I? I am young, with a living to earn and a mortgage to pay. His passengers are old or unemployed and cannot therefore be in much of a hurry.

To prove that buses do nothing but clog things up, you should look at what happened when they all went on strike last year. Many left-wing radio stations predicted chaos would result as everyone took their cars instead of the bus. This is rubbish because people who use the buses don't actually own cars.

In fact, I have never seen the traffic in London flow so well, which is hardly surprising when you consider that huge, red oblongs, each of which is bigger than my flat, weren't stopping every few yards. A great deal of effort is used to dissuade people from stopping their cars, even momentarily, at the side of the road; yet it is fine for vehicles three times larger than even the biggest Mercedes to stop whenever and wherever they damn well want.

As a result of that day, I am of the opinion that *the* biggest cause of traffic congestion in the capital is the public transport system.

One of these days, someone is going to have to get tough; someone is going to have to explain that buses must go, that they are the principal cause of traffic jams and that they have no place in a democracy.

Unless this happens soon, I will move to Moscow where special lanes are reserved for rich and important people such as myself, and not the proletariat scum in their trams.

Cat Lover

I have chopped the word 'free' off one of those trendy stickers they give you in garages so that it now says 'I love lead'. It is in the back window of my Alfa and it is meant to be a joke. But I'll tell you something: people who won't eat meat have no sense of humour.

Now look. I have green armpits and each morning, I wipe my bottom with recycled lavatory paper. Whenever it's humanly possible I buy unleaded petrol and I make all the right noises about elephant hunts and Japanese whaling fleets. I even stopped buying tuna after one of those tabloid newspapers said that each time a bundle of tuna is trawled in, a whole load of dolphins are killed.

But this, according to my vegetarian friends, is simply not enough. I was even described as a half-wit the other day because I wouldn't give those anti-nuclear idiots at Greenpeace any of my hard-earned money.

I simply wondered out loud how, on the one hand, they could want the CEGB or whatever they call themselves now to stop burning fossil fuels and, on the other, campaign for the decommissioning of nuclear power stations.

What do they want us to do? Get the cows we don't eat to work treadmills? Power our CFC-free fridges on manure? The computer I'm using at this moment runs on electricity and I really don't give a stuff how it gets to the plug just so long as it keeps getting there cheaply, efficiently and, if it's at all possible, greenly too.

The trouble is that the loonies who get taken in by this environmental crap lose all sense of reality. And with it goes their sense of humour. Forgetting to take a plastic bag to the supermarket becomes a life or death struggle. Making jokes about the Irish or religion is considered to be acceptable but woe betide anyone who dares to appear on television and poke fun at the greenhouse effect.

What staggers me is how damnably knowledgeable everyone is about the trendy, vegetarian matters of the moment. We all know the name of every Mexican trawlerman who has killed a dolphin; we know exactly how much rainforest is being destroyed each hour; we know how hard it is to recycle super- market carrier bags; and we know just how much effluent there is in the North Sea.

But people who can trot out the number of elephants slaugh- tered a week last Tuesday don't seem to have the first clue about what the difference is between unleaded petrol and catalytic converters.

What with her Greenpeace sweatshirt and her penchant for going on and on about nuclear disarmament, the girl who called me a half-wit is easily the greenest person I know. But when I asked why she bought a Toyota MR2 which doesn't have a catalytic converter, she said, 'I don't need a catalytic converter because my car already runs on unleaded petrol.'

Now, I sat her down and tried to explain that although her car does not produce any lead, it still chucks out 78 lb of unburned hydrocarbons, 50 lb of nitrogen oxides and more than 1000 lb of carbon monoxide in one year. If she had bought an Audi 80, which does have a catalytic converter, then she would be respon- sible for just 7 lb of hydrocarbons, 8 lb of nitrogen oxides and 30 lb of carbon monoxide.

And do you want to know what her answer was when pre- sented with these remarkable facts and figures? Would you like to guess? She said, and this is verbatim, 'That's all very well but the Audi isn't very trendy, is it?'

Somehow, someone is going to have to get through to people like this and explain what the cat business is all about.

A massive advertising campaign seemed to be getting the

message about unleaded fuel across, but along came Esso and messed it all up with their Super Grade Plus or whatever it's called. Even I don't understand what that ad with the white Orion going green is all about.

Saab's elegant campaign with the *Green Wellie* headline was a masterstroke but they spoilt it with a reference, in the body of the text, to a little-known fact that most of their cars are re-cyclable. More than a couple of people have rung me to ask whether 'these reusable catalytic converter wotsits' are worth the bother.

And that Audi television commercial with the man rushing in his catalysed 90 Quattro to see his wife have a baby prompted Beloved to remark that if he hadn't had the cat, he would have got there in time for the big moment! Audi rarely cock up their adverts but, my God, that one was a real mess.

Basically, there's no concerted marketing effort with cats, and some people think they're an alternative to unleaded petrol, while others reckon they take the form of a ball of cotton wool rammed up the exhaust which prevents the car from reaching a speed of over 10 mph. Most, however, have never heard of them.

If and when the message ever does get across and we're as well versed in the functions of rhodium as we are in the antics of Brazilian bulldozer drivers, let's not get paranoid.

I tried to tell a farmer the other day that the funniest news item I had ever seen was that mad cow doing the hokey-cokey. For some extraordinary reason, he did not appear to agree. If the earth does suddenly implode, I'll be the one at the back giggling.

Goodbye to All That

Last night, Robert Dougal, the ex-news reader, stole my car. I came out of the house in the morning and found it had gone but, strangely, this didn't bother me unduly. I simply hired a cab.

Even more strangely, when I arrived at work the car was parked outside the office. All day I sat on the telephone telling people that there is such a thing as a considerate thief.

But then, in the evening, it had gone again. Now this time I *was* angry and set off on foot to look for it. I stomped about for a few hours and eventually wound up in a swampy wood full of mangrove trees and mist.

A car tore by. *My* car. The roof had been cut off and the seats replaced with chairs from a 1.3L, the pretty alloys were gone and every remaining panel was smashed.

There were four people in it, jeering and shouting as it sploshed through the water and careered over the mangrove roots. Then it crashed. I ran over and was horrified to find Robert Dougal trying to extricate himself from the driver's seat. Then the *Today* programme came on the radio, I got up, got dressed and went to work. Puzzled as hell.

Mystic Meg has never once addressed me. Week after week, she fills her page in *Sunday* magazine with messages from beyond the grave and up and down the country people called Brian rip up their sofas looking for the missing millions.

I don't pay any attention to Doris Stokes because I believe that when you're dead, you are a piece of meat which rots and makes a funny smell.

I also don't believe there is such a place as heaven, and anyway, even if there is, Christianity is based on the concept of forgiveness so I shall simply roll up at the Pearly Gates and tell Pete that I'm sorry.

And never mind death, I can't really grapple with the concept of strange mind-bendery when we're alive either. I don't believe in ghosts, the Bermuda Triangle or spoon bending. But what about dreams? There are as many people out there who try to read something into what goes on between our ears at night as there are people trying to read things into what goes on between our legs.

If we dream, it is simply an active mind not shutting down properly. But that said, just recently I have been a tormented soul between the hours of one to five. And I'd like to know why.

Last night I moved house, which would have been a peculiar thing to do as I did it for real only last week. However, before going to bed, I had just watched *The Chain*, so that might have had something to do with it.

Regularly I can fly, and it's really special, soaring over London's proletariat who point and gawp quite openly.

Hell, I have even played table tennis against myself and every time I missed a shot, a piece of purple velvet was pressed by an unseen hand against my face, giving me an electric shock.

I think I might like to have met Sigmund Freud so that he could have explained what it was that made me mad. But as I can't I guess his granddaughter will have to do.

And believe me, I *am* mad, because this is my last column for *Performance Car*.

I began writing for the magazine shortly after it underwent the metamorphosis from *Hot Car*, and that was nearly ten years ago. Since then, there have been two changes of ownership, three editors and countless staff alterations. But I really do believe that, right now, it is a better magazine than at any time in its history and more, that it is a better magazine than any of the others.

I love the way that it flies in the face of current namby-pamby thinking and I constantly use its blossoming sales as back-up in arguments with hideous and spotty vegan types who decry the car along with meat and the free market. Furthermore, these ten years have been happy times. Without *Performance Car*, I would never have been to Iceland. I would never have been in a stunt plane or a Class One powerboat. I would not know how to drive round the Nurburgring or where the heated-rear-window switch is in a Countach. Perhaps most important of all, were it not for *Performance Car*, I would not be on *Top Gear*.

So why am I going? Well, last month a Richard Morris of Walton-on-the-Hill in Surrey wrote a letter to *PC*, arguing that I am unfunny, unobjective, insulting and self-indulgent. He went on, for some considerable time, and ended up by saying that I should give it up. Well, Mr Morris, you win. I am all of the things you say, and I'm leaving. If anyone out there disagrees with him, just contact the magazine who I'm sure will be happy to put you in touch.

Before I go though, I would like to thank the following people who have helped make me rich. Jesse Crosse, the very first editor of *Performance Car* and the man who took me on; Dave Calderwood, for keeping me on when he took over and Paul Clark the current *obergruppen führer* who obviously disagrees with Mr Morris.

Then there is Peter Tomalin, the deputy editor who seems to understand what it is I've been trying to do, and John Barker, the road-test editor, who doesn't. But then he never seems to mind.

On top of all this, there are countless motor industry PR figures who have been tirelessly supportive, even when I've ridiculed their products: John Evans of Mercedes Benz and Peter Frater of Daihatsu, Ferrari and Chrysler lead the charge, with Chris Willows of BMW, Tim Holmes of Nissan and Colin Walkey of Land Rover in hot pursuit.

I cannot forget Jonathan Gill, my partner and Frances Cain, my other partner, whose level headedness has ensured I've yet to see the inside of a libel court.

Finally, there is you lot, the people who have read this column over the years. I did my best and I guess it's just a shame Mr Morris had to go and spoil it all.

That then, is that.

Down, Rover

Round about now, the Rover board will be sitting down to decide whether it is a good idea to start work on a two-seater sports car. A new MG, in other words.

It isn't.

Enthusiasts throughout the land are running around, starting campaigns along the lines of 'kill an Argie, win a Metro' to make them build it. Great bores of today are pointing angrily at the Mazda MX-5, saying that it should be an MG and that if Rover weren't so completely hopeless it would have been.

The fact is, Mazda spent six years developing the MX-5. They started with a piece of paper so fresh it was still a tree and they invested billions of yen and millions of man hours to make sure it was right in every detail. Only the engine has been 'lifted' from current production lines.

Rover could not have started work on such a car six years ago. Back then, under government ownership, they couldn't take the top off a biro without having 23 eight-hour meetings to discuss the implications. They had sod all money and as a result, they were to the world of motor manufacturing what Paddy Ashdown is to politics – completely and spectacularly useless.

If they had started work on a two-seater soft top then, it would have emerged at the right time but it would have had an Ambassador engine and an Allegro-style quartic steering wheel.

There is no doubt that Rover are much leaner these days, but it's too late to start thinking about putting one over Mazda. Besides, lean though they may be, I'm still not absolutely certain that they'd get an affordable sports car right.

The problem is, they are too small to invest what Mazda invested and too big to make a go of it on a TVR or Lotus scale.

In order for economics of scale to work, they would need to make thousands of so-called MGs a week, which means they'd have to be cheap. And if they were going to be cheap, then they would have to be fashioned from whatever is lying around in the parts bin.

That means front-wheel drive, whether they base it on the CRX or the Rover 200. And although I couldn't give a stuff whether a car is front-, rear- or four-wheel drive, I do believe that people who want a sports car prefer the busy end to be behind them.

Then there's the engine problem. Yes, the K series is a good effort but it's hardly a ripsnorter is it? A turbo version perhaps? No no no. Turbo engines are crap. And don't get excited about the possibility of a 3.9i V8 – just think of the torque steer. So it has to be the CRX engine.

But if they do this, the MG purists will be running around, waving their arms and pulling their beards, whinging about how Rover have sold out. If they use the CRX engine and the CRX floorpan, George Simpson will probably end up like Georges Besse. Beardies have the most awful temper, I've always found.

The Rover parts bin is filled to overflowing with some lovely items, but trying to make them into a sports car is like trying to make an origami ice-breaker out of six-inch nails. And if they do the decent thing and design the car from scratch, it will end up being more expensive than the Koenig Testarossa drop head.

The worst thing is that even if they get the green light now and use the best bits they can find, it won't reach the Rover showrooms until midway through 1993 at the earliest.

No one can say for sure what motordom will be like then, but here are a few fairly safe bets. The roads will be chocabloc. Kinnock will be taxing cars like they're going out of fashion. Which they will be. Anything even remotely sporty will be prone to vandalism by marauding gangs of environmentally aware Islingtonites. All in all, it will be a lot more difficult to enjoy a soft-top sports car than it is now.

For heaven's sake, even the Tories are doing their level best to make sure we don't spend our disposable income. Labour will ban anything even remotely hedonistic. Soft tops are a fashion accessory and fashions change.

Now, if Rover could squeeze a car in very fast before the Welshman gets into power and before Sizewell B blows up, maybe they'll make some money out of it for a couple of years. How about lopping the roof off a CRX, fitting an MGish interior and applying some new badges? It would be a pretty horrid effort, I'm sure, but the badge, the engine and the looks would ensure that Mazda had a run for their money in the UK at least. Perhaps in America too.

I'm fearful, though, that if they do go for this type of thing, it will be the new Metro that has the can opener taken to it and not the CRX. I'm also fearful that a not very good convertible would be a lot less desirable than a faster, cheaper and infinitely more practical hot hatch.

The MG of old wasn't a very nice car then, and because of all sorts of things that are way beyond Rover's control, a modern version probably wouldn't be a nice car now. And even if it was nice, it wouldn't be appropriate.

I have a message for George Simpson – don't build a new MG now because you've missed the boat, but the next time an opportunity looks like presenting itself, for heaven's sake, walk around the building, shouting a lot. For now, though, go down to the market research department and ask everyone in there what the bloody hell they were doing six years ago.

History Lesson

Before administering a weekly beating, my headmaster usually took the trouble to sit me down and explain why he felt it necessary to burnish my bottom. I never listened to a word he said. This is because the chair I had to sit in, and subsequently bend over, was quite simply the most comfortable piece of furniture in the world.

And not only that; the room itself was exquisite with oak-panelled walls, 40-watt standard lamps, Chinese wash rugs and exquisite antiques. Being beaten in winter was especially pleasant as there was usually a huge log fire too.

I daresay that if I'd been educated in the comprehensive system, the whippings would have been really rather unpleasant, but at a 450-year-old public school, they were a joy.

Now the reason why I enjoyed my weekly visits to the headmaster, indeed the reason why I would deliberately get into serious trouble, was that his study, his whole house actually, felt absolutely right. From the moment that big front door creaked open, you were in a world of great taste. There was a sense of history and even the smell was right.

This is probably why I like being in a Series 3 Jaguar XJ12. Again, the smell is right; again, it's tasteful; again, there's a sense of history.

No one will buy a car if they do not feel comfortable with it, and by that I do not mean comfortable in the literal sense of the word.

When the door closes, the interior has to feel good; it must be an extension of a person's personality. And when he drives past a shop window, the reflection has to show a man at ease. I do not enjoy driving past mirrors in a Yugo Sana. I will not drive past anything in a Nissan Sunny ZX Coupe.

Now, of course, everyone has different tastes and this, of course, explains why one car with an interior that I consider to be perfectly horrid will appeal to someone who has purple back-lighting in the recesses on their fireplace.

This whole issue was brought to light by a drive in the new Lexus. It was a drive I could not enjoy. Make no mistake: this is one hell of a car, what with its cold cathode ray instrumentation, its quite superb 4-litre V8 engine and a ride that, in Germany at least, was unparalleled.

Anyone who buys a car for its technical sophistication will undoubtedly covet the Lexus a lot. But I wonder; do people buy £35,000 luxury saloons for their technical sophistication? Or do they buy them because they 'feel' right?

The Lexus has been six years in the making and it shows. Just about every single feature has been very carefully thought out indeed, where all the features from Rolls-Royce, Mercedes and BMW have been harmonised in one stately, if not terribly attractive, body.

Yet, to my mind, it does not feel right in the way that a technically inferior Jaguar does.

Toyota unashamedly admit that during the Lexus's development, engineers carefully studied the competition. Good ideas were aped and there's nothing wrong with that. Where others had compromised for whatever reason and Toyota felt they could do better, they did.

But you can't copy a feeling. You can't endow a whole new marque with a sense of history. If you try, and Toyota have, you end up with something that smacks of being *nouveau riche*. This is a motorised equivalent of someone with a whole lot more money than style. A millionaire urchin. George Walker. Mickie Most. Frank Warren.

Do not, for heaven's sake, take this as a criticism of the Lexus.

There's just as much new money in this country as old money. There will be just as many people who will like the pop-out plastic drinks holder as there are who'll hate it. I hate it.

No question that Lexus is a better car than an XJ12. No question that the Jap car's electric seatbelt-height adjuster is well sighted, no question that its thinking four-speed switchable overdriven auto box is so much smoother than the cast-iron three-speeder of the Jaguar.

But if I had to drive past a shop window, I would ensure that I was in the XJ. Gary Lineker, I'm sure, would prefer to be in the Lexus.

The odd thing is that I quite like being seen in a Sierra 4 × 4 yet I can't get into a Granada without feeling acutely embarrassed. I'll happily swan around in a Volvo 740 estate but need a Balaclava helmet before I'll set foot in a T-series Mercedes.

I'll pootle about all day long in a Lancia Y10, wearing a smug 'I know something you don't know' expression. Yet in that little funster, the Charade GTti, I have to have a sticker on the back window telling passers-by it's not my car.

I cannot come to terms with Land Rover Discovery because it has stripes on the side and a blue interior, and I simply will not try a so-called special edition. And could you honestly drive around in a Nissan Bluebird Executive? Of course not. Not unless you had a box on your head.

The point of all this is very simple: people should, and usually do, buy something with which they feel comfortable, irrespective of how clever it may be.

Every single road test report on the Nissan 200SX will tell you just what a great car it is. They will talk of the power and the sophistication of that rear-wheel-drive chassis. They will talk too of the svelte looks and of the great precision in the build quality. But they will not dismiss it out of hand, as I do and you should, because it has brushed nylon seats.

Ski's the Limit

When you are getting on for seven feet tall and you have size nine feet, there are all sorts of things you should not do. Tightrope walking over the Niagara Falls is one of them. Skiing is another.

Manfully, I have been to the mountains twice a year for the past three years in a desperate bid to become good at getting around with planks on my feet. I even bought a primary-coloured anorak.

But until April of this year, I have always failed. In 1988 at La Clusaz, I broke my thumb. In January 1990, at Val d'Isere, I tore the ligaments on the inside of my right knee and buggered up my cartilage for good measure as well.

What makes this chapter of disasters even harder to stomach is that I'm so careful that if I ski on a glacier, it gets to the bottom of the mountain faster than I do.

You cannot begin to imagine how vigorous my snowplough schusses are. You have never seen such fantastically tight step turns. I am capable of getting from an easterly traverse to a westerly one without being on the fall line for more than .003 of a second. I can ski for half an hour and only be three feet further down the hill than when I set off.

And when you remember that I have to stop every fifteen minutes for a cigarette, it doesn't take a professor of pure mathematics to work out that it takes me 1026 hours to do a mile. That's 42 days.

All this has changed now, though. On my last trip to the Alps, to the summer resort of Hintertux in Austria, people gawped in awe as I sped by. Two girls offered me their bodies. A child called me Franz and asked for my autograph. Even the Germans, amazed at the sheer length of my skis, parted like the waters of the

Red Sea to allow me on to the chairs and T-bars without a wait.

Cubby Broccoli has just telephoned to ask if I will do the stunts for Timothy Dalton in the next Bond extravaganza, *007 Kills Some Arabs Because the Russians are OK These Days*.

So how, you may be wondering, has this extraordinary metamorphosis come about?

What happened was that every company in Europe that begins with the letter 'S' got together to organise a late-season skiing trip for members of Her Majesty's Press Corps. Saab provided the cars. Sealink came up with the boats. Salomon handed out the equipment and Servus, the Austrian Tourist Authority, paid for accommodation expenses.

Also on hand were a brace of chaps who coach the British Olympic ski team. I was allocated to John Sheddon, who said it didn't matter how I skied, because there are only two types of turn – left and right – and skis are implements to get you from A to B. My kinda guy. There was none of this 'Benzee knees' nonsense you get from those peroxide poofs with tight red all-in-one suits and six pairs of socks shoved down their underpants.

Sheddon gave me the confidence I needed to make slightly less dramatic turns by telling me to imagine that I had a steering wheel between the skis. He explained, too, that while skiing, my legs were doing the same job as shock absorbers on a car, keeping the skis on the snow. And he told me to steer the skis like a rally driver steers a car on gravel, setting up the skid prior to the turn and powering through to the next turn in full control. By likening skiing to driving, it all began to make a lot more sense.

But not half as much sense as when the man from Salomon poked his Lancastrian nose in.

Now, I have always laboured under the misapprehension that an amateur skier such as myself could not possibly tell the difference between a pair of Ford Cortinaesque rental skis and a pair used by the cream of downhill racers. In the same way that my mother could not possibly know the difference between her Audi and a BMW 750 iL, I figured that switching to a pair of

£375 slalom planks would make bugger all difference. For only the second time in 30 years, I was wrong.

Not only was it possible to tell the difference between my Ford Cortinas and the Salomon jobbies, but it was fairly easy to spot behavioural patterns on the three big-league affairs.

The 1S ski, a gigantic 207, was so stable that it was possible to file your nails while doing 40 mph straight down a mogul field. This is cast very much in the Mercedes 560SEL mould.

The 2S is very much the Golf GTi, being reasonable in a straight line at a cruise but capable of holding its own in the twisty bits.

Then there was the 3S, about which I know very little because I kept falling over. It was dreadfully difficult to handle and quickly became known as the Toyota MR2 of skidom – more so because the Salomon chappie insisted that it was only a handful if it was used ineptly or by cynical journalists.

And even more astonishingly, each one of the three different types is available with a wide range of what Salomon calls power references. An individual calculates his own by scoring a certain amount of points for weight, ability and style.

Howard Lees, the most fearsomely competitive man in history and the deputy editor of this magazine, went for the 8 rating, while I was honest and selected a 7.

The difference was that he spent a day skiing like Killy and I looked smooth and in control. And yet he still won a four-star British alpine ski award, while I could not get past level three. This was only because my right leg was still encased in a RoboClackson-style brace to protect the smashed ligaments. Lees's legs were fine. Very very thin indeed, but fine.

It was in Belgium, on the way home after Lees announced that I had to average 110 mph if we were to catch the 12.30 a.m. boat back to England, that we both decided that everyday skiing is quite a lot more exciting than everyday driving.

So goodbye. We've decided to go to work for *Performance Skiing*.

The One That I Want

A few Fridays ago my horoscope said, and I quote, 'If you think the world is a safe and ordered place, you're in for a shock.'

For once, it was about right.

9.00 a.m. – I opened the post to find a court summons telling me I had no car tax. Frankly, I didn't need officialdom to remind me of this.

11.00 a.m. – my grandfather died.

12.30 p.m. – a major television contract that seemed like a safe bet fell through.

5.30 p.m. – my wife announced she had a crush on a friend of mine and left.

The only reason why my hamster didn't shuffle off the mortal coil that night was because he had done so a couple of weeks earlier.

A lot of people call days like that character building and, do you know, they're right. There are three things that I now know which I wouldn't have done had that Friday been vaguely normal.

One: marriage isn't necessarily for life. When ex-Beloved stood at the top of the aisle promising to love me till death us do part, what she actually meant was that she'd love me until someone with peroxide in his hair, white socks and a crotch the size of a bungalow came along.

Two: Greece isn't so bad after all. You know how you get all your best ideas at four in the morning when you've had two bottles of Australian fizz? Well you'll just have to take my word for it.

Anyway, new Beloved was going on holiday the next day and wondered if I'd like to go too. Seeing as it only meant cancelling two business trips, a dental appointment, a weekend house party and work for the week, I readily agreed.

Twelve hours later, we were on a BA767 to Athens and thenceforth in a rental Fiesta en route to a place called the Peligoni Club on an island called Zakynthos. It's some place.

You live in one of six cottages in the olive groves and, during the day, congregate at the club which is so close to the sea that if there's one more inch of coastal erosion, it'll be in it.

I have never seen such a spectacular bit of Mediterranean coastline either. You can keep northern Majorca and the South of France.

Furthermore, I didn't see so much as a gram of feta cheese and there were no Union Jack shorts, no discos and best of all, no lilo shops. There weren't even any CCs, and if you want to know what they are, broaden your mind and send an SAE.

It was at the Peligoni Club, however, that the most astonishing revelation of all unfurled.

Three: you don't need an internal combustion engine to go bloody quickly on water. I always figured my Fairline Phantom was pretty good fun until I had a go on a Class One offshore powerboat with a boot full of eight-litre Lamborghini engines. And even that was tame compared with a Yamaha 650 Wave-runner. But all three pale into insignificance alongside a Hobie Cat, two of which are available to guests at the Peligoni.

It looks like something those smiley Blue Peter people make out of sticky-backed plastic and two bananas every Monday and Thursday.

What you get are two pencil-thin hulls joined by a piece of canvas and some struts. It is powered by a sail so big that if it were laid on the Isle of Wight, everyone would suffocate.

I shan't bother going into all the technical details about turning and so on because, truth be told, I don't really understand them. If you gybe, it turns very fast indeed, so fast in fact that the boom takes your head off and it capsizes. If you go about, it sticks its nose into the wind and stops dead, hurling you into the water about 50 feet in front of it.

Experts seem to know how to circumnavigate these small foibles but I'm buggered if I do. What I do know is that, in a straight line, it is quite simply staggering.

With a force six creaming the wave tops into what we sailors call white horses, it will whistle along at an easy 18 knots. This would unquestionably be frightening were there not such a lot to do.

You stand on one of the hulls, clip yourself onto the trapeze and, holding the rope that controls the front sail – I think it's called a jib – and a long pole which moves the twin rudders, lean right out with your arse touching the water.

This has two effects: firstly, it stops the whole caboodle from being blown over and, secondly, if you're into S&M, you'll make a mess in your harness.

Get it right and the sensation of speed is awesome. I had it right for about a minute but then, with Albania looming large on the horizon, things went rather badly wrong.

Some say I lost my footing and fell forward, thus pushing the nose of the boat down. Some say there was water in one of the hulls and it sloshed forward of its own accord. I like this explanation best.

Either way, the nose of the boat burrowed into a wave and the back end reared up in a prelude to what became a gigantic somersault.

Forward momentum, as far as the boat was concerned, stopped abruptly. But from my point of view, the world was still whizzing by at 18 knots.

Well, it was until the wire which attached me to the trapeze brought me to a halt. The problem was that the wire was fastened to my harness which was a little tight around the old dangly bits.

Now I'm no scholar of physics but I'll tell you this. You don't measure the pressure involved in bringing a 15-stone male to a dead stop in the space of one inch in pounds per square inch. It's tons per square millimetre. And all of it was borne by my crotch.

And do you want to know what my horoscope said that day? Well I'll tell you anyway.

'Romantically, you're finished for the time being.' Once again, the little sod was about right.

Global Warming

Do please feel free to drool. Last week, as the temperature in Welwyn Garden City reached 102 degrees Fahrenheit, I had at my disposal a Lotus Esprit Turbo SE, a BMW 325i convertible, an Audi Quattro 20-valve turbo mother ****** and a 2-litre Ford Sierra.

In any normal week, you can be assured that the Ford would not have turned a wheel. In fact, it turned all four of them several times.

Yes, I know you can run a Lotus off its 170 mph clock, that you can get a Quattro to generate more than 1.0 g in bends and that, when the sun is shining, there are few better means of transport than a solidly made BMW soft top.

But the sun wasn't shining. There was a haze made up of all sorts of choice ingredients: cloud, exhaust fumes, power station emissions, deodorant spray and so on. The heat was allowed in, and most of it finished up in my armpits, and it simply wasn't allowed out again. The smell was terrible.

And the trouble with the sort of heat we had in the first few days of August is that there was no escape. It was not the sort of hot where you could sit in the shade to escape because it was that permeating, all-pervading hot that got everywhere.

And because Britain can only cope if the weather is 55 degrees and drizzling, the country fell apart. In the same way that every snowplough breaks down just before their drivers go on strike every time it looks like snow, everything designed to keep us cool went west in August.

The fridge in every corner shop was only able to bring Coca-Cola down to the sort of temperature found in the manufacture of glass. British Rail was forced to slow down its trains to 50 mph because the rails had all gone wonky, petrol pumps packed up, roads melted and old women the length and breadth of the land keeled over and died because they'd spent all their hypothermia allowances on two-bar fires and wouldn't turn them off.

And then there was me. The office, so cosy in winter, was a hellhole of fire and damnation and pestilence – mostly as a result of my armpits – and there wasn't even any fornication to liven it up.

Regularly we see that it gets above 100 in Luxor, but let me tell you there's a world of difference between 100 in Africa and 100 here. In Africa you starve. Here you sweat. I prefer starving.

I needed to get home to a cold bath but I didn't want to get into any of the cars outside. I had no way of knowing just how hot it was in the Esprit but there was no way of holding the steering wheel without wearing Marigolds. The Audi, all £33,000 worth of it, had a lift-out roof but the metal was simply too hot to touch; although Audi gives you a spare can to cope with a dearth of unleaded fuel stations, it doesn't provide oven gloves.

I have described the 20-valve Quattro mother ****** as the greatest all-round car in the world. It isn't. It has better ventilation than any Audi currently made but it can only blow hot air out of its vents on hot days.

And the BMW had leather seats which, after three hours in the heat, were capable of melting a pair of Levis at 400 paces.

The Ford, which let's face it can't quite match the competition for outright speed or handling, was provided with a sliding sunroof with a cover for when it's too hot and a windscreen that isn't raked so much that it allows the sun to heat up the wheel to a point where it becomes oval shaped.

It also had air conditioning. Now this was not the best system I've ever encountered, but, nevertheless, it was capable of sucking hot smog from the outside and turning it into cold smog for the people inside.

Rolls-Royce says the air-conditioning plants fitted to its cars have the power of 30 domestic fridges. Ford's has the power of one, but one is better than none. So, all last week, I was the berk in the blue Sapphire with the windows up and the coat on.

And I've been doing some thinking. If the weathermen are to be believed, Britain is going to get warmer and warmer as each year strolls by. I read a report last week which said that, in twenty years' time, temperatures of 107 degrees will be entirely normal during the summer months.

Now, some will say that as the motor car with its infernal catalytic converter is partly to blame, motor-car drivers must be made to sweat. But this is a vegetarian stance.

As a red-meat eater, I see it the other way round. If motor manufacturers are going to heat up the world on the one hand, it is their duty to cool the people who live in it down again.

The air conditioning in my Sierra wasn't standard. After a few minutes' research, I have found that the cheapest car in Britain to come with it, whether you like it or not, is the £13,000 Hyundai Sonata.

The only other mass marketeers to include this life-saver as standard on humdrum boxes are Ford, which sticks it on the Sapphire 2000E, and Nissan, with the Bluebird Executive. And let's face it, these two aren't that much better than the Sonata.

Can it be a coincidence that three of the nastiest saloons you can buy get one of the best extras provided as standard? Maybe not.

What I would like to know is why someone hasn't fitted it to a cheaper car yet? Why, when the trend is towards smaller, faster, more luxurious cars, is the air con ignored? Why can we have a Metro with leather seats, a Charade with a 100-bhp, intercooled, turbo engine and four valves per cylinder, a Renault 5 with PLIP central locking and a Mazda 121 with an electric sun top when we cannot have a small and convenient car that doesn't poach its occupants?

When I asked a Rover spokesman if such a thing might be in the pipeline, he said there was always one rainy day a week in

Britain, that there was no demand, and that the standard of living here was about to fall, that two-thirds of Rover production went to the UK and that it was hard to fit air con to the K-series engine.

In other words, no.

People's Limousine

Now that Nissan and Rover are making some half-decent cars, the motoring headline writers have turned their big guns on Ford who, it is said, wouldn't know what a decent car was even if one jumped out of some bracken and ate the chairman's leg.

Not unreasonably, car buffs are asking how on earth, after spending the best part of a billion quid on it, Ford managed to get the new Escort so hopelessly wrong.

This can be answered very simply indeed. It looks like Ford blundered and built a car that people want.

Instead of getting qualified engineers to sit around a conference table hammering out what is feasible in a family car these days and what is not, they got a whole load of hairy-arsed students to mill about in High Wycombe, doing market research.

It's a fairly safe bet that if BMW had used such a technique, the Z1 would be five times faster and ten times less fun. When asked what they would like to see in a car, people are not in the habit of asking for drop-down doors.

However, Ford felt Mr Average's opinions were important enough and *did* ask what features he would like to see on his next Eurobox. They then compounded the mistake by actually designing the car around these findings and now make no secret of the fact that appearance, quality and price were cited as the most important issues.

Just 14 per cent of those questioned reckoned that performance was important, while handling, according to a spokesman, either wasn't a consideration or, if it was, didn't interest anyone enough even to register on the bar chart.

Irrespective of what may or may not have been technically possible in a car like the Escort, it seems Ford's besuited marketeers went back to its engineers with these findings and told them to design a new car around the results. This means we now have a reasonably attractive, well-priced and quite nicely built car that doesn't handle and can't pull a greased stick out of a pig's arse.

And now, of course, the headline writers are jumping up and down, foaming at the mouth and saying that Ford should have broken the law of averages and given us more. A lot more.

They're quite right too. The Escort is not as spacious as a Tipo. It is not as satisfying as a Rover 200. It is not as nice to drive as a 309 and it is powered by a range of engines so nasty that even Moulinex would not accept them for use in a Magimix.

The trouble is that people outside of motoring magazines will never know just how horrid the Escort is because (a) they will never drive a rival and (b) even if they did, they'd not spot the differences. People, remember, don't care about performance and handling.

I have a Zanussi fridge. I do not know whether it has any CFCs in its engine. I do not know how many horsepower its motor develops and, even if I did, I wouldn't know whether that was a lot or not. I do not know if the light that comes on is ellipsoidal or even if it goes off when the door is shut. I do not know whether it is made out of aluminium or carbon fibre and, more than that, I do not care.

If I were to be stopped tomorrow by a hairy-arsed student with a clipboard and asked what features I would most like to see on the fridge of tomorrow I would tell him that it should keep my milk from becoming cheese, that it should fit under the work surface and that there should be enough room inside for 24 tins of Sapporo.

I do not know if it would be possible to have a solar-powered titanium job that could double up as a food blender cum orange squeezer so I would therefore not talk to the market researcher of such things.

Similarly, a man in the street would not know of radar parking aids or variable valve-timing technology and, as a result, he would not be able to tell Ford's market researcher that he wanted both of them on his next Escort.

Even though it might have been possible for such items to have been engineered in, Ford has obviously made them very low priorities, concentrating instead on value, appearance and quality: things people think the people want.

Of course, people want these things but they want a whole lot more besides. It's just that they don't know what they want until someone gives it to them. My grandfather never used to sit around wishing that he could have a remote-control television set because, in his day, such whizzkiddery was the preserve of sci-fi writers.

My great-grandfather didn't wander through his garden on a hot day wistfully thinking about how nice it would be if someone would invent a white box that would suck in hot air and turn it into cold air, thus keeping his Sapporo cold. And that's not only because he hadn't got a clue what Sapporo was.

You can't want what you don't know exists. I think Sinead O'Connor had some sort of anarchistic viewpoint in mind when she eloquently entitled her album, 'I do not want what I have not got' but the sentiment holds water on a commercial basis too.

It's fair enough to target existing Escort drivers, asking them what features of their current car are annoying. It is fair enough to act speedily on information received, but it is entirely irresponsible to let ordinary members of the public, most of whom went to state schools, decide what the cars of tomorrow should be like.

I can't think of one great breakthrough that has been achieved through market research. Isaac Newton didn't use a single clipboard to find out if we'd like gravity or not. Alexander Fleming didn't commission MORI to see if we all needed penicillin. And NOP had nothing whatsoever to do with the theory of relativity.

The question Ford should have asked itself is this: how can we trust the views of a nation that, according to the market research in which we place so much faith, looks set to let a red-headed Welshman into Downing Street.

Questioning people in the street is only useful if you want to compose a silly article in a silly women's magazine about underarm deodorant.

Radio Daze

If you think that fertiliser is interesting, that Gary Davies is a decent chap and that opera is music, then you will probably argue that Britain's national radio stations do a good job.

However, my idea of the perfect garden is one that needs hoovering once a year. I do not like Gary Davies and I would rather listen to a pile-driver than Placido Domingo.

Traffic jams are now part and parcel of any journey in Britain and, if you get as bored with your tapes as I do, the radio should provide alternative aural entertainment. But on a five-hour journey from Birmingham to London the other day, it became more and more obvious that the airwaves in this country only cater for my mother and Stock, Market and Bankerman. They used to keep Percy Thrower happy too, but he died.

Radio 1 is slick, 'Our Tune' is a good laugh and Steve Wright is a funny man, but it plays sheer, unadulterated rubbish between the chitchat.

If you are more than twelve, there is Radio 2 with its comfortable disc jockeys in woolly pullies and Vera Lynn. Radio 3 does a good job if you enjoy being shrieked at by a fat tart in a tent and Radio 5 is OK for those who want to know what sort of cake the cricket commentators are eating while the turkeys on the field take tea.

That leaves the worst of the lot. Radio 4 only has three programmes: *Gardeners'* bloody *Question Time*, which is fine if you think that greenfly on your clematis is more important than Green Jackets in the Gulf, the shipping forecast, which is of no earthly use to anyone, and *The Archers*, who live in a farm-subsidised world and think postage stamps are fascinating.

I wonder if David Mellor, broadcasting minister, has ever

considered the plight of thirtysomethings who want the Doobie Brothers interspersed with informed comment; a sort of cross between Q magazine and *Channel Four News*, where Peter Sissons does the interviews and Joe Cocker does the singy bits.

At the moment, we either have Radio 1 which occasionally plays an old Beatles song or Radio 4 which, if it can find time between the weather in Dogger Bank and the state of Stefan Buczacki's stupid rockery, squeezes Clement Freud in for a quick joke.

Largely, local radio is terrible too, but in London, where there are twenty stations, we have something called GLR which broadcasts, if ever you're down here, on 94.9FM. Conceptually, it's excellent.

Before it began in 1988 we were teased with a test transmission tape featuring non-stop Led Zep, Bob Seger, the Doobies and Steely Dan.

My appetite whetted, I tuned in on day one and found the disc jockeys were every bit as good as the music. When the radio alarm went off, I was treated to a man called Nick Abbott who rang up public figures every morning and insulted them. They had Tommy Voice, Johnny Walker and Emma Freud too. It was a damn good station.

But, systematically, the decent presenters have been shunted into late-night slots or ejected altogether. Their replacements, complete with horrid regional accents, are bad enough, but chief horror is Janice Long who, along with a sidekick called James Cameron, does the morning show.

Cameron is supposed to play at being Peter Sissons while Long spins the discs. Unfortunately, she can't go for more than a minute without sticking her left-wing nose into the news items.

Every day, I leave Balham rubbing sleep from my eyes and arrive in Fulham half an hour later spitting blood and screaming blue murder. Yes, the traffic on the Trinity Road is partly to blame but worse, much worse, is that woman. I even dreamed about her last night. Things are getting bad.

I listen to her for two reasons. Firstly, there is no alternative for all the reasons I've already outlined and, secondly, I simply have to know how far to the left you can lean on a major radio station without falling over. It has now become a battle of wits: will she get fired before I go barking mad?

A spokesman for the station described her as an 'Earth Woman', saying she is a veggie and a bit left wing. He even admitted that the finger had been wagged at her after an interview she did with that actress woman who wants to be an MP but won't ever make it because she's got bosoms like spaniel's ears.

If Long wants to harp on about organic vegetables, then why doesn't she buy a psychedelic bus and move to Glastonbury where I'm sure the audience would be more appreciative. There is no place for an 'Earth Woman' on a station which is aimed right at the jugular of 25- to 40-year-old 'discerning' listeners.

I wouldn't mind but her brand of socialism has rubbed off on the news staff too. Only the other day, one, probably another 'Earth Woman', was reporting on a demonstration in Wandsworth, home of the lowest poll tax in Britain.

She claimed she had talked to residents who would willingly pay more for better services. Were these interviews broadcast? Were they hell. Did this woman really expect me to believe that there are people who want bigger poll-tax bills just to keep the Janice Longs of this world in odd-shaped carrots.

Then the reporter had the audacity to claim that Wandsworth was at a standstill because of the huge demo. Well, I was there at the time and I've never seen the one-way system flow so freely. The 'huge' demo she was referring to involved six people. Three were women and four had beards.

It seems GLR's traffic reports are politically motivated too. Certainly, they're usually pretty inaccurate. One day soon, Mrs Thatcher will be blamed for the weather.

GLR is still on trial. Apparently David Mellor doesn't like it and unless the audience figures improve soon, the BBC's Board of Governors will close down the only radio station I know that gets close to making life in a traffic jam bearable.

Horse Power

Obviously, in this green and caring land of hope and glory where man's best friend is a dog, one has to be a little careful when advocating the slaughter of an entire species.

But let's face it – what possible good are flies? Have you ever tried to sunbathe when a bluebottle has designs on your arm? And why, when you've wooshed him off 30 times, does he still try to land? Worse, have you ever tried to sleep when there's a fly in the room? Bzzzzzzzzzzzzzzzzzzzzzzzzzzzzzzzz bump. Bzzzzz-zzzzzzzzzzzzzzzzzzzzzzzzzz bump. Bzzzzzzzzzzzzzzzzzzzzzzzzzzzzz-zzz bump. If evolution has rendered the mole blind and turned the seal from a land-based mammal into a furry fish, why can't a fly get to grips with windows?

And what the hell are flies full of? What is that yellow stuff that splatters all over your car windscreen when a wasp decides to headbutt your car?

There are countless dangerous, ugly or just plain useless species which serve no purpose whatsoever; David Attenborough finds a couple of hundred every week. But worst of the lot – worse than an electric eel, worse than a bluebottle, worse than a rat – is the horse. Unless of course it's first past the post in the 3.15 at Doncaster with ten of my pounds on its nose.

When it was fashionable to wear armour, the horse was as important to personal mobility as the Ford Escort. But thanks to the Ford Escort, we do not actually need horses any more. I know they did the Boers a big favour and Custer would have been even more buggered without one, so maybe we do owe them a small debt of gratitude, but in a world of modems and faxes, the only use I can think of for the common or garden horse is as an ingredient in glue.

Things wouldn't be so bad if horsey types were all from the land-owning classes so that at least when they took their stupid animals out for a ride, no one else would be inconvenienced. Unfortunately the middle class, as usual, has stuck its nose in.

And because the idea of land to the middle class is a lawn, it is forced to exercise its infernal pets on roads. That's bad enough but there are some professional bodies which do the same.

If the army has enough money to transport an entire division halfway round the world, if it can afford to buy nuclear weapons which, let's face it, are not cheap, then how come the Blues and Royals are given horses to move around London on. What's the matter with motorbikes?

It is absolutely absurd that I should be held up every morning by one of the world's most respected, feared and best-equipped armies as it plods through Hyde Park on animals that, in the modern world of warfare, are as pertinent as a bow and arrow. I am no military tactician but if I were to be given the choice of a nag or a Challenger in battle, I just know I'd take the tank.

The army aren't the only operation in London to use horses either. One of the breweries – I forget which and I'm certainly not going to bother finding out and give it advertising space in the process – delivers its beer on horse-drawn drays.

Even though it is pulled by two magnificent shire horses of a size that would keep Evostick in business for months should they ever be melted down, it has a top speed of 1 mph.

And don't give me any claptrap about the environment on this issue because I would far rather breathe 0.00000001 mg of nitrogen oxide than slither about in a sea of manure. And if you reckon that the dray holds up 2000 cars a day for an average of five minutes each, that's the equivalent of one engine running at its most inefficient speed for one week.

Commercial operations that use horses on the road are anti-social and as environmentally friendly as the Rother Valley and there can be no excuse. It's just a cheap publicity stunt. But what of the people who ride their horses on the roads when they aren't even advertising anything? Perhaps Evostick should consider melting the owners down too.

The other weekend, I went for a ride on a horse so big it was a bison. Described as a bit frisky, which turned out to be like calling Cannon and Ball a bit not funny, we spooked and skipped our way round some Scottish back roads for an hour.

Most passing cars slowed down by some margin but even when the steel dragons were crawling along at 20 mph, the demon horse jumped about like it was limboing up for an assault on the non-stop pogo dancing record. It was worse if the car was a bright colour and worse still if it went through a puddle while going by.

My leading rein explained that some horses are worth £20,000 and that because this figure was way in excess of what the average Scot spends on a car, drivers should get out of her way.

She pointed out that horses are nervous beasts, rejecting in the process my suggestion that they're daft, and the slightest sign of something out of the ordinary may cause them to bolt. Christ, if they can't cope with a car going through a puddle, I sincerely hope that when the Martians do arrive, they land at Hickstead.

If it were left to her, and others of her ilk, we would all have to buy Toyota Camrys and if we did encounter a horse while out driving, we should do a smart about turn and find an alternative route. I even noticed that the back window of her car sported a warning that she slowed down for horses. When she breeds, and horsey people do, frequently and with much vigour, doubtless she will have a baby-on-board sticker too.

I have to go now because I'm due at Lingfield this afternoon.

Non-Passive Smoking

I like gambling. Just the other day, I relieved a colleague of £10 when he discovered that Eddie Jobson did, at one time, play for Curved Air. Later today, I will win another £10 when I prove to someone else that Tom Stoppard wrote *The Russia House*.

My new wager is a tad more risky. I have bet a leading figure in the motor industry that by 1999, Audi will outsell BMW by two to one on the British market. For the record, BMW currently outsells Audi by the same margin.

My reasoning is simple. Audi is responding to changing public demand better than BMW. Audi was the first to get a baby in its television advertisements, Audi was the first to get catalytic converters standardised across its entire range, Audi was the first to use nothing but galvanised steel and Audi is first off the marks with Procon Ten.

Performance, handling and sheer macho thrustiness have been eschewed by Audi in favour of trees and flowers and having horrid accidents without dying. Audi is on the ball.

BMW is not. The filofax is dead. Nineteen–year–olds on £200,000 a year are no more. Estate agents, praise be to the Lord, are in the mulligatawny up to their scrawny necks and we laugh at people with double-breasted suits and mobile telephones.

So why, if all these have gone, should we expect the car that went with them not to go too? Bye bye BMW. Hello £10.

This probability became a certainty when I noticed, among all the hype about performance, handling and macho thrustiness in the blurb on the new 3-series, a small but vital point. You are able to buy these new cars without any ashtrays.

Well that does it. In recent months, I have become increasingly fed up with the drivel bandied about by hairy-bottomed do-gooders who want us all to take up jogging. And not even jogging on a horizontal basis either, which it seems renders us likely to catch AIDS.

I may however catch cancer or thrombosis or angina or any number of nasties that my packet of Marlboro insists are a virtual certainty should I choose to indulge in the contents.

My simple answer to this is so what? If I choose to cash in the chips early and shuffle off the mortal coil at 60 or so, you clean-living types should be grateful.

I will never buy a pair of those fur-lined boots with zips up the front and I will never get in your way in the post office, failing to get my mind or my arthritic fingers round the hard ECU or whatever currency has replaced Sterling by then.

I will never demand money from the government every time it drops below 70 degrees and I won't clog up the roads in my ten-year-old Maxi with 600 miles on the clock. Dying before you're an old-age pensioner is the most socially responsible thing you can possibly do.

And if you manage to kill yourself in such a way that the treasury benefits, so much the better. On this front, you have two choices: fill up with four star and drive over Beachy Head or, and this is the option I've chosen, smoke 40 cigarettes a day for 50 years.

In today's money, I will have given the chancellor £30,000, thus paying for a hospital ward that I will never use. Now THAT is public spirited.

Also, I will give tobacco companies about £20,000 which helps keep unemployment down and motor racing alive.

At this point in the debate, earth people like Janice Long usually pipe up with the age-old argument about passive smoking and how they, full to overflowing with organic vegetables, do not wish to inhale somebody else's nicotine.

Well, I find football offensive. I do not see why that Paul Gascoigne person has to take up so many pages of my *Sun* every day and I do not see why large areas of Fulham are virtually closed off every time 22 men feel the need to charge around Chelsea kicking an inflated sheep's pancreas at one another.

In my opinion it would be better if they could be persuaded to indulge in this curious pastime at an out-of-town stadium. Football fans, however, point out that they enjoy the game and wonder, out loud and often, why on earth they shouldn't be allowed to enjoy it in a convenient location.

Of course they should. Nice though the concept is, I don't have the power to ban football or socialism or lots of other things I don't like. So who gave the likes of British Airways, LRT and Pizza Express the power to ban smokers smoking?

Just recently, I went for three hours without a cigarette because some Finnish bus company provided a no-smoking coach which took us to a no-smoking shopping centre. From there, we went to a no-smoking airport and on to an internal SAS flight which is also no smoking. It deposited me at Helsinki which, as far as I can work out, is a no-smoking city. And people wonder why Scandinavia has the highest suicide rate in the world.

By offering the new 3-series without an ashtray, BMW must take its share of the blame for job losses in the tobacco industry and big third-world debt problems in tobacco-producing countries. Tax lost from reduced cigarette consumption will be applied elsewhere and the NHS will be swamped with incontinent pensioners who'll live to 150. The suicide rate will spiral and slaughter on the roads will become wholesale as people can't find a way to keep calm in traffic jams. The Tories will be ousted, communism will take its place and how many cars do you think BMW will sell when we all have to call one another 'comrade'.

And what is BMW's reasoning? Well, a spokesman said a car that has never been smoked in fetches more on the second-hand market than one which has a nicotine bouquet.

Someone at Audi should explain to him that these days, quality of life counts for a little bit more than saving a few quid.

S-Classy

Privately at least, the new Mercedes-Benz S-Class has caused a murmur of discontent among certain motoring journalists.

People who can be found running around their offices making gear change and tyre squeal noises have been heard to mutter that the S-Class in general, and the 6-litre V12 in particular, is a rather unsavoury and tasteless exercise in frivolous excess.

Now, I don't understand this. For years, these people, who can be distinguished from normal people by their Rohan trousers, have argued that all cars should have 5-litre turbo engines and suspension systems that are harder than washing-up a Magimix.

So that they have something new to talk about loudly and often in pubs, they want each new car to be bigger and faster and better and more exciting than anything ever before made by anybody.

Mercedes has done that but instead of handing out credit where credit is due, they point to its 2.2-ton bulk, saying that in a world burdened with dwindling resources, there is no place for such a monster. What's more, you even get the impression when talking to Mercedes engineers that if they had begun to design the car yesterday rather than back in the early 1980s, it would not be as it is.

I have never seen such a defensive press pack. Way before you get to engine specifications or that brilliant rear-axle layout there are literally pages and pages of bumph about how environmentally aware Daimler-Benz is.

It even says, and this is the best bit, that only 80 per cent of the car is galvanised because it is trying to conserve the world supplies of zinc. That is called *reactive* public relations.

So let us work out how the S-Class might have looked had it

been designed in the 1990s rather than the 1980s. First, it would not have been blessed with a V12 engine – a lighter, more efficient multi-valve six would have done the job, albeit not as silently or as effortlessly.

It may have been fashioned from thinner, lighter steel or even composites and it may have been built with less integrity to save a few pounds of both the lb and £ variety. Also, if it were built less well, the cabin would be less airtight and consequently, self closing doors would be an unnecessary waste of time. Double glazing would have been thrown out as the whim of a madman.

Air suspension, however, may stay as this uses lightweight electronics and fluid rather than bulky and out-of-date metal. There would be no drop-down vanity mirrors in the back and surely a nice Richard Grant tail fin would do the job of those complex aerials which pop out of the rear wings to help shorter drivers see where the rear of the car is while reversing.

In addition to all this, it would have been smaller by some considerable margin. And cheaper.

In other words, rather than being a jaw-lowering masterpiece which sets new standards in every single area, it would have been just another executive car which, in all probability, would have been no better than a Citroen XM.

When you're talking about the S-Class you can, in all honesty, call it the 'best'-handling big car, the 'fastest' limo, the 'most' comfortable saloon and the only complaint you'll get is from your computerised thesaurus which just won't have enough superlatives in its memory bank.

How can journalists berate Ford in one breath for letting the accountants have too much control over the engineers when, in the very next moment, they are lambasting Daimler-Benz for saying to its engineers: 'Get on with it boys. Show those Oriental chappies that we can grind them into the dirt when push comes to shove. Sod the money, go out there and build the best car in the world.' Or something like that.

Had one eye been kept on the abacus or the Greenpeace

newsletter, the 600SEL would have crept on to the market, as big a leap forward as the potato peeler.

If I were in Merc's shoes right now, I wouldn't be crawling around, half apologising for the masterpiece my back-room boys had created. I'd be on the roof at Canary Wharf, hailing it for what it is: the best car in the world.

The whole point is progress. No one jumps up and down with foam at the corners of their mouth when Ferrari introduces us all to another extravagant sports car. In the real world a Renault 5 GT Turbo is very nearly as fast as a Ferrari but that doesn't mean Fiat should close Maranello down.

Yes, an XM is very nearly as comfortable as an S-Class but that doesn't mean the whole project should have been scrapped, as some heavily bearded people are now saying.

No one seems to mind that we're all expected to replace our album collections with CDs even though the qualitative difference is actually quite small and no one cares two hoots that we have to replace perfectly serviceable clothes each year because something better and more fashionable has come along.

So why the hell should we worry that Mercedes has gone that extra mile to make a car that is head and shoulders above everything else? And damn it all, £85,000 is not expensive when you look at the price tickets in a Rolls-Royce showroom.

I can't help feeling that Rohan-trousered journalists are up in arms about the timing of the S-Class simply because they can find nothing to moan about the car itself. I will admit that the 600SEL has emerged at a rather inconvenient moment but I will never be party to criticism of it as a result.

The brontosaurus met a premature end because it came along at the wrong time but let's face it, the Natural History Museum would be an altogether duller place had it never existed at all.

Would You Buy a Used Alfa from This Man?

If it turns out that a Malaysian customs officer cannot be bribed, I shall renounce Christianity and move to the Orkneys, where, I'm told, everyone is Lucifer's best mate.

Selling a beautiful Alfa Romeo at a fair price ought to be easy even though *Glass's Guide* shows a 1986 GTV6 to be worth 34p whereas I know £7000 is not unreasonable.

I chose to advertise it in one of those *Classic Car* magazines; written BY people with beards FOR people with beards, and the response was good, with five calls on the first day.

Two hours before man one was due to arrive, I decided to make sure the thing actually worked, something that is never guaranteed with a GTV6 especially when it has been sitting in a vegetative state outside my house for nine months.

I pumped up its tyres, cleaned away the cobwebs, ran a hoover over the carpets, topped it up with oil and water, attached some jump leads and crossed my fingers. And it burst into life, the exhaust signalling this emergence from hibernation with a melodious bark.

Man one duly arrived and we stood, poring over the service history and discussing various rust spots for ooh, about ten minutes before deciding to go for a test drive. Yes, it started but no, it would not go into gear. The clutch, after such a long rest, had welded itself to the fly wheel and would not, even when enticed with a 10 per cent cut off the asking price, dislodge itself.

Man one buggered off.

Man two arrived ten minutes later and buggered off five minutes after that, saying that I had wasted his time, and that I was a nuisance. Only he didn't say nuisance. However, he DID say I should call him back when it was working.

Over the next few days, I consulted colleagues like Jeff Daniels and LJK Setright and Citroen's spanner-man, Julian Leyton, to see how a clutch could be unstuck without resorting to brute force or a £500 visit to Kwik Fit.

There was a lot of umming and aahing but in effect, they said it couldn't.

But they were reckoning without my mop. After it had held the clutch pedal down for three days, there was a boinging noise and the GTV6 once more became a fully functional motor car.

Man two came round again, took a test drive, and said he would very much like to buy it but could not until he had sold his own 2-litre GTV. I expect to see him again but I shall be 52 years old.

Man three was an Australian and didn't turn up. I now have 342 reasons for saying that Australia will be the last continent on earth that I visit. And that includes the Antarctic.

Man four worried the life out of me. One, he sounded foreign on the telephone. Two, he was from Essex and three, he said he wanted the car for his wife.

Face to face, things did not improve. His claim that he drove a Lotus Carlton was at odds with both his demeanour and his 'friend' who wore an earring. Alarm bells rang. Even if he had offered cash, I'd have been suspicious but he launched into a remarkable tale about how the piece of paper he was waving under my nose-end was a building society banker's draft. For all I knew, it could have been a dog licence. Now, the BBC is forever getting letters from people who have been diddled when selling cars. I just knew that whatever deal I did with Mr Dodgy, I'd end up on *That's Life!*

So I refused to budge by so much as 1p on the price and he went away.

Then I entered the Malaysian phase. It began when an Oriental chappie rang from Denmark, where he is currently engaged servicing rigs, to see if it would be all right to come over and look at the car. He arranged to catch the Friday-night flight and we'd meet on the Saturday morning.

But on the Friday afternoon, way after it became impossible to stop the Malaysian Dane from coming over, man four turned up complete with salivating chops and a bundle of wedge. He wanted the car and would pay full price. DILEMMA or what?

You know that scene in National Lampoon's *Animal House* where the spotty youth is presented with an available, if slightly unconscious teenage girl at a party? On his left shoulder is the devil advising him to 'go for it' while on his right is an angel, advising him not to on account of her tender years etc.

On the one hand was my moral fibre. On the other, was an overdraft which is not being helped by £100 a month premiums on the car I now had an opportunity to sell.

The Devil said screw the Malay-Dane. My public-school education and sheer Britishness said don't . . . and won. Man four went off in a huff.

The Oriental Viking duly arrived and we spent the whole of Saturday with an Alfa Romeo specialist who pronounced the car to be fit and well worth £7000. This had nothing to do with my advice to the said specialist that if he wasn't forthcoming with a result of this type, I would write about his operation in a derogatory manner every hour, on the hour.

It transpired, after all was said and done, that you can't import a car to Malaysia if it is more than five years old and my GTV6 is, by one poxy month.

Our Tropical Nordic friend is, as I write, trying to grease the palm of a customs official in the hope of getting round this idiotic legislation but holds out little chance of success.

If I had listened to the advice of Satan, the car would have been sold already and I'd be seven grand better off. Because I waited for the Malay-Dane, I feel extremely righteous.

But I can hardly tell the bank manager that my overdraft has not been cleared due to extreme righteousness because he'll think I've gone mad.

Which I have.

A Question of Sports

Away from the world of motoring, just about the only thing that ranks as 'really puzzling' is why on earth anyone votes Labour?

Within it, so many things are *really puzzling*, you'd need a whole bank of Cray supercomputers to work them out.

For example, just what is that car on the cover of Peter Gabriel's first album?

Then there's Ligier and its sponsorship deal with the French government. How come a budget that could finance a small nuclear war or a vast conventional one is not big enough to get one point in Grand Prix racing?

I shall go on. Why is the standard of driving so uniquely atrocious on the M1 just near Leicester? Why isn't there a motoring programme on ITV? Why do some people, usually those with bosoms, find it so difficult to park? Is it true the Celica was designed by a horse? How come Robin Cook is so ugly? That's not really a motoring problem but it needs answering nevertheless.

Then there is the small question of depreciation. Why does anyone buy a BMW 750iL knowing, with absolute certainty, that in a year's time, they'll be twenty grand worse off? If you really must have such a car, why not pop into a casino on the way to the dealer and plonk £20,000 on red? If it comes up trumps, you can cover the certain loss that lies ahead and if it comes up black, you can relax knowing you'd have lost it anyway and that you've saved £100 on road tax.

And that's another thing. Why do motorists have to pay £100 for road tax when 70 per cent of it is spent on ethnic lesbian theatre groups and poison to kill doggies?

Is it true that Stevie Wonder designed Oxford's one-way

system? Why do multi-storey car park stairwells always smell of urine? Why do buses have to be so big? Why is it that whenever three men get into a van together, its throttle jams wide open and the brakes fail? Do dustbin-lorry crews get a bonus every time they knock off someone's wing mirror? And how come Vauxhall is allowed to claim the top speed of an Astramax van is 90 mph when, in fact, it's twice that.

Why do the drivers of all BMWs in south London refuse to turn their headlights on at night and why do all Austin Maxis have tissues and cushions on the rear parcel shelf? It sure as hell can't be anything to do with 'naughtiness' because the drivers are all old and the naughtiest thing an old person does is cheat in a beetle drive.

I'm afraid there is no point trying to work out answers to any of the above because they're all imponderables. It's like trying to establish where on earth mucus comes from or why people have babies or why your toast always lands on the carpet butter-side down.

However, the one imponderable I've been having a stab at just lately is why Toyota sells more sports cars in Britain than anyone else?

And the answer I've come up with is that no one else actually makes sports cars. Which leads us on to another imponderable. Why not?

Yes, I know Lotus, Morgan and TVR will be jumping around at the back now, waving their arms and pointing to Elans, Plus 4s and S3s, but these, let's face it, are small fry compared with the MR2.

Whereas the MR2 is designed and backed up by the world's third-largest motor manufacturer, the TVR S3, frankly, is not. It's a lovely car, you might even call it a great one, but it will never outsell the MR2 and that's the end of it.

However, what I want to know is why Ford or Vauxhall or Peugeot or Fiat do not make a sports car – and I don't mean a rebodied rep-mobile with electric windows and a spoiler that wobbles about; I mean a real, get out of my ****ing way, sports car.

The usual answer trotted out is that there's no demand. Oh yeah, so how come Toyota makes such a success of it? Or they'll claim that one-off projects are not viable. Oh yeah, well how come Toyota did it not once, not twice ladies and gentlemen but, if you count the Celica as a sports car which, grudgingly, I will, three times?

Toyota made the MR2 to be just as popular in Detroit as it is in Nidderdale or the Australian bush or Egypt or Modena or Dublin or La Paz or anywhere, for that matter, where Toyota has an important operation. Which is just about everywhere.

Both GM and Ford are bigger than Toyota but they seem to be incapable of grasping the concept of a world car. Toyota has proved that if the car is right, it will sell everywhere. You don't need one version for the States, one for the Far East and one for Europe. You can make the economies of scale work.

I sometimes wonder if the Western big boys are frightened by the MR2 but I've just spent a week with one and I reckon there's no need for such lilyliverishness. After all, how does anyone know whether it's good or hopeless when no one else makes such a thing?

Maybe, if everyone made a budget-priced mid-engined two-seater, it would be to the class what the Escort is to Euroboxes or what the Croma is to executive saloons.

I am beginning to despair of the European motor manufacturers. Where is the investment? Where is the initiative? Where's the bloody pizzazz?

If Toyota was run by Europeans, its range would include the Starlet, the Corolla, the Carina and the Camry. And that would be it.

But Toyota is run by people who can see their ears and, as a result, there's also the Previa, the MR2, the Celica, the Supra, the Land Cruiser and a whole host of other stuff it doesn't export to Europe because of import restrictions.

Which brings me on to the next 'really puzzling' thing. Why is everyone involved in Western automobile manufacture sound asleep?

Volvo Shock

Before reading beyond the first paragraph of this story, ensure that you are sitting down. Also, loosen all items of clothing, take off your spectacles and remove your dentures.

Volvo has made a good car.

It still has typical Volvoy looks but they disguise the fact that it goes like stink and handles like the sort of dream where you spend six hours making love to Daryl Hannah AND Patsy Kensit.

It is called the 850 and it will be appearing at a Volvo dealership near you early next year. Price-wise, the GLT version I drove should cost about £18,000.

So, you've read this far and you've seen the photograph and doubtless, you're wondering how on earth a car that looks pretty much identical to the old 700 series can be demonstrably better than almost anything else in its class.

Well, for a kick off, it has front-wheel drive. Yes, Volvo has used the expertise gained by making the 400 series and applied it to its new machine – but to make sure it all works properly, a new rear suspension has been developed.

It's so complicated that the press conference needed to explain everything went on for six days. All you need to know is that it's the subject of a Volvo patent, that it works and that it's called the Delta System.

On the devilish piece of road Volvo calls its test track, mid-corner bumps, hideous adverse camber and awesome pot holes failed to unsettle the 850 in any way whatsoever, though a Spanish journalist did manage to turn one over. It has extraordinarily high levels of grip, stunning turn-in, no torque-steer worth mentioning and a ride comfort to rival all but the Citroen XM. You want more . . . good, because there is some.

And it comes in the shape of a new engine. While Ford is busy telling us that you need eight years to develop a new power unit, Volvo is out and about proving this assumption wrong. Just after the introduction of a new 3-litre six with four valves per cylinder, which, incidentally, took four years to get into production, comes a development of that engine – a 2.5-litre, 20-valve five cylinder engine which took even less time to get from the drawing board to reality.

There are no signs, however, that even hint at an abbreviated or rushed development. It's a gutsy unit which produces lots of that stuff real road-testers call torque and which you and I call grunt. Moreover, most of it is available from just above tickover.

Power-wise, even the most ardent BMW aficionado is left gasping. In a body that weighs 300 lb less than a similarly priced 24-valve 520i, there is a transversely mounted engine which develops 170 bhp – that's twenty more than the Bee Em.

It equates to excellent performance. 0 to 60 takes, we are told, 8.9 seconds and on Volvo's high-speed test track, I reached an indicated 216 kph (135 mph), with the sunroof open. In more normal conditions, you can expect 25 mpg from the catalysed motor unless of course you go for the clever four-speed auto.

The other good toy, of course, is air-conditioning which rounds off a pretty impressive list of gizmos. Even the dash, a traditional Volvo weakness, looks solid and tasteful. It even has an LCD computer.

But, when all is said and done, it is a Volvo and that means safety. To that end, there is a new B pillar and a door design which, in a side impact sends much of the energy, that would ordinarily be used to kill those inside, down to the floor.

Knowing this new system was in place and knowing it was backed up with anti-lock brakes and an air bag, I dispensed with the usual Clarkson reserve and found the Volvo to be great fun. And you've never read that much about such a car before.

The new engine sounds more like an Alfa V6 than a humble 'five' but it is the quality of power of delivery that impresses most. The whole car feels like a fluid extension of your limbs, responding to driver input like all performance cars should.

It even excels in town where good visibility, a stupendous turning circle and well-defined corners come into their own. The seats are pretty damn comfortable too.

Equally useful in day-to-day life is the rear seat's armrest which can be converted into a baby seat and the passenger's front seat which, like those in the rear, can be folded down enabling long things to be carried around. It's a simple idea and one that leaves you wondering why no one else has ever thought of it.

Mind you, less clever, is Volvo's product policy. It keeps introducing new cars without deleting anything. This means we now have to choose between the ancient 200, a large estate car, the 700, a large estate car, the 900, a large estate car which looks just like the 700, or the new 850 which, one day, will be a large estate car even though for now, it's only a saloon.

Not only are they all the same size but the new 850 is indistinguishable from the 900. I just cannot understand why Volvo's stylists did this and, having talked to people in the company, it seems, neither can anyone else.

But we can't moan because here at last is a car that looks like a Volvo, feels like a Volvo but goes and handles like a BMW. And that is so astonishing that it just has to be reported.

No Free Lunch

Iceland, Norway, China, Finland, Sweden, Denmark, Germany, France, Spain, Portugal, Hong Kong, Maui, America, Japan, Italy, Sardinia, Sicily, Cyprus, Chad, Niger, Austria, Switzerland, Belgium, Holland and Luxembourg.

In five years, I've been to them all and it's cost me the grand total of no pounds, no shillings and no pence.

There isn't a car you can buy I haven't driven and that small feat didn't cost anything either.

Tomorrow, at Castle Combe, I shall be playing with a Countach, a Miura and a Diablo and then I shall come home in a helicopter. And the bill? Zero.

I have stayed in the Carlton Hotel in Cannes and the Hyatt Regency on Kanapali Beach. I have jet-skied in the Pacific, snow-skied in Italy and skidooed in Finland. I have drunk Mouton Rothschild on the shores of Lake Annecy and Barsac with *foie gras*.

You name an expensive restaurant in Europe, and I mean so numbingly expensive you would be struggling to pay for a lettuce leaf, and I will have eaten lobster in it. Think of your dream hotel and I'll have been there already.

I have been in the sharp bit of a Cathay Pacific Jumbo and helicopters have taken me round the Alps, into the Grand Canyon, from Nice Airport to the Loews hotel in Monaco and over the queues you sit in to get to the British Grand Prix.

Day after day, week after week, year after year, I live a champagne lifestyle that would quiver the shivery bits of even the most hardened Fleet Street gossip columnist. Compared to me, Joan Collins is like a walk-on extra in *Coronation Street*.

I redefine excess. Princess Stephanie is to me what a Fiat 126 is to a Bentley Turbo, what a Peter and Jane book is to *Othello*, what a plankton is (*get on with it* – Ed.).

But do not despair because all you have to do to join me on this caviar and Krug roller-coaster is find a newspaper or magazine which, each week, will give you a column inch or two to write about cars.

Then, motor manufacturers will compete with one another to ensure you write about one of their products rather than someone else's.

It is motor manufacturers who pay for the first-class travel and the helicopters and the fine wines and the *foie gras* and the Carlton Hotel and the trips to China. And then to make sure we all remember our trips, it is motor manufacturers that give us all going-home presents: telephones, briefcases, jackets, fish, whisky and so on.

There are 56 million people in Britain. Excluding those who are too young and those that have begun to wear fur-lined boots with zips up the front, that leaves maybe 40 million. Then take out those that can't read or write and you're left with six. And I doubt there's one who wouldn't sell their children into slavery to do what I do for a living.

Or is there? According to an organ produced by the Northern Group of Motoring Writers, this job is not all it's cracked up to be. More than that, it smells a whole lot worse than an anchovy's wotsit.

It seems that some of my northern colleagues are angry because first-class travel, Barsac and the Carlton are just not enough.

One of their number, who claims to write a column in the *Pig Breeder's Gazette* (no, I'm not) suggests in a recent edition of the Group's newsletter that it is a bloody disgrace that he is unable to get a Ferrari to test for a week. Diddums.

But this little snippet is small fry compared to the front-page lead which begins thus: 'The tendency among PR departments to expect journalists – especially north of Watford – to attend product launches at their own expense is a growing and worrying trend.'

He cites a recent BMW launch, saying that some members

had to get up at 5 a.m. and drive for up to 90 minutes to get to an airport. He goes on to add that lunch was too brief and concludes with the astonishing revelation that many members had an 18-hour day!

So let's look at this 18-hour day shall we. Our man wakes and after a pot of piping-hot coffee, climbs into that week's press car, a Rover perhaps or maybe a Calibra. Either way, it has a tank full of fuel paid for by whoever delivered it. He drives to an airport and boards a plane to Scotland, using a ticket sent to him by BMW. At Glasgow airport, he climbs into a waiting 325i and drives through breathtaking scenery for an hour or so, arriving at Inverlochy Castle. There, he wolfs down some salmon before driving a 318i back to the airport for the plane home.

I don't know how he survived. Ranulph: forget your Transglobe Expedition, forget walking to the North Pole. Just you try being a Northern motoring journalist for a day or two.

This front-page exposé suggests that the manufacturer should pay for petrol to and from the airport (though why the newspaper can't do this is beyond me), that it should pay for car parking and that overnight stays should be incorporated if it looks like being a long day. I thought Northerners were supposed to be gritty.

But the best bit I've saved till last. Our lead writer says he was invited to London by Pirelli for the launch of a new tyre and that to get from Lincolnshire to the capital would have meant a £70 experience on the train or a £120 plane ticket.

It is up to an editor to decide if a new Pirelli tyre is news. If he says it is, he must pay for his motoring writer to attend the launch. If he decides that the good people of Grimsby are able to get by without knowing the tyre exists, then the motoring writer cannot go.

The notion that Pirelli should pay £120 so that half a dozen Grimsby-ites can read all about their new tyre is nonsense.

There is only one thing in the world worse than a whinger and that's a whinger with a Northern accent. And to think I was born there. Eugh.

Are Cars Electric?

I wonder whether history will be kinder to Karl Benz or Council-man Marvin Braude. The man who invented the motor car. Or the man who killed it?

At the Frankfurt Motor Show, the world's motor manufac-turers and assorted secretary birds showed off no fewer than 24 cars powered by electricity.

Ford, Chrysler and General Motors announced that they had joined forces to spend half a billion dollars of their own money and another half a billion from the US Treasury on research into advanced battery design.

And the talk was not of Toyota's new factory in Derby but of the new Chloride plant in Manchester.

The latest Japanese concept car and the usual crop of hopeless Italian design studies were completely ignored. All anyone talked about were electric cars, sodium sulphur batteries, fast charging and other assorted pieces of what bulls do.

Believe me, in twenty years' time, you won't be reading *Performance Car* and even if you are, we will not be writing about how fast the new Nissan goes from 0–60 mph but how fast you can recharge its power pack and how far it will go before such recharges are necessary. And the most important of all, how many miles you can do before you need to spend £2000 on a new set of batteries, and whether it's worth leasing them from the LEB.

And Councilman Marvin Braude is to blame.

Marvin lives in Los Angeles. Marvin is a city councillor in Los Angeles and Marvin doesn't like the fact that children are not allowed to play on his streets because of the smog.

Marvin places the blame for this smog squarely at the door

marked Detroit. Apparently, Marvin is fed up with excuses from Motown so a couple of years ago he instigated the LA Initiative whereby companies large and small from all over the world were invited to design an ultra low-emission car which could later be converted to zero emission. He said it must have freeway performance, i.e. a top speed of 60 mph, that it must have a range of 150 miles and that it should be a quality product aimed at the lower luxury market.

The prize was a sackload of cash from the city of Los Angeles who would also market the car, guarantee big sales and ensure that charging points would be installed throughout the city to cope.

The competition was won by a British-designed vehicle which has a range of 50 miles if you use the electric motor only or 150 miles if you use the 650 cc petrol motor as well. This has two catalytic converters and produces less bhp than a Kenwood mixer.

It has a top speed of 70 mph and 0 to 50 mph takes 17 seconds. It is therefore about as advanced as a Ford Anglia, circa 1961.

Having shown Detroit that such a thing could be achieved, the State of California announced that by 1998 any manufacturer wishing to operate in the world's seventh-biggest economy must ensure that for every hundred cars sold, two must produce no emissions. And that means battery power.

If I was a car manufacturer, my knee jerk reaction would be to pull out of California and let them use the bus but sadly, we can be assured that what happens on the west coast of America today will happen in the rest of the US tomorrow, and in Europe next year.

There is no escape. Every manufacturer has to make electric-powered cars. And to make sure the simply enormous costs can be recouped, they have to be desirable. They have to sell which means they'll have to be as good as a petrol-engined car or significantly cheaper.

Now while every car firm in the world is scurrying around trying to make hitherto untouched technology as desirable as the internal combustion engine, which can trace its roots back to the last century, you can bet your bottom dollar that the amount of investment in the kind of cars we've come to know and love will dwindle to diddly squat.

Take Jaguar for example. Every penny it has must now be poured into the development of a battery-powered car. You can kiss goodbye to the notion of a new petrol engine because there won't be one. The oil industry can pull its hair out until it looks like Telly Savalas but we are facing, right now, the beginning of the end of the internal combustion engine.

And Marvin is to blame.

Now when the world's third-biggest industry is forced into a corner by technology-forcing legislation, you can rest assured that technology will come, and fast. Eventually, we will have cars propelled along by dylthium crystal batteries, cars that can perform just as well as the S-class Merc of today, cars that will go for 20,000 miles between recharges and cities with power points at every parking meter.

And as a result, the air will be cleaner and cities will be quieter, and we'll wear flowers in our hair and not eat meat.

Or maybe not. You see, charging up the millions and millions of electric cars that Marvin hopes will one day roam the roads, will require a lot more effort on the part of power stations which, at present, are responsible for 90 per cent of 'greenhouse gases'.

By running an electric car, all you are doing is displacing the pollution from your exhaust pipe to a power station somewhere else. Even the LA goody-goodies admit this by stating that 64 per cent of the city's power is not generated in the LA basin. In other words, we clean up our act and to hell with those who'll suffer as a result.

Now I don't dispute that LA has a dreadful smog problem because I've been there and I've seen it. Nor do I dispute that motor vehicles are to blame but why is LA's smog worse than anyone else's?

It seems that the prevailing winds from the Pacific are blocked by the mountain range behind LA. Consequently the smog doesn't get blown away.

Rather than make all the world drive around in milk floats, surely Marvin would have been better off seeking the advice of a demolition team. He's already said he doesn't mind pollution so long as it isn't in LA so why doesn't he simply blow up the mountains?

In the prologue to *Look Stranger*, W. H. Auden said: 'Far sighted as falcons, they looked down on another future; for the seed in their loins was hostile.'

Marvin probably thinks he's being a falcon but it might be a good idea if he had a good look between his legs.

Cruel to be Kind

I find myself wondering whether the new Archbishop of Canterbury, the good Doctor George Carey, has ever been scrumping.

Without wishing to sound like Frank Muir, *to scrump* is to break into an orchard and steal apples.

I used to do it. My father used to do it and I'd bet a wedge of Melvins that old George cannot put his hand on his heart and say that, at one time or another, he hasn't climbed over a wall and helped himself to the odd bit of somebody else's fruit.

However, times have moved on and this is what George and all the other weirdos who go on television to talk about 'social issues' fail to understand.

In the fifties, people would queue for hours to see *Way to the Stars*, a dreadful black and white film where people said 'bother' if they trapped their thumb in a door and, apart from people trapping their thumbs in doors, nothing much happened.

Today, youth is not satisfied unless strange metal aliens chop whole limbs off. Furthermore, those who do get de-legged do not say bother.

Then there's sex. In the fifties, the merest hint of an ankle would have the censors reaching for their scissors whereas these days no film is complete unless it features at least six panty hamsters.

Translate that sort of progress into the real world and it becomes a damn sight easier to understand why the modern-day equivalent of scrumping is ram-raiding.

We do not need hairy social workers and do-good churchmen looking for complicated reasons why the youths of Newcastle and Oxford want to steal cars, because it's patently obvious to anyone under the age of 100. They do it because it's bloody good fun.

Why do you think rock stars throw televisions into swimming pools? Why can I not walk past a stack of beans in Safeway without getting a sometimes uncontrollable urge to push it over?

Glass makes a satisfying noise when it breaks but I bet it makes a hell of a more satisfying noise when you've just driven a Range Rover through it.

And I absolutely cannot think of anything which would be more fun than racing a Golf GTi round Woolworths.

George Carey has the bare-faced effrontery to claim that the recent spate of rioting is because of 'social deprivation'. His sentiments, inevitably, are echoed by various beardies who have been invited to wax lyrical on *Newsnight* in recent weeks.

But ram-raiding has as much to do with social deprivation as pork pie. What it does have a lot to do with is risk.

I would steal apples because if I was caught, and the chances were slim, the worst I could expect was a pair of boxed ears. And I reckoned that the thrill of nicking a Granny Smith easily outweighed the possible consequences.

The youths of Newcastle drive Range Rovers into electrical wholesalers because if they get caught, and again the chances are slim when you remember Plod spends most of his time and manpower trying to catch you and me speeding, the worst they can expect is some magistrate applying a metaphorical blackboard rubber to their knuckles.

However, I am not prepared to leave it at that.

Even if the police did begin to understand that speeding is not the most heinous crime and that they are wasting precious resources trying to stamp it out, they still would not be able to patrol every shop, in every town, every night.

And anyway, they've let the youths get away with it for too long. When, as a child, I was told to stop doing something I'd been doing for ages, I'd have a tantrum; that was the way in the 1960s. Tell them to stop ram-raiding and there'd be a riot.

So how do we tackle it? Well, we have to ask ourselves what differentiates those who steal cars on a Saturday night with those who don't.

We have to ask ourselves, also, why scrumping is the preserve of pre-pubescent schoolboys who stop doing it when they get older?

Why don't I nick a car tonight and do some handbrake turns outside the pub? Why don't you hot-wire your neighbour's Cavalier and go for a spin in Currys at the weekend? Why doesn't George Carey nick fruit any more?

We don't do these things because we are intelligent. We understand about the notion of ownership and we can see that if we steal and destroy things, insurance premiums will rise, pushing up the cost of living and thus increasing the chances of a Labour victory in the next election.

Those who do indulge in ram-raiding and hotting handbrake turnery of a Saturday night are incapable of logical thought like us because they are stupid.

And how do you stamp out stupidity? Simple; you don't allow dim people to breed.

What I propose is that at the age of sixteen, everyone has to take a simple IQ test. If they can't name four cabinet ministers, three American rivers and two characters from *Cannery Row*, then it's vasectomy time.

For sure, we won't reap the benefit for a number of years but eventually, when Britain is freed from the shackles of having to support a whole bunch of stupid people, ram-raiding will cease to be. So too will the Church and British Rail.

Carey and his mates at the DSS believe in giving these kids what they want. They say that if a child won't stop nicking cars, he must be given a car and the opportunity to race it at weekends.

Yeah well, I want a boat in the South of France, a flat in Paris, a house in California and while you're at it George, a jet.

An Able Ford

You will never have stayed at the Prince de Galles hotel on Avenue George V in Paris because it is too upmarket, but I was there last weekend, and so was Brigitte Nielson, and yes, they really are as big as they are in the photographs in *Hello*.

Can it really have been a coincidence that the three films available to guests on the pay-as-you-watch video channel were *Tango and Cash, Rocky IV* and *Cobra*? I think not.

Over the course of the weekend we ate in two restaurants that you will not have been to because they are far too expensive and we saw England absolutely stuff the French at a game called Rugby.

But all this is by the by because the best bit is that we drove to and from Paris in the most coveted car sold in Britain.

It was not, however, a Ferrari or a Lamborghini, as you might imagine, and nor did a flying 'B' embellish the radiator grille. And no, it was not an Audi S2, which as you all should know, is the *best* car in Britain.

I am talking about the Ford Sierra Sapphire 2.0i Ghia, complete with air conditioning and compact disc player.

Of course, all of us want a Ferrari 348 in the same way that all of us want a million in the bank, a mansion in the country and a nymphomaniac in one of its bedrooms. But, not to put too fine a point on it, none of us will ever achieve even one of the above. We can only strive for what is achievable. That which is not is a fantasy. Thus, a 348 is a fantasy while a Sierra Ghia is a goal.

If you are a divisional sales manager for one of the major food manufacturers and each day you ply the motorways in your Sierra GL, you can dream all you like about owning a Ferrari, but it will not happen. And nor will you get home that night to find your wife has been transmogrified into a salivating teenage sex machine.

You can, however, strive for the Sierra Ghia because you know that if you could only find a supermarket manager who would return your calls, you'd meet the targets, get the promotion and thus, get the Ghia. It's a hell of a depressing way to go through life, I know, but that doesn't stop thousands of people from doing it.

And as there are more people out there driving humdrum Fords than anything else, there are, logically enough, more people out there striving, day in and day out, to make it to Ghia status than there are people striving to get a Volkswagen Corrado or a Mercedes.

Now, those of you with cars from outside the Ford stable will, by now, be howling with derisive laughter at the small-minded nature of our reppy brethren. You will dismiss the notion of a Sierra Ghia with a casual wave of the hand as you seek to explain that your Corrado will out-corner and out-perform any jumped-up sample-transporter.

Indeed it will, but then the ventilation in your Corrado is not that brilliant is it? And when you put a biro on the front seat, it always slips down onto the floor behind, doesn't it? And there aren't *that* many places in the cabin where you can store maps and chocolates and cans of Coke and fags and so on, are there?

You see, with a Corrado as with all other performance cars, only three things matter: How much does it cost? How fast does it go? Can I pull birds in it?

But repping requires a specialised tool. Over the course of my weekend, I drove the Ford for more than 500 miles and it did not irritate me once. I have never, and I mean never, encountered a better heater, and the driving position is even more perfect than lovely Brigitte's bits.

Now sure, the rev counter should be red-lined at 3000 rpm and if you attempt a corner at anything like breakneck speed, you will probably crash and break your neck. But handling is of no concern to the man whose boot is filled with precious samples.

Go round a corner too fast in a car that must double-up as your office and your cassettes will fly off the dash, your briefcase will fall over and your can of Coke will tip up, spilling its contents all over your polyester suit. Your wife will then be cross with you, reducing still further the chances of her becoming some kind of Lolita.

Same goes for performance. On the rare occasions when you take your Corrado out of town, sure, give it some wellie, but if you drive for five hours a day, five days a week, and you're always giving your car some stick, you run the hugest chance of losing your licence or crashing so often that whatever chance you may have had of promotion evaporates, along with the chance of your Ford Sierra Sapphire 2.0i Ghia.

You can, of course, take a colleague out to lunch in your Corrado, but with the Sierra you can take two of his friends as well.

And though it is of no concern to our friend in the suit-of-man-made-fibres, the Sierra is easy to service, easy to mend, cheap to operate and, if rumour is right, pretty reliable as well.

Now don't think the leopard has changed his spots and that all of a sudden I'm about to claim Ford makes the best cars in the world, because of course it doesn't – Audi does – but I believe that we performance car fans ought to remember that the average car is made up of some 15,000 parts and that the chassis is only a few of them.

On an RS2000, it is probably the most important bit, but on a Sierra Ghia it is less crucial than the upholstery. If you were told you had to drive for 25 hours a week, your major concern, above all else, would be ease of operation.

Stack the Sierra Ghia against any of its rivals in a *Performance Car* group test and it would lose, hands down. But in the real world, it should be, and is, a winner.

So would I ever think about running one? You have got to be joking. 'Hey bird, do you want to come for a play with the heater in my Sierra?' does not sound quite so endearing as 'Hey bird, ever been up a back street at a hundred and forty?'

Does it.

Train Strain

Each Wednesday, I have to make a 120-mile journey from Nairobi, South London to Bombay, near Birmingham.

If I leave at 7 a.m., I am onto the M40 before the London rush hour begins and then I arrive in Birmingham ten minutes after its rush hour has died down.

En route, I can ring people up on a new device I have just bought called a mobile telephone, I can mount huge excavation projects in one or both of my nostrils and I can listen to the radio, or if Greening and Nicholas are on one of their left-wing crusades, play a compact disc instead. It's all very civilised.

If I stick to this schedule I never encounter anything which could be described as a jam but even if I don't there are only three places where things get sticky and, even if they're at their most glutinous, I only need add twenty minutes to my ETA.

However, like the good citizen I tend not to be, I have taken of late to dispensing with the motor car and using public transport instead. Thus when the token veg-head at a dinner party begins to harangue me for promoting death, I can explain that I do my bit for congestion and pollution. Then we all play party games, seeing who can get the fork, which I have inserted into her eye, out again.

But here's the rub. In the last fourteen weeks, British Rail has failed to get me from London to Birmingham, or back again, on anything even approaching time. Yesterday, I'll admit, it was only six minutes late but the week before I was stationary for one hour outside Coventry and consequently arrived at the terminus a staggering 94 minutes behind schedule.

A man kept coming on the public address system, presumably to explain why the train was not moving, but as he had not mastered the art of speaking English, his message was a trifle garbled.

The women who rush up and down the aisles, dispensing salmonella and bashing into your elbows, said they didn't know what was going on and that we should ask the ticket collector, but he was in a terrible temper and explained rather brusquely that it wasn't his fault. Also, his uniform didn't fit.

If this was a one-off, caused by a mad Mick with a bit of Semtex, you might put it down to bad luck and be understanding, but it happens with the regularity of a freshly wound metronome.

The awful thing is that even if it didn't, even if the train was as punctilious as the Queen's Christmas message, it would still take 40 minutes more than a car to get from my front door to the door of my choosing in Barmyhom.

Then there is the cost. Getting to and from Birmingham in a car that costs 15p a mile to run sets you back £36, while if you use public transport there are two £5 taxi bills and British Rail has the bare-faced cheek to charge £44 – none of which it spends on cleaners.

I smoke, quite a lot, and that means I am wedged, with the most disgusting bunch of old fleggers, into half a carriage where the ashtrays are all missing, the windows are caked in nicotine and if you stand on the carpet for more than a minute, you stick to it.

If smoking is going to be allowed, why the hell can't someone pop into the relevant carriage once in a while with some Flash? Same goes for the lavatories, which ought really to have a sign advising passengers that excrement should be ejected in the general direction at least of the small porcelain receptacle without taps.

Even if I could afford first class, I would object to sharing my carriage with people in polyester suits shrieking into mobile telephones. And let's face it, the staff are still just as rude and the train is still just as late whether you have an extra tad of leg room or not.

I have also noticed that, in first class, I always feel sick whenever the train's speed exceeds 100 mph, which thankfully isn't very often. Mind you, this is better than the 'thrifty' carriages, which shake so much the print in your book blurs and your coffee goes everywhere except down your mouth part.

What is required is a class in between first and second (second, apart from being uncomfortable, is also full of mutants). Yesterday, on the way up, a fat girl plonked herself next to me and talked incessantly about retirement homes, thus preventing the massive nose diggery scheme I had planned. On the way back, the man opposite was shamelessly reading the *Guardian*.

A couple of weeks ago, a girl said she was educated at a public school called Abbots Bromley and that she was 29. Yet she claimed not to know any of the thirty 29-year-old ex-Abbots Bromley girls I fired at her. Either she was, in fact, 46 or she did not go to AB at all and she was educated in the state system; like most liars.

The class I'm proposing would not be based on ability to pay but on breeding. Smoking would be compulsory because, in my experience, the only people worth talking to get through at least twenty a day, all the sandwiches would have meat in them, polyester would be banned and so would the *Guardian*. Basically, before being allowed in the carriage concerned, MI5 would have to check your background, you'd be tested on certain U and non-U expressions and you'd have to be proposed by me.

However, in Major's classless society this is unlikely to get off the ground, which means that those of us wishing to be green will get black as we talk to reds.

So why don't I just give up and use the car? Well, the thing is that, for about five miles, the train runs alongside the M1 and even if it's being as asthmatic as ever, it always manages at that moment to be going faster than the traffic.

This gives a false impression of speed and efficiency and for a glorious moment you tend to forget that British Rail couldn't get its leg over in a brothel.

So here is an appeal. If, on a Wednesday, you are heading North on the M1 just near turn-off 17 and you see a train coming up alongside, please, please, please put your foot down.

And make me a very happy man indeed.

Cruising Soundtrack

Last night I returned from America with a cricked neck and sunburned feet to find that someone had thoughtfully left a Jaguar XJS for me outside the office.

Ordinarily, one has to reverse cars to the main road some 200 yards away but, because of the broken neck, I had to make a 67-point turn in a street that is just two inches wider than the Jaguar is long.

This was a nuisance. It was also much, much colder than it had been in Florida. There wasn't enough headroom. The leather seats were like blocks of ice. I knocked my cigarette end out while twirling the wheel. I had jet lag. All in all, the Jaguar XJS, pretty new rear windows or no, was lining up alongside VD in the suitable companion stakes.

And as the very *raison d'être* of the XJS is comfort, I began to consider the notion of abandoning it and using a taxi.

But then, as I finally accomplished the turn, the CD player began, seemingly of its own accord, to fill the cabin with the strains of 'Nimrod', Elgar's most moving excursion to the very furthest-flung corners of jingoism.

And, as a result, I stopped likening the XJS to an enema and began instead to think of it in the same breath as lobster thermidor and, er, second helpings.

I do not consider myself to be especially musical. You're reading the words of a man who fainted while attempting to learn the flute and who reached grade four in piano, but only after failing grades one, two and three.

Yet music is capable of inducing strange mood swings. It can soothe away the aches and strains of a busy day or it can drive me nuts. I even have a compilation tape which I play when I want to get somewhere quickly because all the songs on it, from Bad Company's 'Feel Like Makin' Love' to Bob Seger's 'Long Twin Silver Line', are designed specifically to make me drive much faster than is usual.

I have another tape, well I have a lot of other tapes actually, but there's one in particular I play when the day has been especially awful and the traffic is being especially bad and the pavements are full of horrid working-class people queuing up to spit on me as I drive by. They do this a lot these days.

This one features such songs as Albinoni's 'Adagio in G' and Pink Floyd's 'Time'. There are those who recommend John Martyn and Leonard Cohen, but these guys take things a bit too far. I mean, they go beyond calming you down; they lower you so low you start to hallucinate about gas ovens and vats of Valium.

On the other hand, Katrina and the Waves' 'Walking On Sunshine' or Haircut 100's 'Fantastic Day' prompt a grin bigger than Cheshire. If either is on the radio, I'll even let people out of side turnings. Yet play me anything by Billy Bragg and I'll throw a brick through the Labour Party's nearest HQ. And 'Bat Out Of Hell' makes me dribble.

I don't like foreigners at the best of times, but whenever I hear even so much as a snatch of Elgar, the mild dislike becomes a deal more pronounced. And believe you me, the best place to be at such a time is behind the pencil-thin wheel of a Jaguar.

If you sort of half close your eyes, you can imagine that deeply sculptured bonnet is the prow of HMS *Victory*, the nose of a Spitfire, the protruding snub of a Challenger tank.

If I find myself listening to Elgar while driving along in, say, a Mercedes, I have to get out and sit on the grass verge until it's finished. When you're in a Mercedes, you can only listen to Strauss or Wagner or something that makes you want to bludgeon your way around the Soviet Union, smashing it into small pieces.

You also cannot listen to Elgar when you are driving around in America, because it sounds silly. When you are in America, you absolutely must listen to American music.

A cruise down the seventeen-mile drive south of Monterey in a convertible Mustang to the accompaniment of six spotty youths from Manchester banging on about life in a tower block is just plain daft. Even Squeeze, whose tunes are fine on a wet Wednesday in Clapham, are wholly inappropriate. No, you need Don Henley wailing on about 'Boys Of Summer' and the Doobies with 'China Grove'.

From time to time, I get to air my views about this and that on *Top Gear*, the motoring programme, and while all of it is a giant ego trip, the best part as far as I'm concerned is choosing the musical interludes, the dream sequences where a car is seen whizzing hither and thither to the strains of whatever song we happen to feel is suitable.

Having explained that the Lamborghini Countach was a fairly terrible car, it seemed right that we should play Bad Company singing the song called 'Bad Company'. Similarly, having decided that the Ferrari 348 is just about the finest car made, Tina Turner was drafted in to give us a 30-second slug of 'Simply The Best'.

In the new series that should have begun by now, you will be treated to a seven-minute item about the Ford Mustang. Because I can't think of enough words to fill in for such a long stretch, much of the soundtrack will be down to Andrew Strong and 'Mustang Sally'. Nice of him that; in the same way that it was nice of Prince to do 'Little Red Corvette', and Mark Cohn to do 'Silver Thunderbird'.

We will never be stuck when it comes to choosing music for bits about American cars because American singers find them a source of lyrical romance. 'Cruising in my Mustang down the I5 to New Orleans' is always going to be a better line than 'Strugglin' up the A1 to Rotherham in my Maestro'.

A few weeks ago, a columnist in a rival magazine argued that one tends to make one's mind up about a car within five seconds of getting into it. This is almost certainly the case, but what he didn't say is that whether you like the car or not is dependent on the music that happens to be playing at the time.

Big

So, do the needs of the many outweigh the needs of the few or is it the other way around? Certainly, the needs of people who are disabled, be it through a physical or mental malady, outweigh the needs of those who are able-bodied.

It may cost a business a thousand quid or more to install lavatories big enough to take wheelchairs, but this is something that must be done. If I was disabled and found a shop, hotel or restaurant which did not provide such a facility, I would crap on the floor. On purpose.

However, I am unable to think of any other minority group whose needs should be allowed to inconvenience the majority.

Thus, I have no sympathy whatsoever with these so-called action groups that hang around outside embassies and council offices, waving placards and getting their beards wet.

I do not understand why my poll tax bill in Fulham should be nearly £500 a year when I just know that a huge chunk of that will be spent on weirdos. Like most people, I want my bin emptying, the street lighting on, the schools open and the police doing some arresting. And that's about it.

What we have instead is pot-holed roads, council officials who won't answer the telephone, rampant truancy and a police force which can never get to the scene of a crime because of all the dog turds on the pavement. Oh and some immensely wealthy Cypriot lesbians.

This is absurd. If you happen to be a homosexualist Cypriot, you cannot expect everyone in the whole borough to finance your perversion. The council should let us decide whether we want to spend our money on gay Eastern Mediterranean types or not. Me, I prefer beer.

I like to smoke while eating, but if I am at a table peopled entirely by non-smokers, I will try to limit any cigarettery to periods when food is not in evidence.

So why then do vegetarians expect – demand even – special attention whenever I have them round for dinner? If I am prepared to give up smoking for them, they should damn well be prepared to eat cow for me. It's all give and take in this world and, if you're in a minority, you should bloody well do the giving.

Now, against this sort of a background, I was approached the other day by a chap from something called the Tall People's Club of Great Britain who would like me to become a member.

For two reasons, alarm bells immediately began to sound. First, this is a club and clubs are for the insecure who thrive on the company of the like-minded and like-bearded.

Down at the local golf club, they all give one another idiotic names and abbreviate everything. And they all treat the chairman with some kind of divine reverence, forgetting that he only got the job because (a) he has the woolliest pully and (b) he'd been on the committee for longest. The same goes for the Freemasons. And the Guild of Motoring Writers. And the infernal Round Table.

Secondly, the alarm bells were ringing because this whole 'tall' thing smacked of minority interest behaviour. We've had the race relations board to tackle racism and the equal opportunities commission to bop sexism on the head. I was fearful I was being lured into something which would set its stall out to fight something that doesn't even exist – heightism.

Yes, I'm 6 ft 5 in but some of my best friends are midgets. My girlfriend, for instance, is just one inch tall.

Neither of us has ever been abused, physically or verbally, because of our height and neither of us has ever found it to be a particular problem. What, then, if there is no such thing as heightism, is the point of a Tall Person's Club?

Maybe we'll all get together once in a while and call one

another Lofty or other amusing names. Maybe it would be a chance to meet tall members of the opposite sex.

But no. Apparently, the idea is to lobby various manufacturers, convincing them that they must start taking us into consideration. Or else.

The club wants taller door openings. But I was brought up in a seventeenth-century farmhouse and it never bothered me. The club wants higher kitchen units. Why, for Christ's sake? Find a sink that comes above your knees and the last excuse you have for not doing the washing up has gone.

And, needless to say, the club wants more space in cars. Well, at 6 ft 5 in, I'm just about at the very edge of reasonableness and yet the only car I absolutely cannot drive is a Fiat X19. Again, no bad thing.

Sure, in an F40, my head is on the roof and, in a Renault 25, my knees have to adopt a position which is most unladylike, but not at all unreasonable for a man. Come to think of it, not unreasonable for a woman either.

What I'm trying to say is that of the 750 cars on sale in Britain today, all will accommodate someone my size. Indeed, most will readily accommodate those of an even taller disposition. I even saw Herman Munster in a Mercedes 190 the other day.

Now, fair enough, some people are more than 7 ft tall and I would imagine that finding a car when you're that big is just about impossible.

And I'm afraid that it will stay just about impossible because car manufacturers simply cannot be expected to organise an interior for a seven-footer.

Or, if they did, can you imagine the problems of fitting the necessary equipment to make the same interior suitable for someone like my girlfriend, who, as I said, is just an inch tall.

If you are born long and freaky, then by all means join a club but don't expect it to answer your prayers for an easier life. Because it most certainly won't.

Far better, in the current environment, to move to Fulham

where the council will give you a specially converted Cadillac limousine. Or two, if you have a predilection for members of the same genital group.

What to Buy?

Today, my desk is freed from the burden of supporting a computer and assorted in-trays. In their place there is a pot of *foie gras* and a glass of Dom Pérignon. The whole office is bathed in an almost ethereal light while outside, beautiful young people are flouncing by, smiling in the spring sunshine.

The stock market has registered its biggest single jump for five years, leaping 130 points in just fifteen minutes, and there is talk of interest rates coming down.

For the fourth time in thirteen years, Britain has elected a Conservative government. Though it was clear by 2 a.m. that the forces of good would triumph, I stayed up until four so that I could watch that man Kinnock squirming in defeat. It was a glorious sight.

With a bit of luck the recession will now screech to a halt as business rejoices but just in case the economy needs a kick-start, I have taken steps.

First, I have instructed an estate agent to sell my flat so that I can get something a little more palatial, and secondly, I have taken the curious step of ordering a car.

Not a rash decision this as I've been chewing over the concept of just such a move for the best part of a year now. The question has fluctuated between: do I really need one and if I do, what sort should it be?

With the concept of Kinnock and his sidekicks getting into office, I felt that buying a car before the election would have been just plain stupid.

With his programme of spending money on social services and the National Health Service, anyone with a job would have been squeezed until they bled. And then squeezed a little more.

And then, men would come round and take away our video recorders to give to the poor, who under Labour, would have become the very rich.

I therefore needed my savings more than I needed wheels, but conversely I don't think it's right that a motoring journalist does not own a car. Many do not, arguing that there is always something new to test, but I hardly feel we can pontificate about motoring when we don't have firsthand experience of it.

Until you've queued for a tax disc and wondered why you can't apply through the post, or until you've heard an insurance broker suck air through his teeth when you said 'GTi and no, it won't be garaged', you don't really understand what's what. Anyway, now that I know my savings will be left alone, the time has come to do buying. But what?

First to fall off the short list was the old pagoda-roofed Mercedes SL. Lovely car and all that, but cars I own often spend months on the street without ever being called into service and my experience of really old cars is just when you need them the most, they are at their most stubborn on the starter-motor front.

Mercedes are engineered like no other car in the world but when something is 25 years old, it doesn't really matter how well it was built, it will just be unreliable.

Second to go was the BMW Z1. Though this would be absolutely perfect because it's modern enough to be reliable and different enough to be fun, they are still too expensive. Hunt hard and you can get one for £16,000 but £16,000 is an awful lot of money to spend on what would be street furniture for 360 days a year.

The Porsche 944 Turbo was lasting well on my list because here is a beautifully engineered, well-made car that you can now buy for less than £10,000. It is exceptionally good fun to drive, remarkable to look at and I have no doubt that it will be a Michelangelo's David when it comes to standing the test of time.

But there's something prattish about a Porsche. Urban yobs enjoy converting them into De Loreans and I sort of know why.

I'm not really the type of person who indulges in the art of gobbing on people but the temptation is strong when a Porsche struts by.

And that just about covers all the cars in which I'd be even remotely interested. I'd love an XJS but they really are too big for London, and too thirsty. Same goes for the Range Rover. And yes, I know a 325i or a Golf would be sensible but hell, that's like being nice, or balanced, or reasonable. I despise reasonableness with the same gusto that I despise socialism.

I'll tell you something else as well. Excluding all exotic nonsense I don't really like new cars. They're too sanitised and adonised and, oh the hell with it, I can't think of another word that ends in '-ised', but boring will do.

I just can't whip up any enthusiasm for the worthy Rover convertible or the Citroen Volcane. All those roadtests saying it was once king but it handed the crown on to the 19 16v which has subsequently passed it on to the Tipo have the same effect as a Mogadon 'n' whisky mix. I even borrowed an AMG-tweaked 24-valve Mercedes coupe the other day and nodded off in it.

However, there is one exception that proves the rule. It is made by Ford but don't bother hunting behind the pot plants down at your local dealer because they won't have one. It is a convertible with a powered hood. It has air conditioning, cruise control, electric seats, windows and mirrors and it barrels along at speeds up to 125 mph thanks to the installation of a 5.0-litre V8 engine, which makes all the right noises.

It is a Ford Mustang GT and I have discovered that you can buy one-year-old examples in America for $11,000. Ship one over, pay your taxes, insure it for a year and you still get change from £10,000.

It will undoubtedly be reliable because that engine is not exactly overstressed and I will, for the first time ever, have a convertible so that I can enjoy the sunshine.

And believe you me, there will be sunshine this summer, even when it's cold and wet. There will be sunshine in my heart because while the country in which I live overcharges for its cars and then sells a whole load of nasty ones, its people, for the fourth time since 1979, have, to use a footballing expression, done good.

Thank you Basildon. Thank you Portsmouth South.

All Change

Darwin's theory of evolution is a weighty tome but, in essence, it suggests that we all began as amoebas, then we were fish, then we were monkeys, then we were men.

And whenever we were going up the wrong path, nature gently inserted something like an ice age. This would kill off the evolutionary mistakes, like dinosaurs, allowing the rather more successful species to survive.

Undoubtedly, this will happen again one day soon, and all the socialists and car-stereo thieves will be swept away in a maelstrom of locusts and acid. Nature takes its time with this evolution game but, over and over again, it is proved to be right.

Look at the avocado pear. When nature discovered that avocado and prawns made a wholesome double act, it began, bit by bit, to enlarge the stone so there'd be space for the filling.

So it goes with the seal. Originally designed as a land-based mammal, it developed a penchant for fish and, as a result, nature has spent the last 200,000 years turning its legs into flippers and its lungs into hot-air balloons. Doubtless, by the year 4992, the seal will have gills, so that it never needs to surface at all.

According to some recent research, man is getting bigger. In 1992 we are, on average, one inch taller than we were in 1892, and one has to wonder where this will end. Perhaps nature has decided that we should all be 200 feet tall, but feels that there will be chaos if we suddenly start producing 16-foot-long babies. So it's being done nice and slowly, allowing us to get used to our new-found stature, an inch at a time.

Now, let us for a moment compare this state of affairs to the alternative put forward by those ancient scribes who wrote the Old Testament. God wakes up one morning, cleans his teeth and decides: 'I know. I'll make a man and a woman today.' So he does. In a matter of hours, the woman's had a fling with a snake, given herself up to the devil and had two children, one of whom eats the other and climbs into bed with his mother, claiming that if she doesn't come across, it'll be curtains for humanity.

Either way, there's bugger-all point tracing your family tree because, if Darwin got it right, your great-great-great-great-grand-father was an amoeba and, if the Old Testament was right, you stem from someone who ate his brother and pulled his mum. Even if, en route to this discovery, you find that you are a direct descend-ant of Richard the Lionheart, it really is only a small consolation.

But this is a peccadillo, a momentary loss of the thread. The point is that evolution may be time-consuming and boring, but it beats the crap out of revolution any day.

Look at the world of politics. The Greeks, somehow, invented democracy, the only real rival to which, excluding the excellent concept of feudalism, has been Communism. But a prerequisite for Communism is that the population like eating cabbage and being shot, so it didn't last very long – except in Cuba, where they're all on drugs anyway. Then there's the world of cars.

Nothing is guaranteed to send me scuttling for the door faster than when a well-scrubbed engineer, with a biro he lost two weeks ago stuck behind his left ear, announces that his company is about to unveil an all-new car. It begs the question: 'What the hell was the matter with the old one?' But no one ever asks because everyone is crossing and uncrossing their legs, barely able to contain their excitement at the prospect of a new gearbox.

Take the new Honda Prelude. This is a stunning-looking car, and I will pat the back of anyone who says they were even slightly involved with its styling, but for heaven's sake, did it need a new engine, a new floor, a new interior and a new four-wheel steering system too?

If you are going to change everything you run the risk, as Russia did in 1917, or as God did in the Garden of Eden, of getting something horribly wrong.

The Rover SD1 was unreliable but, instead of concentrating their efforts on quality, the designers came up with the all-new 800, which had a hole the size of France in its torque curve.

The original Toyota MR2 was beginning to look a little dated but, instead of a mild facelift, we got an all-new MR2 which, by all accounts, had the handling prowess of Bambi. Then there was the Celica. A few tweaks would have kept the eighties version as fresh as lavatory cleaner but no – in came something that looked like an extra in a Vincent Price movie.

And Subaru. For years it's made solid, dependable farm vehicles, but does it stick to its specialist subject? No, it invents the SVX, which is to the world of coupes what vomiting on the Queen's corgi is to your chances of getting a knighthood.

Now compare these revolutionary cars to those which have been gently evolved: the glorious Jaguar XJS, the characteristic Porsche 911, the Rolls, the Morgan.

And best of all, when it comes to illustrating the point, the Range Rover. Though the silhouette remains the same as it was in 1972, it has been evolved gradually, taking on four doors when it was deemed necessary, adopting a 3.9-litre engine when a 3.5 was no longer enough, sprouting anti-lock brakes, leather upholstery and various other toys, as market forces dictated.

The end result is a contemporary machine with the familiar cosiness of tradition. And because Land Rover has limited itself to a few choice alterations every year or so, not only have the development costs been pared to the bone but the chances of making a mistake have been virtually eliminated. Actually, the Range Rover is very probably the most developed car you can buy.

Now at this point the engineer with the errant Biro will point out that production techniques have changed considerably over the past twenty years and that, comparatively speaking, it costs a fortune to make a Range Rover. To which punk rock had an answer: 'We Don't Care Grandad.'

Sex on Wheels

Judging by the wall of anoraks down at my local newsagent's, there are a great many people out there who absolutely cannot wait to introduce their trouser snakes to the Viper.

Ever since the first sneak photographs of this new Dodge began to appear in British magazines, sales of *Club International, Razzle* and *Fiesta* have plummeted. Apparently.

They're calling it the horniest beast ever to emerge from the world's motor manufacturers and, although I personally find it extremely difficult to become aroused by a car, I do sort of know what everyone means. Indeed, just the other day I was to be found explaining to a young boy who works on one of the other motoring magazines that Julia Roberts and Sharon Stone are sexy, but the Dodge Viper is not. He couldn't grasp it at all but, then again, he wears Rohan trouserwear.

What the Dodge Viper is, is exciting. Not since yesterday tea-time have I looked forward to driving a car quite so much. Now, why should this be so? Why am I not bothered about the Ferrari 512 or the Maserati Shamal? Why am I able to sit here, with the keys to a Syclone on my desk, wondering which taxi firm to call when I go out tonight? What makes the Viper any different?

Well, first things first; it is not a sports car. Sports cars need to be small and nimble, and I'd like to bet a wadge the size of Devon that the Viper is neither. In a sports car, handling is everything. In a Viper, handling is the addendum.

It is not a supercar either. In order for a car to graduate to supercar status it has to be mid-engined, but as I always say, if God had meant us to put engines in the middle, he wouldn't have given us bonnets. Also, a supercar needs to look exactly like a Ferrari, and the only thing that looks less like a Ferrari than the Viper is my left lung.

No, I'll tell you what the Viper is. It's a muscle car. As curvy as a curvy thing, it has a huge engine in the front and rear-wheel drive, and that's it. Doubtless we'll all be reading soon about how a Carrera 4 will out-corner it, and how a Delta Integrale is faster point-to-point, but would you like to know something, I couldn't give a toss.

I'm fairly certain that, in a 100-metre sprint, Colin Moynihan could beat Arnold Schwarzenegger, but who would queue to see a film with Col the Doll in it? If Sylvester Stallone had been equipped with a body like mine – which, by the way, is terrible – no one would have been to see *Rocky*. And he would have no money, and neither would Brigitte Nielson, and there's another case in point(s).

People like powerful things. We like the majesty of a 747 taking off. We like the Destriero because it has 60,000 horsepower. We like crash, bang and wallop. We like finesse in the kennel and brute force on the kitchen table. Well, I do anyway, and if you don't your sexuality must be seriously open to question.

Now, I hope you're starting to understand why the Viper holds such appeal. What makes it so special is that it's unique. There are no other big-engined, rear-wheel-drive muscle cars on offer in this country. And no, the Griffith, in comparison, is about as muscular as the Princess of Wales, who is, incidentally, the world's prettiest person.

The trouble is that the European and Japanese manufacturers that follow this timeless and classic design philosophy tune the end product for comfort, creating a GT car in the process.

The Jaguar XJS has a huge 5.3-litre engine and rear-wheel drive. It has a bonnet so big you could play baseball on it, and more curves than the Pompidou Centre. Also, has anyone else noticed that, from the driver's seat, those front wings look just like the legs on the lions in Trafalgar Square? No? Well I did.

The trouble is that Jaguar decided to go for the Darby and

Joan brigade, so in came sound deadening and the automatic gearbox and the silken ride, and out went the wide-eyed 'oh-my-god-we're-going-to-crash' excitement. Fine if you're 50 – annoying if you're not. And I'm 32.

However, it does not take much – about £15,000 actually – to turn a five-grand XJS into the British answer to Viper. From a distance, the Hands Hyper XJS looks like the sort of car that delivers escorts to your door, day or night. The rental kind.

But, if you actually get down on your hands and knees, you begin to understand that it only looks like a tartmobile because it looks like a customised XJS. Forget you ever clapped eyes on an XJS in the first place, and it looks absolutely bloody marvellous.

The front wings are flared outwards by one inch and the rears by two. The resultant gaps are filled with giant 16-inch pepperpot wheels, and then the whole car is lowered by two inches. To bring it even nearer the ground, a spoiler and skirts kit is added. This little lot turns the rather svelte, gentlemanly standard item into a car that looks as aggressive as a gorilla forced to wear evening dress for the first time.

Mechanically, the engine is bog-standard, but the gearbox is not. Designer Paul Hands explained it all to me time and time again, but I still can't get it. He's taken something called the torque converter out, I think, which means you get some more horsepower, but you have to move the stick if you want to change gear.

The bits underneath are finished off with some stainless-steel exhausts and new manifolds, which help up the output to 340 bhp. Nice.

What you're left with is a truly splendid car to drive. Yes, it handles and yes, the steering is quite superb. The interior's not bad and the gearbox is probably clever. The looks are what you'd call horny, and what I'd call angry, and the fuel consumption is strictly for Mr Rolex.

But the best bit is that when you put your foot down on the

accelerator, it goes whoooooooooooooooooooooooooooooooooo-ooooooooooooooooarrrrrrrrrrh. A lot.

Yours from the funny farm.

In a Car Crash

The sun was out, the roof was off, the revs were right up against the red line and Northumberland had never looked, sounded or felt better. The road, a sinewy grey ribbon, darted this way and that in a frantic attempt to run alongside the babbling brook.

The car was Honda's latest CRX. With its new soft suspension, that clever roof and the extraordinary 158-bhp VTEC engine, this was a seriously good machine.

The driver was me, and I was having the sort of fun I didn't think you could have in a car any more. I've argued time and time again that no driving experience could ever get close to sex, but this was close. Damn close.

But then, like the husband coming home or the headboard snapping, as I rounded the bend, there was a car parked, broadside, right across the middle of the road, blocking it, ruining my fun.

Now this is not a story about the advantages of anti-lock brakes. I am not going to tell you in great depth how I hit the middle pedal, hard, and was still able to steer round the car, because this did not happen.

Nor is it the story about how rural interbreeding has rendered the average country bumpkin so stupid that he will park sideways on the blind side of a bend when I am coming the other way.

You see, it didn't take a great deal of time or intelligence to work out that the offending car was, in fact, upside down.

Initially, I imagined that, after a pissy lunch, someone had had a bit of a whoopsy with the hedge and had walked home, where they were now sleeping it off, unconcerned with the consequences of their accident.

So I was angry. Angry enough not to have noticed that the thing reeked of petrol and that trying to pivot it round, single-handed, would result in either a broken back or a bloody big explosion.

In fact, neither of these things happened because, after a deal of pushing and shoving, the car had moved exactly no inches. By this time I was really angry and had set about the hedge on the basis that privet is more manoeuvrable than Ford.

While attempting to uproot a particularly stubborn bit, I had to get on my hands and knees, which enabled me, through the wonders of peripheral vision, actually to see into the car. Where there was a young girl.

Only two days earlier I had harangued a friend who said he was going to first-aid classes in case someone next to him had a heart attack. This, I argued, was the sort of thing a bearded person would do, and that it's a dog-eat-dog world. 'If someone next to you has a heart attack,' I said, 'nick his wallet.'

It was a joke with a cruel twist in the tail, because here I was in the middle of bloody nowhere, peering at a girl who was either unconscious or dead. And I had absolutely no idea what to do.

Somewhere, deep inside the furthest reaches of my memory bank, I recall someone once saying that you should not attempt to move them but, as I did not wish to stand in a coroner's court explaining that I had been at her side for a full five minutes before the car blew up, I decided to get her out. Now even I could work out that, the instant I released the seatbelt, she would drop on her head and that, if her back wasn't already broken, it sure as hell would be then.

But I managed, and once she was far enough from the car, I decided to see if she was alive or not. And that, believe me, is not as easy as it might sound.

I did not want her to come round to find me fiddling with her chest, something you have to do in order to test for a heartbeat if, like me, you can't even find you own wrist pulse. And for the same reason, I did not want to stick her lips to my ear to listen for breathing.

Eventually, of course, I threw caution to the four winds, went for a quick grope and determined that she was indeed alive. Happily, there was no sign of blood, otherwise I too would have been out cold.

But then what do you do? Drive off and leave her? And anyway, we're talking Cheviots here, not the Marylebone High Street, and for all I knew the nearest phone might have been 30 miles away. The next time someone calls my mobile (yes, the one I'd left at home) a pose, I shall insert it in them.

Thankfully, while deliberating, a brace of locals emerged from the undergrowth and, between us, we decided that one should go for the phone, one should stay with the girl and I should go and get her parents, who lived nearby.

It's a laugh, let me tell you, knocking on someone's door in the middle of the afternoon to explain that their daughter has crashed her car and is lying unconscious in the middle of the road.

It's even more of a laugh when you are wearing a biker's jacket and ripped jeans, because you know that they think you caused the crash in the first place.

And boy, did I split my sides when they said it was her nineteenth birthday. The punchline was still to come though, because both Mum and Dad wanted to come with me in the CRX. In those few short moments, there was enough material for an entire ITV sitcom starring Richard Briers as the fast-talking father, Adam Faith as the yob and June Whitfield as the tearful mum with tea towel. Not.

By the time we made it back to the scene of the crash, the ambulance, the entire Northumberland police department (Eric and Reg) and lots of people with straw in the mouth were there.

But the best bit was that the girl was whimpering and moving her feet, suggesting that if anything was broken, it wasn't too serious. She was carted off into the sunset for what I sincerely hope was a happy ending.

Except for one thing. This time I was lucky, but next time I find a car crash, the person may die because of my hopelessness. So, since all this happened a couple of weeks ago, I have been feverishly studying human anatomy down at the library.

And I've been doing some practice as well. Last night I amputated my next door neighbour's leg and sewed his wife's spleen on to their daughter's left ventricle.

Today, when they arrested me, I was wearing my underpants on the outside of my trousers.

Speed Kills

I have made no secret in the past that I do not like the *Guardian* which, I've always reckoned, is a paper for hirsute vegetarians and Christians *who care*.

It is a paper written for those who like to think they can make a difference. It is a paper for fools, except on Mondays when it is a paper for people who choose to wear bigger spectacles than is actually necessary.

Now, I do not buy it and nor do I speak to anyone who does, but every so often people fax me extracts. Normally, they create a little mirth in the office and then they go in the bin. But now this has all changed because an article appeared recently that is not at all funny, not even if your sense of humour is as warped as Windsor Castle. It was entitled 'Live Fast, Kill Young' and not since Julian single-handedly foiled a massive smuggling operation in *Five Go Picnicking* have I ever read such drivel. Believe 'Live Fast, Kill Young' and you'd be down at the bottom of the garden, looking for fairies.

It begins with the tale of Shaun Gooch, who lost control of his Ford Escort while pursuing a friend round the streets of Swindon at speeds of up to 90 mph. He killed four children outright and another died later.

Almost immediately, it quotes the editor of *Fast Lane* magazine, Andrew English, claiming that 'speed is fun', and that there is 'an enormous amount of prudism about the whole thing'.

So now every bearded Christian in the land has English pegged as a stupid person who gladly condones the behaviour of those who drive around Swindon at 90 mph, killing people. I know him, and I can tell you he isn't like that at all. He, like just about

every other right-thinking person in the land, would like to see
killer joyriders hung up by their dangly bits.

Anyway, the message the *Guardian* is trying to get across is
that speed kills. Specifically, it says that 'excessive speed is a
principal cause of fatal accidents'. Unfortunately, a caption on
the next page says that the English police do not compile any
speed and accident statistics. Without data, it is damned hard to
work out how anyone can make the link, and it's even harder
when the small piece of information you do have is wrong.
Another caption says that road deaths in Germany increased by
18 per cent when the country abolished speed limits on the
motorway. This is not true because there have never been speed
limits on German autobahns.

OK, so the facts are either wrong or based on incorrect data,
but does this interrupt the flow? No, it does not.

Gavin Green, sometime editor of *Car* magazine, is quoted as
saying that the Escort Cosworth cocks a snook at pleasure haters
who are trying to take the fun out of motoring, and that Ford
must be admired for making it.

The *Guardian* asks whether we really should admire a company
that makes a car so hugely capable of breaking the speed limit. It
says it *knows* that people who buy the Cosworth will break the
law. I know that people who buy Astramax vans will break the
speed limit too, but do I hear calls for the Astramax to be banned?
No, I do not. Sure, I've got a Cossie and I drive at 80 mph on
motorways, which is illegal. However, the point is that I like
driving Ford's winged wonder not because I like to drive fast,
but because people who know it can go fast stare at me.

'Live Fast, Kill Young' calls the Cosworth 'pointlessly' over-
powered, but if someone who buys one gets his or her leg over
as a result of its gutsy motor and exec jet looks, then that makes
the purchase point*ful*, surely?

Anyway, with the Cosworth well and truly dealt with, we are
told all about the people who will buy it. Me. Apparently, we

are suited bullies who test our cars alongside poorer, but equally menacing drivers in ex-post-office vans. This, it seems, makes driving a problem for everyone else. Well, in the last two weeks three of my friends have been involved in city-centre accidents, and on each occasion the blame lay fairly and squarely at the door of the dithering gits who pull out of junctions without looking and stutter round roundabouts.

Fine, I might be doing 80 mph on a motorway in my pointless Cosworth when a woman, distracted by two screaming kids in the back, pulls out unexpectedly. Sure, if I had been doing 70 the crash might not have had such dire consequences, but similarly, if she had been paying attention it wouldn't have happened. Same goes with caravanists. If I encounter a queue of cars behind a caravan which is dawdling along at 20 mph and I crash whilst attempting to overtake, is that *only* my fault?

Yes, I am an impetuous young fool in a souped-up Escort who should exercise patience and restraint, but then the caravanner is a selfish idiot who doesn't understand human nature. If he'd made his journey at night, or better still, had worked hard enough to have been able to afford a proper holiday, there would have been no crash.

Besides, speed is essential. In today's profit-motivated world we need to get hither and thither quickly. We want jets that can get us to America in five hours and trains that can get us to work in twenty minutes. And fast cars. Yes, this must be balanced with safety, but the cost of accidents must be weighed against the cost of going down the *Guardian*'s ozone-friendly route and buying ox carts.

I would never condone the behaviour of those who drive recklessly, but there is a world of difference between that and doing a ton on the M1 once in a while.

The trouble with the *Guardian* is that it just doesn't understand the real world. War is awful, but you absolutely can't stop it happening. It is unfair that Paul Raymond has more cash than he could possibly need while poverty drives thirteen-year-olds into prostitution, but in a democracy that *will* happen. Aids is terrible, but you can't spend two hours looking for an all-night chemist when you want sex *now*. Speed does kill, but no matter how many articles appear in vegetarian newspapers people will continue to drive their cars quickly.

It is not the most heinous crime in the world.

What's That Then?

When I was two, I used to have a book called the *Ladybird Book of Cars* and on long winter evenings my mother would keep me amused for hours by covering up all but one bit of a photograph and then asking me to tell her what sort of car it was.

She'd show me the tiniest bit of rear-light cluster and I'd know it was a Triumph Herald. When confronted with a grooved hubcap, I'd bounce around the room, clutching my part and talking loudly about the Rover 2000.

OK, by current standards this is a fairly tame way of passing the time, but we didn't have Super Mario Game Boys in the early sixties. Today, of course, the only bit of a car that most two-year-olds can identify is the steering lock.

But that has little to do with the decline of moral standards or the breakdown of family units and quite a lot to do with car design.

There is no way a Triumph Herald looked like anything (on earth) in the same way that no other car on the road had grooved hubcaps like a Rover TC. No one ever mistook a Ford Corsair with its pointy and very shiny nose for a Ford Classic. Volkswagen Beetles had about as much to do with Vauxhall Vivas as Vauxhalls did with anti-corrosion treatment.

I've harped on about this before, I know, but even as recently as a year ago I had no idea how bad things were going to get, and how soon they were going to get as bad as they have. In short, they are now dreadful.

For the first time since I was two, I cannot tell you what every car on the road is at a glance. The eyes may be getting a bit piggy as the years and the beers take their toll on the fleshy bits, but they still work fine. The cars, on the other hand, do not.

I noticed this for the first time last week when I was following a K-reg hatchback up the M40. For the first 30 miles, I thought it was a Mazda 626 but then, when things got very boring indeed, I started thinking about it a bit harder and realised it didn't have that funny rear spoiler.

So I reckoned it must be a Toyota Carina and went back to 'Our Tune'. However, when that finished, I realised it was not a Carina at all and that it had to be something else. It was with a Benny Hillesque slap to the forehead that I finally realised what it was. What it was was a new Mondeo. Definitely. Probably. Perhaps. Nope, it wasn't that either.

At this point, I began to get a little angry. This was something that had never happened before.

I have always prided myself on a sure-fire certainty that if I ever witnessed a crime, I'd be able to give the police a perfect description of exactly what sort of car the thieves used, what sort of engine it had, what level of trim it featured and where the knob for the heated rear window was.

But here I was, following a car up the M40 and I had no idea what it was. Shergar could have stuck his head out of the boot. Lord Lucan could have waved from the back seat and, later, I'd have had no idea at all what sort of car they'd been in.

So I closed right up to have a look and found to my horror it was a Renault Safrane, a car I hadn't even considered.

The next day, in the pub, while discussing cars with a colleague, I told the tale and he simply pointed over my shoulder and asked me to name the estate car that was pulling out of a side turning. I knew it was Japanese and reckoned it was a Nissan Sunny. It was, in fact, a Mazda.

So I was half right.

Since then, I have been counting the number of cars that I can't name. And there are bloody hundreds.

This is going to have repercussions because one of these days

I am going to review a car, be it in *Performance Car* or even on *Top Gear* and I shall spend the entire time talking about the wrong model. Hell, maybe it's already happened and the Vantage was in fact a Wartburg.

And even if I don't and it wasn't, how the hell am I going to find anything interesting to say about it. If car A looks exactly the same as car B and both have the same equipment levels, the same sized 16-valve engines and the same price, how can anyone form any kind of decent reason for buying one rather than the other?

The next time someone asks me whether the Nissan Primera or the Ford Mondeo is the better bet, I shall have to respond with a rather unhelpful 'Haven't a clue mate'.

If anyone asks me what the Nissan Sunny estate is like, I shall have to admit that I simply don't have the faintest idea.

But here's the deal. There is nothing we can do about it because cars are simply catching up with everything else in the world.

I've just bought a house which is exactly the same as the houses on either side of it and indeed as every other house I've ever been to in London. The estate agent described it as unusual because the bathroom roof slopes a bit. Wow.

Go to the City and see if you can find anyone whose haircut is anything other than sergeant-major neat or whose suit is anything other than suitish.

I was out last week in a sort of West End singles-bar type place called Caspars where every single man who wandered into the place had half a tub of what looked like lard in his hair. Every girl had had her clothes sprayed in place, but this, on reflection, wasn't so bad.

And although I'm sure they're all very good, I can't tell the difference between any of the new generation of Hollywood stars. Who is Kiefer Sutherland and why is he any different to Emilio Estevez or Charlie Sheen?

Fridges all look the same. We all look the same. Everything is the same as everything else. So small wonder that car designers are responding by making our cars all look the same.

Tomorrow, I'm going to wear my Levis back to front. And I will paint my fridge green.

I Had That Geezer from *Top Gear* in the Back Once

Word is that Prince Charles will never be King. However, this has nothing to do with his marital difficulties, even though anyone who lets Princess Diana go is obviously barking mad.

Nor does it have a great deal to do with his predilection for talking to trees or his alleged obsession with tampons, or even the fact that Brenda might cling on to the crown jewels until he's got a bus pass.

And then the cost and pomp of a coronation would be wasted, bearing in mind the little time he'd have before William could take over the orbs.

No, the reason Charles will never be King is this: the way things are going, there will be no such title. He may, however, become Emperor.

In this role, he could preside over a nation where it is an offence not to be yellow and Westminster Abbey sells raw fish to passers-by at weekends.

You may have noticed, over the years, that I am fiercely proud to be British and that I hope the Maastricht Bill ends up where it belongs: up Jacques Delors's backside. But I am also a realist.

I know therefore what is coming. The Queen's head will be lopped off the stamps, the pound will be replaced with an ECU, peanut butter will be renamed peanut sauce and sausages will be banned.

But this isn't so bad. At least we understand the Europeans; we know, for instance, that the Germans have no sense of humour and that the Greeks are completely useless. We know also that the French are rude, the Italians are mad and the Dutch are a bunch of dope-smoking pornographers.

We can maintain our sense of English aloofness, obeying the *letter* of Maastricht but none of its *spirit*.

Far worse is the concept of Great Britain becoming Japan's third island.

We should, I suppose, be deeply grateful that Japan's car makers have chosen to invest their billions here – though we should never forget that Ford has nearly 30 per cent more tied up in the Land of Hope and Glory than Honda, Nissan and Toyota combined.

But I don't understand the Japanese. I don't know what makes them tick and cannot easily understand how they've been so successful in such a short period of time. Not to put too fine a point on it, I'm scared shitless of them.

That's why I want someone to call a halt. We have their hi-fi factories and their car plants and their shops on Lower Regent Street. We have courses for businessmen in how to speak Japanese and restaurants that serve fish that are still wobbling. This is enough, thanks.

But no, even the institutions are now under threat. According to a report in my local newspaper, The London Taxi Drivers' Club, open to anyone called Reg, Sid or Archie, is asking the carriage office – its licensing department – if it can use Nissan Serenas instead of the black cab.

This is by far and away the most stupid thing I've ever heard anyone say.

Chairman of the club, Jim Wells, is reported to have said that he wants to be in a position where he can buy a vehicle and, within a year, sell it on the market for the same sort of money. Hey, Jim, don't we all mate.

He also says that a black cab costs up to £22,000 and that a Serena is £7,000 less than that. And finally, he points out that a Nissan people carrier is able to carry eight passengers.

Which it can't.

Let's look at that bit first. If Archie is behind the wheel, he doesn't want anyone next to him so that front can, in fact, carry no passengers at all.

Behind, there is space for five but there is no way those in the very back can get out unless those in the middle make way. In a normal London cab, there is space for five and anyone can get in or out without anyone else having even to twitch.

Then there's the turning circle. A London cab can do a U-turn whenever and wherever it wants. A Nissan Serena can also do a U-turn whenever and wherever it wants, providing it is in a field at the time.

And where does the luggage go in a Serena? In the driver's mouth? And what about wheelchair access? And how would everyone else who buys a Serena feel about being flagged down every 30 seconds each time they come to London.

Now these are practical reasons why the Serena has about as much to do with taxi cabbery as a cauliflower.

But then there are emotive reasons too. In my experience, London is unique in offering specialist cabs. In Milan, for instance, a taxi can be anything from a Fiat Mirafiori to an Alfa 90, while in Geneva it is as likely as not to be an S-Class Benz. Just about the only clue you really have is the light on the top and the colour. In London, you can make a cab look like a newspaper (and they do) but you know immediately it's a cab, even if you've never been here before.

Americans are constantly amazed by the way our cabbies know everything, and how they let you know they know everything by talking about everything all the time. Certainly, I don't feel like I've had a good day unless a black cab has carved me up at least twice. I love the way you can flag them down, and how they absolutely will know where you want to go and how the rules say that if it's in London, they MUST take you there.

This is a peculiarly English thing and that's why no postcard of Westminster Bridge is complete without one big red bus and two cabs in it.

People come here from all over the world and when they get

here they want to go in a black cab with a driver who knows, without being told, where their hotel is and how to get there. They would not find the concept of a ride in a Portuguese-built, Japanese-designed people carrier quite so 'quaint'.

The first time I was driven in a black cab, I was an eight-year-old Yorkshire boy, and I got an erection with all the excitement. The first time I went in a Nissan, I was 24 and I was sick.

Part 2

Acceleration Times are a Bit Nonsensical

I spent half an hour in a computer shop this week and only when the salesman said 'goodbye' did I realise he hadn't been talking to me in Norwegian.

I don't know what DOS is. I don't know how many megabytes this Mac has and even if I did, I wouldn't know whether it was a lot, or not. They say I need more Vee Ram. Gosh.

There is nothing wrong with this of course. Every group of like-minded people always dreams up a new language so that lesser mortals can't understand what they're on about.

Police people can have an entire conversation and you wouldn't recognise a single word. They call cars 'vehicles' and they never walk anywhere. They 'proceed'. Doctors are as bad, solicitors are worse. And then there's the world of film and television. I know what 'Roll VT' means and you don't, so I am brighter and cleverer than you.

I also know that a car which can get from 0 to 60 in five seconds is fast. And that a car which takes 14.7 seconds is likely to be a Volkswagen.

You cannot be a car person unless you understand what 0 to 60 actually means. You need to be impressed when friends tell you that their new car does it in 6.9.

Basically, the metrestick was dreamed up in continental Europe where road testers measure the time it takes for a car to accelerate from 0 to 100 kilometres per hour, which near as dammit, is 0 to 60 miles per hour.

Similarly, we've always rejected the American habit of referring to the standing quarter, a stupid system which comes from their drag-racing scene. When someone says they have an eleven-second car, they mean that it gets from rest to a marker post a quarter of a mile away in eleven seconds which, incidentally, is pretty fast.

But it's myth-exploding time again because judging a car on its ability to get from 0 to 60 is completely daft.

First of all, you have to be absolutely brutal with the clutch and the gearbox in order to get the best possible time. And no car can stand treatment like that for long – the mile straight at the Millbrook proving ground in Bedfordshire is littered with broken drive shafts and gearboxes and the air hangs heavy with the aroma of cooked clutch plates.

You see, what you do to get a car going quickly is build the revs up to, say, 4000 rpm and then you just move your left foot sideways off the clutch pedal. This means the full power of the engine is applied, very suddenly indeed, to the rest of the moving bits.

I once did six full-bore take-offs in an Aston Martin Vantage, whose undersides are tougher than the hinges of a seventeenth-century barn door. And on the seventh attempt, the diff exploded.

Now the Vantage has rear-wheel drive which is what you need for a fast start on grippy tarmac. Getting a powerful front-wheel-drive car off the line quickly is harder because if you drop the clutch pedal with too many revs, the wheels just spin. Too few and you're not going to get the best time. Too many attempts and something will break.

But let's just say you do manage to get rolling without a mechanical mishap; you are then faced with a gear change. And what you do here is simply wrench the lever from first to second without using the clutch.

Now come on, are you really going to do that sort of thing with your own car? Of course not, so you look in the back of a car magazine to find out . . . and it says your car does it in, say, 7.6.

Well, a few points spring to mind here. First of all you need to know whether the track was wet or dry when the road tester tried it because dampness underfoot can add a second and a second in the world of 0 to 60 is a light year.

Second, there may have been a bit of floor mat behind the throttle pedal when the run was timed.

Third, how many gear changes were needed? Some cars can do 60 in second gear whereas others need another shift to get into third.

And finally, it doesn't really matter whether your car does it in 7.2 or 7.7. Just look at the second hand of your watch and tell me that half a second is a long time.

Top speed is equally meaningless. I regularly test cars on the two-mile runway at Greenham Common and you wouldn't believe how much difference a slight breeze can make.

In a Lotus Esprit, I coudn't make it go faster than 120 mph when going from east to west but the other way round, it damn near went off the clock. So what is the car's top speed? Haven't a clue.

Quite apart from the wind, I'm fairly sure the runway isn't completely level and anyway, I was relying on the speedometer which almost always lies. When my old Escort Cosworth said it was doing 140 mph, it was, in fact, travelling along at a mere 129 mph.

So, if the 0 to 60 time is meaningless and you can't achieve your car's potential without breaking something, and if the speedo can't be trusted, and if a little wind can affect top speed so much, what measurement should we use?

I suggest four simple categories: terrifying, fast, average, and Volkswagen Diesel.

There are other advantages to this system too – non-car people will understand what we're on about.

Adverts Versus the Truth

Every fortnight, Alain Prost hurls his Williams Renault around some race track or other, taking 90-degree bends at the kind of speeds that most drivers will never, ever experience, even in a straight line.

His car, equipped with an 800 brake horsepower engine, active ride, traction control and computer telemetry back to the pits is, without any question or shadow of doubt, the ultimate driving machine.

A BMW 316i is not. It has a top speed of 119 mph, it accelerates from 0 to 60 in a glacial 13.9 seconds and while it handles neatly, its tyres and brakes would be absolutely shattered after fifteen fast laps of a race track.

And while that automotive blancmange they call the 850i is faster and better able to stand up to race track use, it is still a long, long way behind the Williams as a technological tour de force.

So how come BMW is allowed to litter its advertisements with the stark and bold claim that they make the ultimate driving machine?

A spokeswoman for the Advertising Standards Authority said, 'Well, it's subjective and we consider it to be obvious advertising puffery. If BMW made a verifiable claim, then that's different.'

So what then of Saab's latest 'claim'? They say that their new engines are capable of pumping out cleaner air through their exhaust pipes than they sucked in through their inlet manifolds.

For sure, some of the nasty poisonous stuff which hangs around in places like LA and Denver is eliminated by the Saab's clever engine management system and catalytic converter but if you attempted to live in a room full of the gases from a Saab, or indeed any car, you'd last about 45 seconds.

Strangely, Saab seem to be a little out of kilter with current automotive thinking. We went through the so-called 'green' phase a couple of years ago when unleaded fuel was all the rage.

Every single manufacturer busied itself for months, telling us how their cars would run on lead-free petrol and therefore, the days of children being born with two noses were over. Every single manufacturer except Peugeot, that is.

Peugeots couldn't run on unleaded so their ad department came up with the idea of getting Jack Nicholson to be photographed while pointing a gun at the head of a cute baby seal. Below it said: 'Buy one of our cars or the seal dies – and no, they don't run on unleaded.' Oddly, the campaign never made it past the drawing board.

Then we had a brief flirtation with the notion of recycling, when everyone was running around explaining that their car could be turned into something else when we had finished with it. Hmmm. I thought that's what scrap-metal dealers had been doing since the dawn of automotive time.

Just six months ago we moved into the baby phase. Everyone from BMW to Hyundai was using some hideous child to hammer home the point that we were into the caring nineties and that the vulnerable and adorable baby, like the vulnerable and adorable car, was symbolic of the need to go around kissing old ladies and becoming scout masters.

Vauxhall, however, no longer feels the need to show us an infant dropping to all fours when presented with a slope, so that we'll understand how four-wheel drive works. Peugeot has fired the kid driving a toy car round the kitchen to spell out the advantages of its advanced chassis.

Even safety is no longer absolutely essential. No longer do you have a huge head-on shunt in your Audi and walk off smiling. Besides, Vauxhall has used research to show that if you even so much as mention the word safety in an ad, never mind show a dummy flying through a windscreen, people will assume the commercial is for Volvo.

Today, the car you buy must give you a low profile. It must have beauty with inner strength like, say, Ford. It must be so rare that you will never see another on the road, like Rover. Renault go further. They stress, inexplicably, the importance of stealth.

Is that, I wonder, why they made the Safrane look exactly like every other car on the road?

Or are they just trying to distance themselves from that fantastic 1980s advertisement for the 25; the one where that idiot in a sharp suit was explaining to his wife how he was going it alone, how he had the bank and a colleague on his side and how everything was going to be a barrel of beer and skittles from now on; except the company car would have to go. Wifey was not best pleased.

Neither was I because I simply couldn't work out how he'd managed to set up an entire, and seemingly major business deal, without bothering to whisper a word of it to Mrs Yuppie until the very last moment.

Perhaps she was the woman who turned up later, in VW's ad for the Golf, smiling and laughing her way through a divorce. In the world of advertising, they may be able to fool some of the people some of the time, but image and puff will not sustain an inferior product for long.

For proof, see Mercedes. While motoring journalists and engineers will always be able to pick holes in a slick but drivel-filled 30 seconds of prime time TV – I can, for instance, easily resist the Renault 19 – we get stuck when Daimler Benz tell us their products are 'engineered like no other car in the world'.

Because they just are.

Politicians and Style Motors

Adolf Hitler set something of a trend when he decided to use a Mercedes Benz because today, every single government in the entire world owns at least one car with a three-pointed star on the bonnet.

Indeed, in Swahili, African bigwigs are named after the cars they invariably drive – Wabenzi.

Of course, for official functions, politicians from car-producing countries are forced to use models that are actually made by their people; thus Mitterrand has a Renault Safrane, Yeltsin has a Zil and Clinton has a Cadillac to go with his own 1964 Ford Mustang.

At the recent London G7 summit, Mrs Major kept the trend going by arriving in a beige B-registered Montego with a dent in the door. We're talking here, I think, about a real woman of the people. And a real patriot too.

Edwina Currie has tried to follow in Norma's footsteps, opting for a Toyota, on the basis that the company's Burnaston plant is in her constituency. Unfortunately, the factory makes a model called the Carina while she uses a sporty Corolla GTi which has about as much to do with Britain as sake.

Not only is it important for politicians to drive something jingoistic but also, it's important to ensure that it is safe. John F. Kennedy, for instance, probably regrets the moment he said, 'Honey, let's get a convertible.'

His brother Teddy went for a saloon but should really have gone for something with better road holding. Or if he hadn't been forced to buy a Yank tank, he could perhaps have opted for the British-made amphi-car.

A Nigerian government minister was almost certainly as sore

as hell that he hadn't done something about Lagos's appalling traffic problem, as gunmen riddled his car with bullets while he sat in a jam.

In Italy, where they're all good enough drivers to get across bridges without falling into the water, they are plagued with the nightmare cocktail of bad traffic and terrorism.

To get round the problem, Italian manufacturers deliberately make their top models look dull and uninspiring. They believe that gunmen will expect their targets to be in something big and flash and will not dare open fire on something so ordinary as a Fiat Croma.

Hmmm.

Do the British Love Cars?

In Italy, every single male, and most females, between the ages of five and seventy-five, loves cars. They love driving them, touching them, admiring them, and most of all, talking about them.

Drive a new model around the streets of an Italian town, and it doesn't matter whether it's a Ferrari or a Fiat Punto, you will be swamped at every set of lights. They'll want to know how fast it goes, whether it corners well, whether it's quicker off the mark than their car.

I have driven a great many new models in Italy and it's always the same. You are pumped for information like you have just come back from Mars and the simple fact that I only know two Italian words – mussels and bitch – doesn't seem to put them off.

Things are different in England. Drive a car that no one has ever seen outside the pages of the specialist press before and you may as well be on foot, in a grey Marks and Spencer suit with shoes to match.

And even if passers-by are forced into conversation about the new set of wheels, the questions are quite, quite different to those that are fired at you in Rome or Milan or Taormina. In Barnsley and Birmingham, they want to know how much it costs to insure, why there are only two doors and how much fuel it uses; practical, sensible, dull things.

Things that are intended to make you, the driver, feel decadent and extravagant and stupid.

In Italy, if you drive a fine car, you are revered. In England, you are a parasite.

Back in the sixties, Pinin Farina, one of Italy's top designers, found himself driving a Ferrari through an anti-Vietnam march.

The protesters banged on his window and roof, demanding to know how fast it could go. In a poll-tax riot here, they would set you, and your car, on fire.

Even Britain's more affluent road users are strangely indifferent when it comes to a new car. Keep your head pointing forwards but swivel your eyeballs to the left so far that it begins to hurt. Now swivel them a little more.

You have just done a passable imitation of the driver of a 7-series BMW who knows that I am alongside in a Z1, a two-seater Bee Em with no doors. He absolutely will not let me see that he is interested. It is not the done thing. It is not the British way.

And this is odd because according to the Society of Motor Manufacturers and Traders, one working person in ten in this country owes his or her job to the motor industry.

Furthermore, Britain is unique in the world for its specialist car makers. Our major players may have been decimated but AC, Morgan, TVR, Aston Martin, Rolls-Royce, Lotus, Caterham, Westfield, Marcos and a host of even tinier outfits continue to thrive.

Outside the UK, there are no tiny car firms. Here, there's nothing but.

Then there are racing cars. Take a look down a Formula One grid and count the cars not made in Britain. You'll only need one hand.

There is nothing so American as an Indycar race except for one small thing. Every single car in the series is made in Britain. The car Nigel Mansell used to win the title uses a chassis from Huntingdon and a Ford Cosworth engine from Northamptonshire.

Even Ferrari, the greatest racing team of all time, has been forced, after a four-year spell away from the winner's rostrum, to employ a Brit, John Barnard, as chief designer.

In the world of rallying, the all-conquering Subaru Legacy upholds Japan's honour, but it was built in Banbury.

There must be a deep enthusiasm for cars in Britain but is it buried even deeper than the vast number of classic cars we own?

Just the other day, I needed to borrow a Ferrari Daytona – like you do – and as I was in Italy, I figured they would be ten a penny. After two days, I gave up trying to find even someone who knew someone who might have one.

In England, after two hours on the telephone, I had ordinary people from ordinary places queuing up to lend me one. They use a Sierra most of the time but in their barn, they have 'just a few classics'.

So why, against a background like this, is it considered poor form to talk cars in public? Why, when there are 132 different car magazines on sale in Britain, does the biggest seller have a circulation of just 130,000? In Norway, Norway, for Chrissakes, one car mag alone sells to a million people a month. And why are there so many people in this country who'll gladly tell you they don't like cars?

I'm not talking about the bearded environmentalist types who have just cause but about normal people, like my mother, who actually says she hates cars. Is this not like saying that you hate tables, or light fittings or plants? How can you hate what, at worst, is an inanimate object?

Any why get so hot under the collar about cars being sold for £5 or £10 million when you don't care two hoots about someone buying a painting for £22 million?

To the heathen, a painting is a piece of canvas with some oil on it, and a car is some metal. But to the enlightened, both are art forms. I'm amazed that rare cars, which are both art forms and tools for moving around in, don't fetch more than paintings.

But this is a sentiment rarely heard in Britain these days. And I have a sneaking feeling that our company-car mentality is to blame.

Because 50 per cent of cars sold in Britain are bought by companies, people don't bother talking about or ogling cars because they have what they're given.

In other countries, people buy their own cars, with their own money, so they need all the information they can lap up. They will stare at new cars in traffic jams, because who knows, next time round, they might buy one.

But in Britain, why read a car magazine when next year you'll get another Cavalier whether you like it or not? Why aspire to a Mercedes Benz when you just know your company will never buy you one, and you don't need one anyway because you have the Vauxhall for free?

Why talk about cars with your friends when all you learn is of no real importance?

And of course, because company cars are such a huge thing in Britain, the manufacturers target fleet buyers, enticing them with things that matter most on the company balance sheet: fuel economy, residual values, insurance ratings.

These things don't make a car look or feel good. They don't make it sexy or fast. They make it dull so who can blame the people who drive it for not taking an interest.

Of course you won't talk cars down at the pub if you have a horrid beige box parked outside. It's a functional tool like your washing machine or fridge and such things do not make for lively conversation.

Underneath it all, the British have a deep-seated love for motor cars; they must do because Britain, not Germany or Italy or even Japan, is the capital of cardom.

The RAC rally is still the country's biggest spectator event and *Top Gear* still pulls enormous audiences, but unless the company car culture is stamped out, the concept of watching people driving cars around, and finding it interesting, will eventually become positively weird.

Lancia Out of the UK

It was inevitable really, but we go into 1994 with a major omission from the list of new cars you can buy in Britain – Lancia.

Founded in 1906, the company built up an awesome reputation with its sporty yet luxurious motor cars but by the late sixties, it was in financial trouble and had to be rescued by Fiat.

Things got worse. In the late seventies, horror stories began to appear in the British press about Lancia rust protection and how there wasn't any. This culminated in a much-talked about campaign on the *Nationwide* programme which served to decimate sales.

In Britain in 1978, Lancia shifted 11,800 cars but from then on in, it's been downhill all the way. In 1993, excluding December's figures which aren't available yet, they sold just 569.

That isn't enough to pay for a full-page advertisement in the *Sunday Times* and it certainly isn't enough to keep the 46 dealers happy.

'We just never recovered from that rust problem back in the late seventies,' said a spokeswoman. 'And we couldn't because of journalists,' she added.

It seems that us lot always began every piece we wrote about Lancia talking about how the cars didn't go rusty any more, thus ensuring that the words Lancia and rust remained as inexorably linked as Wimbledon and strawberries.

Now, back in the seventies, this wasn't so bad because after we'd finished talking about the rust, we'd go on to say how pretty the cars were, and how the engines were lusty and how the design was clever. Remember the old HPE? Half estate, half sports coupe and 100 per cent drop-dead gorgeous.

So what if it fell apart after twenty minutes. They'd be twenty great minutes, twenty minutes you'd always remember.

Then there was the Integrale. This was based on the old Delta and is one of the most successful rally cars of all time. With a 2.0-litre, 16-valve, turbocharged engine and four-wheel drive, it afforded the keen driver the sort of thrills that normally go hand in hand with a Ferrari badge.

Yes, the last time I drove one, the centre console came off and pinned my right foot to the throttle, which was a bit unnerving, but hey, until then, I'd had a great time with it.

But this is the rub. In recent years, the Japanese have taught the world's car-buying public to expect total reliability.

Other car manufacturers caught on but Lancia did not. And that was fine because they had pretty, clever cars with lusty engines and there was always a band of enthusiasts who'd want one.

Even in 1990, they sold 308,000 units throughout Europe and that was pretty good. But by then, they had stopped making pretty, clever, lustful cars and the enthusiasts simply gave up. You could have a pretty, clever, lusty CRX from Honda, the people who powered the McLaren F1 cars.

What chance did the Dedra have? Built on a Fiat Tipo platform, and with Fiat Tipo engines, this car felt, unsurprisingly, just like a Fiat Tipo when you drove it. But it looks like the dinner of a dog and the name Dedra lacks any kind of cocktail-party prestige.

The Thema too had its work cut out. As it was basically the same as the stunning Alfa Romeo 164, anyone after a luxurious Italian express bought the Alfa. And anyone just after a big car remembered *Nationwide* and bought a Toyota.

The Y10, or white hen, as it became known, made a brief appearance and I liked its quirky charm and suede-look trim but I was alone and it was retired two years ago.

And now the rest of the range has followed suit. Oh, you can still buy one with left-hand drive, but that's just another reason for not buying one. And there are too many of those already.

The really worrying thing is that in Europe, sales are now

down to just 214,000 and at the present rate of decline, they'll be below 100,000 by the turn of the century.

Then, Fiat may just pull the plug and use the name Lancia as a badge on upmarket Fiats, like Ford do with Ghia.

Damn shame. Damn damn shame.

So What's the Big Deal with the Beetle Then?

With the exception of a few child molesters, Nazi memorabilia tend not to feature very highly on anyone's shopping list.

Jackboots have an appeal, for sure, but only in the sort of clubs frequented by government ministers and television personalities. Iron Crosses are collected by people with beards, which is fair enough. And panzer tanks intrigue children at military museums.

But none of these things are sweet, or cuddly, or nice. Normal people collect thimbles, or teddy bears, or the numbers on the side of trains; harmless things. It takes a special kind of person to be interested in a vicious bunch of sadistic murderers led by a man with facial hair.

So what, I wonder, went wrong with the Volkswagen Beetle?

Here is a car that was designed by Ferdinand Porsche in 1933, which gives it some pedigree, but only after he'd been ordered to do so by Hitler who wanted a people's car – literally, a volkswagen.

By rights then, it should be remembered with the sort of fondness we reserve for Dachau and the Blitz. It may have been designed by a genius, but it was the vision of a loony.

It was nearly a short-lived one too. After the war, the factory in Wolfsburg was a bombed-out ruin, but to keep the locals busy, the allied powers appointed a British major, Ivan Hirst, to get it going again.

Things once again looked good for the Beetle even though Lord Rootes, Britain's head motoring honcho, apparently told Hirst he was a 'bloody fool' for attempting to make what seemed to be a silly car.

Henry Ford thought it was a foolish idea too, and very nearly bought the factory for his own rapidly expanding operation. He pulled out at the last minute because he felt it was too close to the fast-closing Iron Curtain.

So, miraculously, the Beetle survived, and here we are, in 1993, smiling when a Beetle clatters by. Students sit around discussing the merits of anarchy and the evils of Thatcher, and then drive home in a Nazi staff car.

Woody Allen, a man who has more cause than most to have a problem with the Nazis, used a Beetle for laughs in his film *Sleeper*. He even had a flattering word or two for the people who made it.

But it was not *Sleeper* that turned the Beetle around. It was Herbie. That little white car with the number 53 on the doors and a superimposed screen going on outside the windows transformed the image of the Beetle. No longer was it a Nazi staff car. And nor was it a living testimony to British military stupidity. It wasn't a car at all in fact. It was a cuddly puppy dog.

The kind of people who like to give their car a name – people who have musical lavatory-roll dispensers, usually – fell for the Beetle hook, line and sinker.

Despite the rudimentary suspension, despite the air-cooled engine, despite the wayward handling and despite the fact it performed with all the gusto of continental drift, it sold incredibly well.

To date, 21 million have been made which makes it the best-selling car ever, and by a huge margin. By comparison, there have been just 5 million Minis.

Not only that, the Beetle is still being produced in Mexico and Brazil and is by far and away the most popular car in the distinctly un-Aryan continent of South America. Especially so in Paraguay where the local importer is a Mr A. Hilter.

That's a masterstroke for VW. When Morris finished building the Oxford, they sold the rights and the manufacturing equipment to Hindustan of India. Today, it stills sells well but the original creators get nothing in return.

VW owns its operations in Mexico and Brazil and making a

car designed more than 50 years ago is very nearly as profitable as South America's only other big industry.

The Beetle, then, has been a good thing for VW who, because of the *Love Bug* films, managed to fool all of the people, all of the time.

And the charade looks set for another few years yet because at the Detroit Motor Show earlier this month, VW unveiled a new concept car.

It is brand new from tip to toe, but it doesn't take someone with a degree in car spotting to work out what inspired the Californian designers.

The engine may be at the front, and the passenger compartment may be an air-bagged and -conditioned palace but this is a Beetle. VW themselves say it is a back to the future concept car.

It's been born because by 1998, VW, along with every other major car maker must ensure that 2 per cent of all the cars it sells in California produce no emissions.

The trouble is that if you put an electric motor in a normal car, no one will buy it. The end result looks like a normal car but performs like a wheelbarrow, costs the earth and takes six weeks to recharge every 50 miles.

If we are going to have electric cars, VW believes they must look different to normal cars, which is why their designers looked back to the Beetle. Half the battle's won already because most of the people who like the relic are the kind of souls who sport shoes made out of potatoes, and would actually want a planet-saving milk float.

No firm commitment has been made on what sort of engine it should have, but three alternatives are being examined. It seems VW likes the idea of blending diesel and battery power. Oh my God. Mogadon will be bankrupt in a week.

The man who headed up the operation to make this snooze-mobile says the original Beetle offered innovative technology when it arrived in the States in 1949 – 'An air-cooled motor, unusual shape, no grille, motor in the back.'

The design team wanted to blend modern technology with VW's heritage and the finished product reflects, he says, 'Everything we have always stood for — simple, honest, reliable, original.'

And a desire to annex the Sudetenland. But he forgot that bit.

Just What is It about the BMW?

A Rolex watch may well be exquisitely crafted and priced accordingly, but there is no way I'll be convinced that it tells the time any better than my Casio.

And furthermore, my Casio is capable of operating in space, 4000 metres under the sea and even after it's been dropped from a 747. Battersea, then, is a breeze.

Nevertheless, at parties, the people with Rolexes are known to check the time more often, and more extravagantly, than those with Casios.

That's because Rolexes are expensive. People who spend their weekends looking round show homes do not have them. People who go fishing don't either, unless they're moored off Mauritius, after marlin.

But what if Rolex were to introduce a bargain basement, pile 'em high, sell 'em cheap, battery-powered jobbie with a nice plastic strap? Sure, they'd ruin the image of the ten-grand versions but in the short term, before the name lost its exclusivity, they would be a huge success.

Which brings me neatly on to BMW.

There was a time when the blue and white aero-propeller badge meant something; usually that the driver was a jumped-up twit who drove far too fast in built-up areas, but that's not the point right now.

BMW has always made affordable cars, but these tended to be quite sporty and quite different to the run-of-the-mill competition. And anyway, they were always overshadowed by the race cars and the more expensive offerings.

But today, on the race track, BMW is very much yesterday's news. Sure, they currently hold the British Touring Car

Championship crown but towards the end of last year, the Ford Mondeo was by far the quickest car in the field. And if you want my tip for this year, bet on Ford again.

And what of the upmarket image creators? Well, there's the out-of-date 7 series and the almost completely pointless 8 series. I mean, if you're going to blow upward of 75 grand on what is effectively a two-seater sports car, most people with their heads screwed on the right way round would go for a Ferrari.

This point is amply proved by the sales figures. Last year, 1400 people bought a 7 series and just 150 went for the 850.

Today, BMW seems to be concentrating its efforts not on image but on volume and boy oh boy, is it working.

In 1983, BMW sold 25,178 cars in the UK. Ten years down the line, they shifted 40,921. In the coupe sector, the 318iS outsells the Vauxhall Calibra and round here, in south-west London, there are more BMWs on the road than there are dog turds on the pavement.

BMW say exclusivity has nothing to do with rarity and that their cars are still exclusive because it's hard to find the same sort of experience anywhere else. That might have been the case last year but now the new 3-series Compact is with us, it isn't any more.

This three-door car is effectively a normal 3 series with a slightly altered rear end. It will appeal, say BMW, to company-car drivers on a budget or as a second car, for, dare I say it, wives. Keen drivers will like it too because unlike any other car in the class, it has rear-wheel drive.

It is not, however, a fast car. The only choice you have under the bonnet is from a brace of four-cylinder units – either a 1.8 which is quite slow and a 1.6 which is glacial. Both engines are super smooth though.

Early versions of the 3-series BMW were thrown together by playschool children and some reports suggested that the average warranty cost per car sold was running at £800 per year. But the children have now been fired and all is rosy in the garden once more. Your new BMW is likely to be a reliable companion, and because of that hatchback rear end, a practical one too.

But the best bit is the price. Though not official yet, it seems likely the 316 will sell for around £13,000 which puts the new boy in direct competition with the Maestro, another BMW product now, of course.

With the Maestro, you get five doors rather than three and because only 7176 are sold each year, you also get some of the exclusivity that is missing from BMW these days.

Where's All the Style Gone?

It's interesting to see that there may be some changes to the way Britain's pop charts are organised.

Seems you only need sell 5000 copies of a single to make it into the hit parade and that you could get a higher placing than a song which, in the previous week, had found 150,000 homes.

The industry, already up to its neck in manure, is up in arms but it only has itself to blame. I heard, last week, of a boy who has been selected to front a new group whose name has gone from my mind. He can't sing and he can't play an instrument. For God's sake, he can't even read music.

He's been chosen because he can dance a bit and because he has the looks of an angel which, he says, will give him equal appeal among homosexuals and young girls. For this reason, his 'right-on' contract expressly forbids him from going out with women in public.

He, then, is a machine which has been created by other machines to sell a noise which is made by machines on machines. And then everyone runs around waving their arms in the air wondering where the next Rolling Stones are going to come from. For heaven's sake, another Golden Earring would be better than what we have in the charts now.

The car industry should watch this state of affairs very carefully. And they should take note that the really big hits these days are from established old-timers like Meat Loaf and Bryan Adams. A trudge round the Geneva Motor Show last week revealed the usual crop of dreary no-hopers which will flicker briefly in people's lives, when they are advertised on television, and then die. Does Mitsubishi still make the Lancer Estate? Does anybody care?

Hey, Volkswagen has chopped the roof off its Golf to make a convertible version but wait a minute, didn't I just see exactly the same car with an Astra badge on the Vauxhall stand?

And yes, there's the Fiat Punto or is it the Seat Ibiza? Both companies explain that their new cars were designed by Guigaro of Ital Design and claim that they're not the slightest bit bothered that he seems to have flogged them exactly the same drawings.

Renault had the Laguna – a new mid-sized car – and their designer, a genius called Patrick Le Quement, said it looked refreshingly different to all the other cars in that sector. He's right too, except for one small thing. It doesn't.

This is surprising as we're talking here about a company that dared to be different with the Twingo. But then again, maybe it isn't because they haven't the guts to launch this stunning little one-box town car in Britain.

Over on the Volvo stand, the magically charismatic chief designer, Peter Hallbury, was explaining just how difficult it had been to get his board to approve a new yellow paint scheme on the wonderful new T5 estate.

He wasn't talking about fins like Concorde's wings or a three-tiered bonnet in kevlar. It was only a new colour for heaven's sake. Even so, the suits were twitchy.

There was, however, one ray of hope and it was sitting, curiously enough, on the Volkswagen stand, next to the new Astra. It was curvily modern and equipped to match with air bags and catalytic converters and all sorts of things which, if they were food, would be ready to eat after ten seconds in a microwave.

And it was being likened to the Beetle but even if there had never been a Hitler or a people's car, the crowds would still have been ten deep. The convertible version especially, which was finished in metallic peach, looked absolutely stunning.

Rolls-Royce had pulled the covers off a brand-new, £100,000 four-seater Bentley convertible which will kick the SL Mercedes to hell in a handcart, but the big story was on the VW stand.

Here was a brace of cars which combined modern-day safety and emission technology with something called style. Here was *Pet Sounds* on DAT.

VW says it will gauge public reaction to their new cars before deciding whether to put them into production.

Which is a bit like the Beatles waiting to gauge public reaction to recent press reports before deciding whether to make another record.

Just get on with it.

Hondas are Bought by Old People

The inside lane of a motorway is where you'll find all the flotsam and jetsam; huge 42-ton trucks mix it with yesterday's news: an alarming cocktail of rust, mustard paintwork and peeling vinyl. Automotive lugworms like Cortinas and old Datsuns crawl along in what they see as the shallows, safe and protected from the rough waters of the outside lane, its sharks and its broken heroes on a last-chance power drive.

The inside lane is not where you would expect to find some of the fastest and most exotic cars in the world. And yet, it's where they all live. I'm talking about Hondas.

You will never find a Honda playing cut and thrust in the outer reaches of motorwaydom. These guys never mix it with the suits in the Cavaliers. Even the cheapest little Honda is so technically clever, it makes an F-16 jet fighter look like some kind of barn door, yet it will never even attempt to play ball with a Mondeo.

In terms of automotive time, Honda is still very much a new boy. Until 1963, this world-renowned motorcycle manufacturer had never even made a car. But then came the little S500 – a two-seater sports car that could rev to 8000 rpm.

In just 31 years, Honda has grown so vast that it now has plants in Japan, obviously, Swindon, obviously, Canada and in Maryland, Ohio. In 1989, 1990 and 1991, the Honda Accord was the best-selling car in America. The young upstart had bloodied the noses of Ford, GM and Chrysler and then, this Colin Moynihan of an operation had kicked them all in the testicles for good measure.

And it was the same story in Formula One. Honda had a brief

flirtation with this megabuck sport back in the 1960s, but then lay dormant until 1984.

No one really thought they'd be serious players until 1986, when they lifted the world constructor's championship. A fluke? No, not really because they did it again in 1987, 1988, 1989, 1990, and 1991.

Having beaten Ferrari on the race track, Honda decided it was time to beat them on the road too and, in 1990, launched the NSX, a two-seater supercar that simply didn't play by the rules.

Lamborghinis, Lotuses and Ferraris are hard to get into, hard to see out of and harder still to drive. You need thighs like redwoods to depress the clutch (though calling it names sometimes works), a neck like a birthday cake to stop the G-forces ripping your head off and the strength of Samson, pre-haircut, to make the steering wheel move. On top of all this, the gear lever feels like it's been set in concrete.

You need to be brave and talented to find out just how fast cars like this will go. But though the Honda NSX looks like a supercar and goes like the very devil, it is no harder to pilot through a crowded shopping street than one of the company's mopeds.

The steering is power assisted and the visibility good. The headroom is fine, even for beanpoles like me, and the pedals are so softly sprung that to operate them is no harder than treading in some dog dirt.

And yet when you press the one on the right, all hell breaks loose. The six-cylinder, 3.0-litre engine hurls the horizon right through the windscreen, and through your Wayfarers too if you're not careful.

Now a 3-litre engine doesn't sound all that impressive when you remember the new McLaren is hustled along by something with twice the volume and twice the number of cylinders, too. But thanks to what Honda calls VTEC technology, the smallness doesn't matter. At low revs, the NSX is a normal car but as the revs pass 5000 per minute, the four camshafts shift, and begin to poke the valves with big, spiky, high-performance lobes. Clark Kent becomes Superman and Dr Jekyll all rolled into one.

Honda were so pleased with VTEC that it is now available on the stunning Prelude, the CRX sports car and even the little Civic – by far and away the most stylish of all the little hatchbacks.

What's more, Honda is now using the VTEC system to improve fuel economy. The Civic VEi is more efficient with the jungle juice than most diesels, so you can save money without giving every pedestrian a face full of carcinogenic smoke and a lung full of asthma.

So, Honda has proved itself on the tracks and the lessons it learned there have been passed on to you and me. On top of all that, the cars are fun to drive, good looking and comfortable.

And yet, despite all this, I passed a Civic VTEC yesterday, its super-advanced engine spinning at maybe 3000 rpm and its aerodynamic body cleaving the air at all of 55 mph – on a motorway.

Behind the wheel was a man who had bought his suit from Alfred the Great. He was thousands of years old.

The trouble, it seems, is that Hondas are perceived, above all else, as reliable which is the one thing, above all else, that a retired couple wants.

I ran a CRX for five years and even though it was never serviced or even washed, it never went wrong. That suits the oldies just fine. They want a car that will outlive them. They want a car that will never break down, that will never need to go to a garage and which will never cost them more than the price of a gallon of oil once a decade.

They are not concerned with style or image. They would buy a wheelbarrow if they thought it would get them to the post office every morning. They want cast-iron reliability and they get it from their Hondas.

And word gets around. At beetle and whist drives the length and breadth of the land, people in brown suits talk about their

Hondas and other people in brown suits go out and buy one. Until very recently, the average age of a CRX driver was 47!

So, even though you may crave that VTEC engine, you would not buy the only car that can give it to you because you don't want to be labelled as an old git.

Privately, Honda people will admit they're concerned but when asked about possible solutions you just get a shrug. One said, 'Short of telling everyone our cars break down all the time, we're stuffed.'

Shame.

Why Do People Drive Differently All Over the UK?

There is nothing quite so funny as watching an American trying to drive in Italy.

Fresh from a fourteen-hour flight, they squeeze their voluminous backsides into what they think is a toy and then set off for an appointment with Mr G. Reaper.

I have seen grown men crying at Italian service stations, explaining to anyone who will listen that they have been rammed and that while doing 55 mph, a nun drove along an inch from their tailgate, waving and flashing her lights.

Pick up any American guide to Europe and it is littered with huge passages in big, bold type advising US citizens to use public transport in Italy. The two car cultures are like Baileys and lime juice. They just do not mix.

For all sorts of complex reasons, each nation drives differently. In France, it's not uncommon to see people hurtling down the autoroute with their left foot resting on the dashboard, but pass into Belgium and it stops. There, everybody eats while driving. Keep going and you get into Germany where they are like the Italians only faster, and more arrogant.

Doubtless, they all find Britain as odd as we find them but I'd love to know how they generalise about our driving style, because it seems to me that it's completely different depending on which part of the country you're in.

Down at the seafront in Brighton, it is perhaps the most explosive cocktail since someone said, 'Hey, I wonder what would happen if we put a sugar lump in this fertiliser.'

Brighton is a town for the very young, who all seem to have 9-million-cc motorbikes, or the very old, whose idea of a high-speed thrill is a Richard Briers monologue.

I alternate between almost uncontrollable rage as yet another Honda lurches out in front, and then meanders down the prom at 4 mph, and stark fear as yet another bike roars by at 4000 million mph.

Then there's somewhere like Doncaster which must rank as the most law-abiding town on earth. If you want to turn left at a roundabout, you will get into the correct lane and queue for five miles, even though the other lane is completely empty.

It never occurs to anyone that they could scream down the wrong lane, go round the roundabout once and then emerge, at the front of the queue, and with the right of way.

I can think of only two reasons for this. Either people are very stupid or no one is in a hurry.

Everyone is in a hurry in Oxford but that is because Oxford has quite the most idiotic one-way system in the known world. Arrive from the east and you are forced to go through all sorts of outlying villages, like Torquay and Keswick, before you're allowed to head for the town centre, where there are no parking spaces.

Coventry's ring road also has all the precision of spaghetti. There are people there today who popped into town for a packet of fags in 1973.

But it could be worse. It could be Birmingham. Get off the M6, go down the Aston Expressway and you are herded into a tunnel which spits you out again in Kidderminster. Turn round, try again and you'll be back on the M6. Every driver in Birmingham looks like forced rhubarb.

Bournemouth has by far and away the most sensible system I've ever encountered with all the street names clearly signposted in large letters, and Braille, on every ring-road exit. Even the staggeringly old population in their Austin Sevens can get from whist drive to beetle drive without ever getting lost.

But Scotland in October is perhaps the best place in the UK for making progress. Everyone up there is used to dealing with the two greatest hazards on our roads – ice and caravans – so when neither is in evidence, they're like dogs off the leash. I have never, ever been inconvenienced by a Scottish driver, even though rather too many of them seem to have Ladas.

Even when I'm in England, I'll hang on to the back of any Scottish-registered car because its progress will be neat, fast and safe.

Unless it's in Norfolk. No one can make neat, fast or safe progress in this moonscape because the farmers think they have a right of way everywhere. You can be plunging down an arrow-straight piece of asphalt, hurrying to keep an appointment with the horizon when a huge tractor will just trundle into your path, its trailer weighed down with all those EC subsidies and its tyres leaving great gobs of glutinous mud all over the road.

Never be tempted to drive quickly in Somerset either, because every other road user will be drunk out of their minds. This is the spiritual home of the Ford Escort RS2000 which is driven by people who like bits of twig in their drinks.

And forget Wales, because none of the road signs have any vowels in them. It's also worth noting that no one in Wales knows the way to anywhere. Pull over and ask the directions to Llyllghll and they always start by saying 'er' – which is your cue to move on.

Stick around and they'll have you circumnavigating the corn exchange till kingdom come.

Now in any of these places, the one common bond is that every driver thanks God he doesn't have to live and work in London.

London scares the hell out of everyone and to complicate it still further, there are little microcosms like Fulham where everyone works in banking, estate agency, stockbroking or insurance. They all wear suits. They all worship Gordon Gekko and they all drive BMWs. None of them will ever, ever, ever let you out of a side turning.

Head east to Southall and you can see how Octav Botnar made

his millions. Everybody drives a Nissan so spectacularly badly that you wonder how anyone is left alive.

In Camden, cars are few and far between because everyone is at home, smoking dope and thinking of new ways to be PC. The car up there is Beelzebub, Hitler and Myra Hindley all rolled into one.

Plus the council does its best to keep them out by digging up the roads. This is a Labour local authority trick – everyone thinks you're doing roadworks but in fact, you're simply employing people to keep cars out. You never have any intention of actually opening the road, ever again. Clever stuff.

Wandsworth, of course, is not a Labour council which means they never do any roadworks at all. And explains why I've spent all morning on the telephone, trying to hire a crane to lift my car out of a pot-hole it fell into last night.

London is a melting pot, a cramped labyrinth where the locals all do things differently and where they still have to mix it with people from all over the world; Norfolk farmers in town to get some more subsidies, Italian playboys, and tourists who've never driven on the left before.

We should be surprised, not that it doesn't work very well, but that it works at all.

You Can Tell What People Drive by the Shoes They Wear

She doesn't eat meat and though she has a television, she makes a point of explaining that she never watches it. She lives in Islington and she cares, she really cares.

When she was asked, reasonably enough, whether the chap over by the fireplace was her boyfriend, she replied, somewhat haughtily, that she can do without stereotypes thank you very much, and hurried off into the kitchen for some more mulled walnut and dill.

Actually, hurried isn't quite the right word because she was wearing the daftest trousers I've ever seen. They were so baggy that as she walked past an open window, the breeze caused a significant course deviation. Plus, she appeared to be wearing eight shirts.

She was a very ugly person but was not wearing make-up because war paint is sexist and the fascist companies that make it use guinea pigs as beagles. Or something.

But it was the shoes that confirmed what I'd suspected all along. This girl drives a Citroen 2CV. Her footwear looked like a cross between a battleship and a coal scuttle, which was stupid enough, but the soles appeared to have been fashioned from potato skins.

I am fascinated by shoes; the idea that old people walk into a shop and though faced with a wide range of alternatives, actually choose those felt booties with zips up the front. Or that young and pretty girls will happily pay a wad of Melvins for a pair of canvas shin-high boots with crepe soles nine inches thick . . . and then go dancing in them.

Except they don't of course, because by the time you've done all the laces up, it's time to come home again and because the only dance you can do while wearing nine-inch platforms is called 'the man who's just about to topple off a cliff dance', which is not very elegant.

You can drive with platform shoes on but you must expect to be stopped by the police who, with some justification, may feel that your car is being driven by a committee.

The sort of person who chooses to wear platform shoes either has a height complex or is so wrapped up in what's in and what's not that they will put up with great discomfort to look good. Either way, they will drive something very showy, and very loud, and something with all the refinement of a baboon that's been forced to wear evening dress for the first time. Something like a TVR in fact.

Then there's the sort of person who wears stout ankle-length boots with elasticated sides. Inevitably, they're a sort of orangey colour and of course, they are made from good, hard-wearing leather. We're talking dairy farmer here. We're talking Daihatsu Fourtrak or Subaru.

Gentlemen farmers wear brown leather brogues with a dimple effect which they bought in 1972, a week after they bought their first Range Rover.

The brogue is popular in the City but on the streets of EC3, it is never brown, it is black. And you can always tell which of the brokers, bankers and Lloyd's-men are ex-army by whether the heels are strengthened with segs.

Ex-army men like to let you know they're coming and consequently feel the need to make a huge, metallic clicking noise as they pound up the railway platform on a morning.

At home, all city boys have BMWs. And you can tell which ones are ex-army city boys again because the carpet in the driver's side footwell is ripped to shreds.

BMWs are also popular in SW2 but only after they've been stolen a few times and have intergalactic mileages. So, any pre-C-reg BMW is almost certainly being driven by someone who appears to have a pair of massive white bouncy castles on each foot.

The rather less extravagant training shoe belongs under the wheel of a Ford Capri while the good old-fashioned Green Flash tennis pump suggests the person wearing it is not the slightest bit bothered by fashion. They play tennis and need reliable and steady footwear. They need a reliable and steady car so they have a Honda.

Volvos, too, are reliable and steady (apart from the T5) but as all of them round these parts are driven by 35-year-old women, every time I see a blue court shoe, I can't help thinking of Sweden.

Unless it's being worn with a mini skirt in which case she's less than 35, has no children and therefore owns a Golf GTi. If it's a micro skirt, she's 19 and has a Peugeot.

Odd to think, then, that all of these people, one day, will have a pair of those fur-lined booties with zips up the front, a tartan shopping trolley and a husband with a Rover 2000. We all will. One day, all of us will wear brown shoes.

Even people who, today, wear grey ones. Now remember, in American spelling, gray is an anagram of Gary so no prizes for guessing what sort of a car My Grey Shoes drives. If the shoe in question is from Dolcis and worn with a white sock, he is a photocopier salesman and has a Vauxhall Astra. If it is cut low at the sides, fitted with a tassel and worn with a pale grey silk sock, he is a footballer and has a Toyota Supra.

The footballer's girlfriend, a model called Denise, drives an Escort Cabriolet. How do I know this? Because her shoes have heels like ice picks and are red. If there's an ankle bracelet too, she doesn't have a car at all. She rides around in Gary's Astra.

This is a rule. And it comes from the same book that says all geography teachers wear shoes which look like Cornish pasties. That way I just know when a beige, crepe-soled piece of plastic footwear shuffles by, the man is on his way to a Triumph Acclaim.

I also know that when I see someone in wellingtons on a hot day, in the middle of a town, I am in the presence of an idiot; which means he must have a motorbike.

But the worst sort of shoe is the half desert wellie, the suede ankle boot with two lace holes on either side. Now I've noticed that everyone who has a pair of Jesus boots like this also has a Nissan Micra. Worryingly, I've also noticed that everyone who has ever been charged with child molesting turns up at court in a pair.

But here's the icing on the cake. Every time I've been to church, I've noticed during the sermon, just before I've nodded off, that all vicars wear them too.

So, next time the police need to interview someone about a nasty piece of child molestation, they only need find themselves a Nissan-Micra-driving vicar. Cuts the list of suspects down to about two hundred thousand.

The New Ferrari 355

The road from Modena to Lucca is well known to British holiday-makers, who use it as a scenic route from the industrial heartland of Northern Italy to the tranquil beauty of Tuscany and Umbria.

It's smooth and fast all the way to Abetone, but from there on down, it's intestinal and difficult and treacherous. And that's on a quiet day, in your Volvo.

But on a not-so-quiet day, there is an added hazard because this is the road that Ferrari, Lamborghini and, to a lesser extent, Bugatti use to test their 200 mph supercars.

They take them to special tracks for specialised development work but no circuit in the world provides feedback quite so well as a real road in the real world. Not until you've actually overtaken a British-registered Volvo on a blind bend will you really know what it feels like to overtake a British-registered Volvo on a blind bend.

The locals know that at any minute, their rear-view mirrors may fill with the ground-hugging snout of a supercar, and they're always ready to pull over and let it fly by, but the cars from out of town are not. And the test drivers don't know which is which until they're close enough to read the licence plate. And that, at 150 mph, is pretty close.

Furthermore, when the Ferrari test drivers run into their adversaries from Lamborghini, they just can't help racing. 'We try to slow down in the villages,' said one. 'To about 100 mph,' he added, smiling.

This made my Adam's apple wobble a bit because we were just about to set off with a Bugatti EB110, a Lightweight Diablo and my steed for most of the trip, a brand-new Ferrari F355 Berlinetta.

And sure enough, we did some truly incredible speeds up that mountain. Up front, the rear wheels of the mighty Diablo were constantly spinning, its tail wagging from side to side as its exhausts barked the bark of a large and angry dog.

Twice we whistled past police cars whose occupants merely leant out of their windows to urge us onward. In the villages, children came running out of their houses to cheer. They're used to seeing one supercar go by but not three and not doing the ton.

Now you may moralise and tut but this is Italy, and Italians love to see fast cars being driven quickly. They cannot see how such a thing could be a crime. And besides, this is a peasant farming district whose only claim to fame in the outside world is the fact that three of the planet's five supercar makers are based there.

The car they liked most was the £300,000 Bugatti, a remarkable looking brute with a 3.5-litre V12 engine that is force-fed by an incredible four turbochargers. When they cut in, you really do need the four-wheel drive because the whole car seems to squirm under the onslaught.

But they don't cut in until the engine is past 4000 rpm and that can be a huge nuisance. Truth be told, the Bugatti left me feeling a little bit cold.

The Diablo, on the other hand, did not, because it was 94 degrees in the shade and its air-conditioning system had the same effect as someone blowing through a straw.

Couple that to non-power-assisted steering, a gearbox that blistered my hand after half an hour and a clutch that appeared to have been set in cement and you will understand when I tell you I very nearly drowned in my own perspiration.

This, too, is an expensive car at £175,000 but it comes with no creature comforts at all. Everything that is not essential has been thrown away to save weight so that the 5.7-litre V12 has less work to do for more rewards.

It's a 200-mph car but that's all academic because it is so damn frightening and noisy and vibratory that only the terminally insane would ever dream of keeping the throttle hard down for more than a second or two. It's fun for a while, like a roller-coaster ride at Alton Towers, but day in and day out: thank you, but no thank you.

There are no such problems in the car I drove for most of that two-day thrash. The Ferrari 355 is, without any question or shadow of doubt, the most complete sports car I have ever driven. Nothing even gets close.

Visually, it looks pretty similar to its predecessor, the 348, but there's now a little spoiler at the back, a completely flat undertray and some beautifully sculptured air intakes. Pininfarina has made a pretty car ravishing.

The engine is still a V8 so you can still potter around town in fourth gear with no fuss, but it now has five valves for each of those cylinders so that it will reach 9000 rpm with absolutely no drama at all. Of course, it is nowhere near as fast as the other two – with a top speed of just 183 mph – but then it is nowhere near as expensive either. It's yours for around 80 grand.

The interior is trimmed in leather with all the switches on the centre console, clustered around the six-speed gear lever. And it all works just fine, though you still have to sit with your arms outstretched and your knees three feet apart.

It's a small price to pay though because this car just flies. Through the bends, I could see the Bugatti driver struggling to keep the turbos spinning and the Diablo was wandering around all over the road, but the Ferrari just grips and goes.

When a bend tightens up more than you think it will, you just turn the wheel some more and there isn't even a chirp of protest from the tyres. Floor the throttle too early, and the tail swings wide, but it's a slow, graceful, easy-to-catch response that will not baffle even the most butterfingered driver.

You can flip the suspension on to a sports setting but even Nikki Lauda says this is a waste of time on normal roads.

I pushed that car with the sort of vigour I normally reserve for vegetarians at dinner parties yet, unlike the beardies who only need one prod to fight back, the Ferrari just kept on taking the punishment, hurling itself from bend to bend as though it had been fired from a steam catapult. It was dynamically perfect.

Ordinarily, I treat supercars with a certain amount of admiration but they tend to be a bit like Chinese food. Delicious when you're in there but perhaps a bit forgettable. I'll never have a Diablo or a Bugatti so who cares what they're like.

But the Ferrari costs less than a house and is therefore realistic. It is now my only real goal in life. One day, I shall buy a 355.

Sitting on a Porsche

The more you pay for a car, the less reliable it will be.

And it's not just cars either. My old Casio watch used to be second perfect, week in and week out, but the Breitling that's replaced it sheds nine seconds a day and sometimes stops completely in the night.

My £8 Zippo is capable of lighting cigarettes in a hurricane but the Dunhill I take out on posh-frock nights refuses to ignite if someone on the other side of the room is waving their arms around a bit.

I have an Umberto Ginocchietti jacket which has worn through at the elbows in less than a year, yet my Lee Cooper jeans are unburstable.

And so it goes on. I read about a woman the other day who has enjoyed 120,000 trouble-free miles in her Daihatsu Charade, yet the new McLaren, which costs more than half a million pounds, broke down on its first-ever journalistic road test.

Prince Charles suffered the ultimate ignominy the other day when his brand-new £150,000 Aston Martin Virage Volante conked out, rather conspicuously, on the Cromwell Road.

We may all drool over a Ferrari but if you used one every day, its engine would go out of tune and then break altogether. You would grow to hate the steering which is more stubborn than a dog which doesn't want to go to the vet's, and the gearbox, which is heavier than a washing machine.

But this is part of the appeal. You've got to be some kind of triangular-torsoed he-man to drive a Ferrari, and you have to be rich enough to have another car for the other six days in a week. You only take the Ferrari out on special occasions – that's what makes it special.

If you have a car that you can use every day, it will be an everyday car; humdrum, and tedious. Unless it's a Porsche.

Porsches are unique as they, like no other cars made, blend quality with sophisticated get up and go. And I have to say that some of them, these days, are pretty good value for money.

The 968 Club Sport does not have much in the way of creature comforts but you find me a more invigorating coupe for less than £30,000. And all you lot at the back with your Mazdas and your Toyotas can put your hands down now. They are not in the same league.

The 911 too is something of a bargain. I recently spent the weekend with an egg-yellow Carrera convertible which can haul itself from 0 to 60 in five point something seconds. It sounded great. Yobs spat at it. Taxi drivers asked if I'd swap. And yet it costs a mere £59,000 which is £20,000 less than the equivalent Ferrari.

Now, I'm no great fan of the 911. It's 31 years old and in some ways, you can tell. The dash was put together during a game at a children's tea party, and a blindfold was involved. And I reckon the new suspension is a triumph of engineering skill over a flawed design. That engine simply shouldn't be where it is.

Furthermore, the latest version, which was launched six months ago, has a pair of headlights which make the whole car look like a startled rabbit. And it's just too easy to drive; the steering's too light, the clutch is no harder to depress than a member of EXIT and changing gear is no harder than stirring soup. The end result is a car that just doesn't feel special enough even if you have just gone round a corner at 150 mph and all the girls in the street are trying to leave their phone numbers under the windscreen wipers.

Me, I've always preferred the Porsche 928, the Big Daddy. At £73,000, it is reassuringly expensive and it is capable of achieving speeds far in excess of what is practically possible.

It also has a proper engine where engines should be – at the front. Lift the bonnet and you are greeted with the sight of a huge 5.4-litre, quad-cam, 32-valve monster which sends 350 brake horsepower to the back wheels through a rear-mounted five-speed manual gearbox. Or, in my case, a four-speed automatic. This is all good beefcake stuff.

And when you climb inside, it gets better. Whereas most cars have measly pieces of wood which aren't big enough to make a pencil, this has two dirty great slabs, like upended coffee tables, on each door. And the massive, swooping dash is just delightful.

There are, of course, plenty of toys but it's what controls them all that I love – knobs the size of ice-cream cones. To turn the lights on, you grab a great fistful of rubberised plastic and give it a big old twist. Perhaps that's why there's no CD player – too fiddly, too high tech: not beefy enough. I'm surprised it doesn't have an eight track.

So far then, it's like motorised rock music: big, honest, down to earth and heavy. That body – a familiar sight now that it's been around for seventeen years – is just enormous; so wide that parking meter bays are too narrow by 18 inches, and long too.

Sitting inside, you feel cocooned so you find yourself trying to squeeze into spaces that turn out to be five feet smaller than necessary. It's a good job that bumperless front end is damage resistant because you just can't see it, or the back, or the sides. The last time I drove a 928, I crashed it, and driving this new one, I can see why – you can't see where its enormous body stops.

Happily, the engine is powerful enough to make light of the resultant weight. Prod the loud pedal, and immediately, the rear wheels chirp and lose traction, only being brought back into line by the various silicon chips. A green light comes on to tell the driver when the traction-control computer has just kept him out of a hedge.

The first time I went out for a spin, I dived into a small gap on the Wandsworth Bridge roundabout and such was the almighty leap forward, I couldn't help whooping out loud.

I've driven faster, more nimble cars but what I love about the 928 is its old-fashioned muscle.

Fair enough, the ride is far too hard and the steering could do with a bit more 'feel', but when you put your foot down and that raucous engine begins to sing its good ol' V8 song, you tend to forget about the various shortcomings.

Who cares about the microscopic boot or the joke rear seats. The back may well sing tenor but the front sings baritone.

And though £73,000 is a lot of money, it's important to remember that this is half what Aston Martin charge for the similar, though even more brutal, Vantage and £60,000 less than a Ferrari 512TR.

With that in mind, I began to formulate a pretty good case for the German equivalent of Giant Haystacks, until I remembered the Corvette. Here is another 2 + 2 coupe with a big V8, a hard ride, and prodigious power which is now available with right-hand drive for £45,000.

There's no doubt the Porsche is built to higher standards than the Chevrolet and that, curiously enough, is where my argument falls flat on its face.

The more you pay for a car, the less reliable it will be. Unless it's a Porsche.

Clarkson's Highway Code

The Highway Code is a very useful document but only if you accept that all other road users are friendly, cheery, obedient, Dixon of Dock Green type characters. Which they aren't.

So here is a Highway Code for the real world.

A flash of the headlamps

Confusing, this, as it could mean any of four things:

Hello, I am a friend of yours. Please feel free to pull out in front of me. Get out of your car and let's do pugilism. Look out, there's a police radar trap ahead.

The horn

Much easier. If it's a series of short toots, then someone friendly is trying to attract your attention. Your response is an omni-directional wave. If it's a prolonged burst, then someone some-where thinks you're an onanist. Put your foot down and get out of there.

Indicators

When the car in front is indicating left, beware. If it's a Datsun, with a large floppy aerial on the boot, then you are behind a mini-cab driver who is lost. A left-hand indicator could mean that he is going straight on or right or even that he is not, in fact, going anywhere at all. What it definitely means is that he is NOT going left.

Lane discipline

In towns, when at a multi-lane junction with traffic lights, never, ever, ever pull up behind a Nissan Micra. The driver will still be searching for his long-distance spectacles when the lights go green. Then he will forget to depress the clutch before trying to select first. Then he won't have the strength to disengage the handbrake.

Pedestrians

Run them down. Pedstrians must learn that they don't pay road tax and have no right to be milling around on something that isn't theirs.

Cyclists

Run them down and to make sure, back up and run them down again. Cyclists must be taught that they should stick to the side of the road and not try to weave around in the middle of it. Some even believe they're so fast that they're not being an inconvenience. Run them down to prove them wrong.

Trucks

Always give way to any vehicle that's larger than yours.

Speed cameras

When you encounter a sign saying speed cameras are in operation, you can be assured of one thing. There are no speed
cameras for a hundred miles, just a few grey boxes with flash
guns in them. Drive very, very fast indeed to prove to the locals
that the experiment isn't working.

Buses

Never follow a bus because you will be asphyxiated by the fumes
from its badly maintained diesel engine. Never try to overtake a
bus either because just as you're alongside, it will lunge out and
ram you. Bus drivers believe they can do this because of the tiny
signs on the back of their vehicles advising other road users to let
the bus go first.

Bus lanes

Always drive in them, even when there's no real need.

Mobile phones

When a policeman apprehends you for using a phone while
driving, explain that you can't talk right now because you're on
the phone.

Yellow cars

Never go to bed with someone who has a yellow car. Anyone who has walked into a showroom and, from the vast range of colours available, selected yellow is not normal. For the same reason, give yellow cars a wide berth when overtaking them.

Vans

If, on a narrow street, a van is coming the other way, it is your responsibility to get out of the way. Right out of the way. Unless you mount the kerb on your side of the road, and then park up in someone's garden, the van will remove your door mirror.

If this happens, don't get out of your car. At best, the van won't stop in which case you'll have wasted your time. At worst, it will stop. Then four baboons will climb out and beat you up a lot.

Speed limits

In town, drive around at 15 mph, ignoring the irate faces in your rear-view mirror. You're on the moral high ground.

On motorways, the traffic is never light enough to permit 70 mph. It was set in the days of Austin Cambridges and Dixon of Dock Greenery. Stick to 50 mph and then you'll hear the quiet bits in the plays on Radio Four.

Yellow lines

It's OK to park on these for a little while.

Red lines

It's OK to park on these too, but be safe and post a look-out man.

Tow-away lorries

Do absolutely everything in your power to make their life as difficult as possible. When collecting your car from the pound, be abusive. Make these people feel that being on the dole is preferable to their brand of government-sponsored, legalised theft.

Why aren't Car Ads Aimed at Old People?

As far as the blue-spectacled advertising copywriter is concerned, old people are simply not worth the bother. They have no disposable income and what little change is left at the bottom of their purses each week is spent on cat food and tinned salmon.

That's assuming, of course, their arthritic fingers are able to deal with the new money.

Yet in recent weeks, the television has played host to Mr Werthers Original Man, resplendent in his angora home-knit cardy doing what old people do best; talking about the days when they weren't old.

With that sepia tint to the film and the soft burr that goes hand in hand with knackered vocal cords, you can bet that pensioners the length and breadth of the land have been dying of hypothermia, and that sales of tinned salmon have plummeted.

This is because all of them will have been turning off their bar fires and spending their money instead down at the newsagent's, on old-fashioned sweets for their grandchildren – who, sadly, would much rather have been given some Evo-stick.

My mother-in-law – bless her – actually buys those commemorative plates which litter the advertisements in Sunday's colour supplements. She swoons over the frilly dolls called Emily. She is misty eyed at the snowstorm paperweights. And it's really only a matter of time before our new child is sent a nice packet of those sweets she saw on the bioscope.

So that's all well and good on the sweet front, but what about everything else? Why is Werthers Originals Man so unique? Why are all other advertisements on the television presented by people whose teeth shine so brightly it hurts? Be it for a pension or a washing powder, the images, the music, and the script are very obviously aimed at the under-forties.

And nowhere is this more apparent than in the world of car advertising.

In every commercial break, a huge finger leaps out of the screen and a deep, booming voice announces, 'Hey you – yes you with the tartan shopping trolley and the stupid slippers with zips up the front. Don't you dare buy one of our cars.'

BMW is slightly more subtle but the message is the same. Whether they're explaining how perfect weight-balance improves handling or how ellipsoidal headlamps let you see further at night, we are being told that BMWs are fast cars . . . and are therefore no earthly use if you only want to go to the post office once a week.

Volvo has a bigger problem. In the queue for stamps every Monday morning, the talk centres around crime, osteoporosis, the Blitz and how the Volvo 340 is the best car ever made.

There's space in the boot of any Volvo for a tartan shopping trolley and a dozen Zimmer frames, but is this the message we get from their TV ads? No it is not.

Instead we have rock music, a man in a T-shirt and a sinister-looking all black T5 hurtling across the Corinthean Canal. I now have a T5 and wherever I go, young men point approvingly. Old people tut.

Both Honda and Nissan have announced, in public, that they worry about the average age of their buyers so both are now engaged on a crash course in wooing teenagers.

Have you seen that absurd commercial where a group of improbably tanned youths ring up a group of impossibly lithe girls, asking if they'd like to go to the beach? 'They're on,' exclaims our hero.

We're then treated to the rather far-fetched scenario of these ridiculous people loading up their ridiculous Nissans with beach furniture. The last time we saw such a blatant attempt to woo people who still have need for Clearasil, it was called the Hitler

Youth, but there is a happy ending. The average age of the Nissan Micra buyer continues to climb.

Or how about Mazda. They ask us to video the commercial for their new 323, knowing full well that no old person in the land knows how to use a VCR.

Then there's Volkswagen, with its hurtful divorce campaign. You may have noticed that everyone who's cheering on the courtroom steps is young, and that the only disapproving look for the recently unbetrothed woman comes from a pensioner.

But all is not lost for the old people because Ford, always the first to spot an opportunity, has stepped in with the 'Which is right for you?' ads. No squealing tyres here. No mini drama. No cunning twist at the end where the man turns out not to be an adulterous bastard after all.

No, Ford tells us straight how much the car costs and what features it has. And I couldn't help noticing last night as I drove past my local dealer that it was full to overflowing with people in brown suits, asking for the price to be converted into old money.

Ford's marketing team may have been the first car-industry people to realise what has been staring everyone else in the face for about two years – young people burdened with a mortgage are unable to meet the monthly repayments on a car, let alone the awesome insurance bills.

And that the only people out there who can afford to buy and run a car these days are in their seventies.

Don't be surprised then if, in the very near future, Papa is borrowing Nicole's car and if BMW start telling us that the centre console cubbyhole between the two front seats is the ideal place for storing incontinence bags.

The New Range Rover Looks Like a Taxi

I was out for dinner last night with two couples, both of whom currently drive Range Rovers.

It's the natural choice, as both live in south-west London, both have one child, and both go shooting every now and again. One of the cars in question even has a silver dog on the bonnet. And bull bars for those tricky moments when the oncoming mini-cab just won't back up.

The old Range Rover looks so damn right too. Styled by Spen King when all his mates were at Woodstock, it has weathered the vagaries of fashion well and, if anything, looks even more pertinent today than it did back in 1972.

Certainly it's a whole lot more regal than any other large four-wheel-drive supertanker. Especially in that sort of olive-greeny colour, with matching wheels.

And strangely that is still true today, even with a new Range Rover in town.

Much has been written and said about this new technological wonderwagon but here is a simple fact: I tried to hail one on Regent Street a couple of weeks ago.

It was black and in the half light of a British winter afternoon, it was almost completely indistinguishable from the Metrocab.

I was a little jaundiced then, even before I took a test drive, and now, I rather look like I've caught yellow fever. I'm sorry, but the new Range Rover just doesn't seem to cut the mustard.

I'll admit, I have only driven the top of the range, 4.6-litre HSE model, and only briefly, but it was enough to demonstrate that it is neither one thing nor another.

And it's not hard to see why this should be so. The original Range Rover was conceived as an off-road vehicle, which after a day in the forests could be hosed down and used for a trip to the theatre.

Over the past 24 years, the emphasis has gradually changed. Recently, most Range Rovers have been used, largely, for trips to the theatre and then occasionally, very occasionally, they'd go off road; sometimes you'd see them with both nearside wheels on the pavement outside Fortnum's.

I was a huge fan of the original car and even today, I stare wistfully at those great V8 monsters as they burble by. I love that lofty driving position and the way they rock from side to side when you dab the throttle.

I also loved the fact that if I felt so inclined, I could take my air-conditioned, luxuriously carpeted car up the north face of the Eiger.

But I will recognise that, on the road, they left a lot to be desired. My father had wanted a Range Rover for twenty years, right up until the moment he actually drove one. He pointed out that it was slow, thirsty and that in corners, it felt like a small kitchen chair balanced on a vibrating water bed.

And in a sort of gritty, look after the pennies, Yorkshire way, he said that because he would never, ever take it off road, he'd stick with a BMW.

There are thousands more just like him too, and it is these people that Land Rover needed to woo with its new car.

But they couldn't just ignore their old customer base, the people who also never went off road but who revelled in the knowledge that they could if the mood took them. And they certainly couldn't ignore the motoring publications who would dance naked round a burning Rover Group effigy if, when they tested the new car, they found it fell over on to its side every time it saw a puddle.

So the new car had to feel like a Jaguar when it was on the M1 and a Land Rover when it was just off the M1, up to its door handles in a peat bog. This is impossible.

But that didn't stop them trying. For a few years now, the old

Range Rover has had air suspension but the new model goes so far into the realms of Arthur C. Clarke, that I was completely confused.

You can make the car rise up, squat down and for all I know roll over onto its back so you can tickle its axles, but all I wanted to do was go to the pub. Pre-flight checks have no place outside the cockpit of a commercial jet liner.

And while I'm sure the new 4.6-litre V8 chews fuel like a 737, I do not want to be bothered with a big bout of button stabbing before I go anywhere. Especially the pub.

Once I'd had the whole thing explained, I set off to see whether the taxi lookalike really can perform the impossible. And guess what. It can't.

The steering and the tendency to roll in the corners are massively improved over the old car, but it's no Jaguar. It can't be. It's too tall, so the centre of gravity is too far off the ground.

Plus, this car rides like a dream over ploughed fields – I know because I did it – and you can't have suspension that soft which will keep a car taut and level through a tightening right-hander. Land Rover has done a spectacularly good job, technologically speaking, but to what end?

My Dad would have hated all those buttons – he couldn't even turn the radio on in his car – and he would point out that on the road, the new Range Rover is still no match for a BMW.

So, the new car isn't clever enough to woo new buyers, and to make matters worse, I fear it's too clever for the old fans, like me. Certainly, neither of the couples with whom I had dinner last night will be buying one.

First there's that styling. Land Rover tried hard to make sure it didn't just look like a large estate car, and they've succeeded, but only in as much that it looks like a taxi. I don't like the square headlamps and it all goes wrong at the back too.

Yes, it's aerodynamically better but comparing new to old is like comparing a bungalow to a wardrobe.

The interior is a huge improvement though. It's bigger and

the dashboard is a joy to behold – apart from all those silly suspension controls.

It is also faster but compared to a basket of similarly priced saloons, it's almost glacial. Yes, it's fast for an off-roader but if you feel the need for speed, may I point you in the direction of the supercharged Jaguar.

Yes, the top of the range Range Rover is a staggering £45,000 and for that, you get a tall driving position, the ability to tell people at dinner parties that you could, if you wanted, drive home across the fields, and A-level suspension.

If you want more than that, you could have an Audi A8, or a Jaguar XJR or a V8 BMW or a big Mercedes, or anything you damn well want. That sort of money is going to steer a lot of people back into four-door saloons.

Or maybe not. Because Land Rover, almost as though they know they might have a problem with the new car, are still making and selling the old one.

It's called the Classic, which, ominously, is what Coca-Cola called old Coke when they launched the disastrous new variety.

I'm not saying the new Range Rover is disastrous because it isn't. Technically, it's better than the old one but in terms of style and price – things that really matter – it just isn't.

Princess Diana Drives Audi Sales Up

When Audi launched a convertible version of the mid-sized 80 saloon a couple of years ago, I drove one and thought it nice; like shortbread with the vicar.

It wasn't especially fast and, though it was handsome, there was no glint in its eye. Small boys did not clutch their private parts as it slithered past.

I seem to recall that it was quite pricey too and as a result, I figured that anyone with a bit of nous would opt instead for the Rover or the Golf and that anyone with no common sense at all would continue to buy the BMW cabriolet.

But I was counting without Princess Diana's social conscience. How was I to know that she'd swap that most conspicuous of things, the Mercedes SL – for the equally German but far less obvious Audi?

And how was I to know that she'd be photographed with the infernal thing every two hours, and that the shots would appear on the front of every national newspaper, every day?

Her clothes may change – from a leotard at the Harbour Club to a baseball cap for her liaisons with strange men in Chelsea – but the car is constant. And this association with the most glamorous royal of them all has done nothing at all to harm its sales.

So far this year, Audi has sold 931 80 cabriolets whereas in the same period last year, before Diana bought one, the figure was 508.

Ever since BMW came to stand for Black Man's Wheels, Haslemere's Vyella and Valium brigade have been looking for a replacement and now Diana has served it up to them, gift wrapped, and on a plate. She alone has turned what might have been just another nice car into by far and away the coolest and most-sought-after four-wheeled status symbol of them all.

And it didn't cost Audi a penny.

This product-placement business normally costs rather more than that. When Cliff Barnes arrived at the Oil Baron's Ball in Dallas in a new Range Rover some years back, it was rumoured at the time that Land Rover had forked out upward of £10,000 for the privilege. And Barnes, remember, was the loser, the no-hoper, the wally who was forever outwitted by the Ewing boys, both of whom had Mercs. As did their wives, their parents, their children, their mistresses and, though it was never made public, their dogs.

Nevertheless, Land Rover's US operation must have figured it was worth it. I guess it was the same deal in Britain with Lady Jane in the *Lovejoy* series.

In this country, Ford is the biggest player on the product-placement scene, ensuring that all the right people are seen in their cars. Ever since *Z Cars*, the televisual boys in blue have had a matching oval badge on their wheels – it gives the whole range a nice 'n' cosy feel.

Even today, Ford is always ready with a Mondeo should the producers of *The Bill* need some wheels. And do you remember *The Fourth Protocol*, the Freddie Forsyth flop? Ever think it was strange that everyone in the whole film was running around in Fords, clean ones too, with all the extras?

Ford supplies the royals with cars too, though like all manufacturers, it's tight lipped about the association. But a spokesman was willing to admit that free loan cars are currently out with David Bellamy and Dame Kiri Te Kanawa.

Oddly, Dave only gets a Mondeo while the Dame has a Scorpio; the old one I presume. The new one would scare all her audiences away.

Ford also ensures that Britain's top players on the motor-racing scene drive their cars. Jackie Stewart has one, as does his son, Paul. The entire Benetton team has used them all this season, as does the Andy Rouse racing stable. Even Michael Schumacher has one. And so, until recently, did Jeremy Clarkson.

The man at Ford says that before despatching a car into the hands of the rich and famous, a number of things have to be taken into account, like: is this the sort of person we want to see in one of our cars? Timmy Mallett, for instance, would struggle to prise an XJS out of Ford's luxury division at Jaguar.

Surprisingly though, when asked if they'd give Rod Stewart a Fiesta, the man ummed and ahhed. 'Well, we'd have to look into it.' Sorry Rod, I tried.

Mr Stewart, of course, is well known for his long association with Lamborghini. Open the trade pages of any secondhand-car newspaper and anyone selling a Countach or Diablo will claim that Rod used to own it.

At least Chris Eubank has the decency to make sure his used Range Rovers never get into the secondhand columns. Though, worryingly, his current car, a 6.3-litre Aston Martin Virage, is still up and running.

This is the trouble. When a celebrity actually hands over a wad of their own Melvins for a car, there's not a whole heap that a manufacturer can do.

And that can lead to all sorts of trouble. BMW desperately tries to cultivate that clinical, sharp, efficient image and doesn't mind one bit when George Michael is spotted outside the River Café with the top-of-the-range 850.

The man's albums are produced with the same sort of clinical efficiency. *Listen Without Prejudice* is exactly what BMW would expect their customer base to slide into the CD player before they go for a drive.

Derek Hatton, on the other hand, is very probably the sort of person BMW would not want to be seen in their car. Yet we all know that at one time Degsy did indeed waft from council meeting to property deal in a 635.

Jaguar too is in the same boat. I'm sure they're absolutely delighted when senior government figures are seen on the news, whizzing down Whitehall in an XJ6, but how happy were they, I wonder, when the Duchess of York bought a soft-top XJS?

Reliant is another case in point. When Princess Anne used to rush from horse race to magistrates' court in her old Scimitar GT/E, it gave the car some street cred that might otherwise not have been forthcoming for what was a Ford engine wrapped in plastic.

When she sold it, the car was doomed and now Reliant is left with its three-wheeler which was quite funny even before Del-Boy Trotter bought one.

And famous people can do a lot more than enhance, or dent, the reputation of a car. They can, in some cases, make or break it.

Since Rowan Atkinson stopped writing in *Car* magazine about his love affair with the Lancia Delta Integrale, the importers have packed up and gone back to Italy!

In all seriousness, Aston Martin might not have survived into the seventies were it not for James Bond. The DB5 was an absolute pig to drive, but 007 gave it class.

Not being a football fan, I'm not sure whether this works or not, but every time another overly coiffeured manager is fired, we're always treated to shots of him climbing into the very latest, most expensive Mercedes coupe. Is this a rule? Must all football managers have Mercs in the same way that their charges all have Toyota Supras?

Is this a good thing? Certainly, I would never buy a Supra or a Mercedes coupe because of their association with hooliganism. Nor would I buy a Mitsubishi Shogun either. Dave Lee Travis has one.

Bryan Adams has a lot more taste. His chosen four-wheel-drive car is a Land Rover, which appears in every photograph of him as surely as Diana's Audi.

Chris Rea goes even further. Though a complete Ferrari nut, the man who made goatee beards popular long before Take That were into short trousers has a Caterham Super Seven, which, he says, is the sort of car Ferrari should be making these days.

It's simple and uncomplicated and liver-crushingly fast and Chris loves it so much, it's a regular fixture on his album covers.

Finally, there's Volvo. Now here we have a company that is so desperate to change its image that I fear Penelope Keith would be ordered from one of its showrooms. I'm surprised the new range of adverts – 'more turbo than diesel' – and – 'drives like it's alive' – don't, at some point in the text, order women in head scarves to get lost.

Volvo is spending a million pounds on its racing programme – hell, even I have one now, but this, of course, is not enough.

Randall and Hopkirk is back on air – and what happened to Humber after one of their Super Snipes killed Hopkirk? So what Volvo needs to do is pay for someone to rerun *The Saint*.

Star Car – Alfa Romeo Spider

Usually, when a car goes out of production, there are no tears. There are no announcements in the papers and nobody sends flowers because nobody cares. One day you can buy a Ford Sierra. The next, you can't, and life goes on.

Occasionally, though, a car goes to that great scrapyard in the sky and people do care. One such car is the Alfa Romeo Spider, born in 1966. Died June 1993. Flowers to the crematorium, please.

These days, European cars stay in production for six or seven years, Japanese cars last only four, and so the Alfa has indeed managed something of a feat by lasting, virtually unchanged, for 25 years.

On the face of it, a car designed before anyone had even heard of Sergeant Pepper is going to be technologically challenged in 1993. Compared to the Mazda MX5, the Alfa is slow, rattly, rough, cramped, and blessed with truly awful handling characteristics.

I took one last drive in this relic last week and was horrified to find that the rear tyres always squeal when pulling out of side turnings and that negotiating a roundabout gives you the impression of being involved in some sort of rodeo championship.

Left turns are out of the question too, if you're tall, because the driving position is so awkward.

In the year when Donald Campbell died, the Spider was probably superb. But today, it is terrible.

Except for one small thing. *The Graduate* is a fondly remembered film for a number of reasons: the sex scene with Anne Bancroft, the Simon and Garfunkel score, the smouldering beauty of Katharine Ross and the birth of a new superstar in the diminutive shape of Dustin Hoffman.

But while a few of the details have become a little hazy, everyone remembers what sort of car he drove. A red Alfa Spider. The impact was enormous. Indeed, today in America, the car is called the Alfa Graduate.

Because of that film, the Spider is by far and away the most loved, cherished and sought-after sports car in the world. Everybody, especially women, turn and stare when it lurches by. Everyone I know wanted to borrow it. Old ladies cooed. Old men went all nostalgic. Young men looked at their Golf GTis and wondered.

They say that image doesn't sustain an inferior product for long but the Spider shows there is a serious flaw in this argument. You might not like the car very much but the idea of it makes people go all gooey.

When Marianne Faithfull announced that at the age of 37, Lucy Jordan had never been through Paris, in a sports car, with the warm wind in her hair, everyone knew the sports car in question would have to be an Alfa Spider.

She'd smash her teeth to bits as she bounced over the cobbles and yes, it would probably break down, but if you are after stylish motoring, the sort where your hair is held in place with a Hermes headscarf, the Alfa runs rings round a flashy Ferrari or the Mazda MX5 with all the personality of a Sony Walkman.

Of course, the Spider isn't the only car to have been elevated to deity status by careful product placement in the movies; where, for instance, would the Ford Mustang have been were it not for Steve McQueen, San Francisco and *Bullitt*?

Sure, this was the fastest-selling car of all time when it was launched in 1964 – a record that still stands today – but when push came to shove, it was nothing more than an American Ford Capri.

It would probably have fizzled out by 1973 but because Steve McQueen showed us all what it can do, greatness was foisted upon it. Because of *Bullitt*, the Mustang survived long enough for Michael Douglas to use one while chasing a Lotus, again through San Francisco, in *Basic Instinct*.

He had to. Cops, California, car chases and Mustangs are now inexorably linked, like sewers and Mini Coopers.

And quite apart from Mini Coopers, *The Italian Job* promoted both the Lamborghini Miura and the E-Type Jaguar to way above their stations.

Then there was the VW Beetle. Do we remember it as a piece of Nazi war memorabilia? Is it a stupid Woody Allen gag? The Beetle was one of Hitler's creations like the V2 and the gas chamber but do pensioners stone them when they clatter by? No.

We all go 'ahh' because the Beetle is Herbie, as cuddly and as loveable as the family spaniel.

In the 1970s, John Thaw spent his time chasing Mark Two Jaguars with bank robbers in them. In the 1990s, he completely changed our perception of this old car by using one himself in *Morse*.

If you drove an old Jag in the 1970s, everyone assumed the boot was full of baseball bats and loot and that you were on your way to some blag or other. Today, people see you are a learned, stately sort of soul. And drunk.

Reagan forced the value of old Jaguars down but thanks to *Morse*, and despite the downward spiral in classic car prices, the Mark Two is now a rapidly appreciating asset.

The right film and the right character can make a car. It can give it cult status and ensure global sales in greater numbers and for a longer period of time than its designer would have dreamed possible.

Thus, if I was running Proton, I would have made damn sure that the T Rex in *Jurassic Park* drove off at the end in the new 1.5-litre Aeroback.

Routefinder Satellite Technology

Hello: this column is coming to you on my new, digital mobile phone whch m usng on the M40 just wr t geeeeks thgh th shored putting.

Hey, this is groovy. No fizzing or crackling, just a digital interpretation of what it thinks I'm trying to say, with blanks for the bits that are too hard.

I don't understand mobile phones. The first one I bought, about ten years after they first caught on, was bigger than my washing machine and heavier than a photocopier. It had to go when my car's suspension broke.

The second was much smaller but after a stupidly short space of time, the '2' button jammed down which meant I could only call the person whose number is 222–2222. Sorry mate.

Then there was the Sony which, thanks to its tiny dimensions, was nearly thrown away with all the fluff at the bottom of my pockets every week.

Plus, because it was so tiny, there was no read-out and therefore no way of knowing what number I'd actually dialled. I even called the man at the local launderette Mum the other night.

And now I have the digital, pan-European Ericsson which enables me to make and receive calls from a boat in Monaco harbour. Well, it would if I had a boat in Monaco harbour.

It works in Australia and the Middle East too, but not Eastbourne, or High Wycombe which, frankly, is a nuisance because I spend much more time in Buckinghamshire and Sussex than Dubai.

When it's not receiving a signal, it can do tricks like diverting incoming calls to my home number and making tea. I've just got to the bit in the instruction book where it explains how, if I press the hash button, it becomes an AK47. Useful.

But like all my phones, useless when it comes to finding a transmitter.

And what makes this especially irritating is that no one else has the same problem. My phone sits on a table in the pub, casting its tentacles out and only finding pylons, while someone else's, on the same table, is bulging with signal.

If I may be permitted to liken these phones to people, I always seem to end up with Kenneth Williams while everyone else has a Chippendale.

I sat in a traffic jam last night, desperate to call my wife with a progress report but the Ericsson just sat there, its signal sac empty and wizened. And yet, in every other car, other people were laughing and joking with far-away colleagues and loved ones. I could almost hear them: 'I'm alongside that bloke from *Top Gear* and he's got no mates.'

It's the same story down at the autobank. Why is it that whenever I get to the head of the queue, it is unable to mate with the computer in Doncaster, where my account is held. The card comes back and as I walk away, people are saying: 'There's that bloke off *Top Gear*. He's got no money.'

And now, my new Philips Routefinder is playing up. The idea is that you give this small black box your starting point, and where you want to go, and it gives you the best route.

But it doesn't. I live in Battersea and after fifteen years in London, I know the best way to the M1 is straight up through the middle of town unless it's rush hour, in which case, you go through Hammersmith, Shepherd's Bush, Willesden and Cricklewood.

But the Routefinder reckons that no matter what, I head out of town on the A40 and go round on the North Circular.

The only people who go on the North Circular are people who are frightened of the M25 and stark staring terrified of

Central London. It's bad enough having people think I have no mates and no money without being labelled a tourist.

My electronic jinx even struck the computer this morning. The screen had become a bit boring so I was staring at the washing machine and couldn't help noticing that all my computer discs were busy being washed. Can computer discs walk? Do they get BO? Can someone write in and tell me.

Oh, and while I'm on the subject of writing in, thank you to all the people who say the number plate PEN1S was issued. It wasn't – you've all seen PEN15 which belongs to Steve Parrish, the truck-racing driver.

And thank you too to the hundreds who wrote to say that we shouldn't buy Korean cars because the Koreans eat dogs. There's another reason too – Korean cars are crap.

The Pickup Truck Phenomenon

Deep in the Florida Everglades, where the men are men and the crocodiles are frightened, a chap called Wild Lyle runs an air-boat rental company.

Wild Lyle's stomach is considerably larger than his vocabulary. He spits more than he speaks and he only eats what he runs over. He wears a camouflage jacket and likes guns. Naturally, he drives a pickup truck.

In rural America, everyone drives a pickup truck. Kids from the Montana flatlands to the dusty plains of New Mexico can walk right past a Ferrari but will stop and drool quite openly when the latest flat-bed Ford burbles by.

The best-selling car in America is the Ford Taurus but even its huge sales are eclipsed by both the Ford F series pickup and its Chevrolet competitor. Between them, these two alone found nearly a million buyers in 1994.

Indeed, 'light trucks' now account for a staggering 40 per cent of the total car market in America, and there just aren't that many rednecks. So who the hell is buying them all? And why?

It all started back in the early eighties when a minor oil crisis forced the American car makers to start building small-engined, four-cylinder saloons. They gave good 'gas mileage' but you can't tow a boat behind a small car. And in America in 1981, 12.5 million people owned a boat.

And then there were those with snowmobiles, and horses, and gliders.

When the cars became 'pony assed', everyone turned to the more powerful, go-anywhere rough-and-tumble pickup truck. Lob the skis in the back, hitch up the boat and in two hours, you're on Lake Tahoe.

The pickup truck still sells to Wild Lyle and his cyclopic ilk, but today, Wall Street buzzes with the things. Tom Clancy has one. Arnold Swarzenegger has one. Bob Seger has one. Last time I was in San Francisco, I saw Barbara Bush arriving at the Fairmont in one.

Norma Major, on the other hand, does not have one. And nor does Gary out of Take That. In Britain, a pickup truck is what your plumber drives.

Pickup trucks, in Britain, just don't sell and having spent a day or two with what's supposed to be the latest and the best, I can see why. They're horrid.

And pointless. In Britain, if you have a boat, you are a criminal and you live in Spain. If you have a horse, you are wealthy enough to have a Range Rover. And if you have a glider, then you tend to fly from place to place, rather than bounce.

Pickup trucks do a lot of bouncing. P. J. O'Rourke once described the pickup as a back porch with an engine but this is not fair. To back porches.

The average pickup truck has no suspension and the sort of steering that's only familiar to the masters of very large super-tankers. They are also crudely finished, noisy and uneconomical.

Now that's fine for a redneck, because they only ever drive when drunk and as a result, don't notice, but an investment analyst from Long Island wants more.

And that's where the Dodge Ram comes in.

This is not, for instance, happy to be mildly uneconomical. No, this baby would need the back-up of a medium-sized government to keep it moving.

You can't see the fuel gauge going down as you accelerate, but that's only because it moves too fast. Start up. BAM. You're out of gas.

This Ram features the 300-bhp 8000cc V10 engine you would normally find under the hood of its sister product – the awesome Viper.

Trouble is, in the Viper, there is very little bodywork to move around. In the Ram pickup, there is a lot. That not only makes it a single-figure mpg specialist but also, surprisingly slow.

Floor the throttle and the engine roars the roar of an enraged lion. Hell, this baby sounds like it's creating its own weather but a glance down to the speedometer shows that you're actually accelerating very slowly indeed.

And that's because the rear wheels are spinning uselessly. There's no weight out there at the back so when a great gob of torque suddenly arrives at the aft end of the prop shaft, they just rip up the tarmac. It's fun, until the council comes round with a bill for repairs.

Of course, you can engage the four-wheel-drive system which removes the wheel spin, and the fun, and all the petrol in the tank.

But all this is by the by. The single most in-your-face aspect of the Dodge Ram is its sheer size. Compared to this, a Range Rover looks like a Corgi toy. To park, you need to find two adjacent bays, and even then, the road needs to be wide too. And I mean really wide.

All inner-city width-restriction poles are too close together for the Ram so you have to go the long way round, which you can't because it keeps running out of petrol.

My wife cannot even see over the top of the radiator grille. Each one of its spotlights is the size of a supermarket trolley. This thing is just huge. Big, like two Pavarottis.

But there's the funny thing. Despite the sheer acreage of road space, it only has two and a half seats, which, as you would expect from the Americans, are finished in the finest vulgalour.

There's no shortage of equipment, what with the electric seats and the drink holders and the auxiliary power socket for your phone. The top-flight pickup, then, has been through the Range-Roverisation programme. With the addition of a few toys and a dash of pleblon here and there, it has become a country car for city folk.

Except for one small thing. I'm sure I remember reading

somewhere that they have thieves in America who like to steal things.

Last Saturday, I did some retail therapy on the Tottenham Court Road and was able to return home with all the boxes stored away in the boot. If they'd been in the pickup, every one of them would have been nicked the first time I stopped at a set of lights.

So not only is there no space up front, but the back, though big enough for a couple of volleyball courts, is nigh on useless too.

America has a history of being able to convert a working man's tool of the trade into a fashion icon – the Zippo, Rayban Aviators and Levis spring to mind – but they'll have a job with the pickup truck.

An American marketing person may try to explain the Dodge Ram is a distinctive, eight-litre, four-wheel-drive two-seater. But it isn't. It's a lorry. And lorries are not, and never will be, trendy.

Safety Measures – Who Needs Them?

In a little over a hundred years, the motor car has killed more people than every single war that has ever been waged.

Stacked up against the car's adroitness at wholesale slaughter, the Somme begins to look like a Sunday School outing.

In India alone, where cars haven't even caught on properly, nearly 50,000 people a year are killed on the roads. In just one state, 16 people are killed every single day, and 97 are injured. Out there, one in every 42 cars on the roads, at some stage, will be involved in a serious accident. It's so bad that in the 5 to 44 age group, car accidents rate as one of the biggest killers.

In the West, the car is still a murdering blaggard but at least the picture is a little more rosy. Indeed, while the number of cars on the roads goes up every year, the number of people they kill is falling.

But I fear that this statistic is about to be filed under 'history'. I fear that within the next five years, the number of people being killed will rise sharply all over Europe and North America.

And I blame the air bag.

Earlier this year, Mercedes Benz unveiled a new concept car which is basically a bouncy castle on wheels. Hidden away, in little recesses all over the interior, are no fewer than seventeen air bags.

Quite apart from the usual places like the steering wheel, they're located under the dashboard to save your parts, in all four doors, between the front seats, in the roof and in the headrests. There is even an air bag in the back of each front seat so that should the driver crash while you're in the back, working on a laptop computer, you won't emerge from the wreckage with qwertyuiop[] stencilled on your forehead.

At the moment, this is at the concept stage but we can rest assured that something along similar lines will soon find its way into ordinary cars for the road.

Volvo is already advertising its seat-mounted air bags which pump themselves up should anyone be foolish enough to drive into the side of one of these Swedish tanks.

Now you must remember that Volvo already has its Side Impact Protection System (SIPS) which transfers all the energy of a crash into the roof and the floor, and away from the poor souls in the car.

Then there's Audi with Procon Ten. Run into something bigger than you are – a Volvo for instance – and at the same moment, the seatbelts are tightened as the steering wheel is pulled forward, away from your head.

This is the cutting edge of safety in cars, and it comes on top of anti-lock brakes, rigid safety cells, traction control and any number of other devices to keep you alive, should everything turn pear-shaped.

And therein lies the problem. Very soon, people are going to realise that they can have huge crashes, at any speed they choose, and walk away.

They'll be careering into buildings, pedestrians, lamp-posts and people in older, less-well-protected cars, knowing that they are immune from injury. This won't do.

So if car manufacturers are really interested in promoting safety on the roads, rather than introducing new measures about which their marketing departments can crow, they should ditch all the new ideas.

Rip out the air bags, and in their place, fit titanium spikes which, in the event of a crash, will leap out of the centre of the steering wheel, and impale the driver on his seat.

And hey, Mr Audi, instead of pulling the steering wheel forward in a crash, why not give us something which shoves it back into the guy's face – hard.

And Volvo, forget SIPS. Better to fit a small nuclear bomb in the back of the child seat which is triggered to go off should the car receive a significant jolt. Crash and your baby is blown into such tiny particles, you won't even need a coffin.

With these sorts of features in all cars on the road, I think it's safe to assume that the number of deaths on the road would fall, in an instant, to zero.

Right now, people are quite happy to hurtle down the outside lane of a motorway, in thick fog, at 100 mph because their anti-lock brakes will keep them out of trouble – they'd better go too – and that even if they don't, everything else will.

Well, they'd think twice if the car was nothing more than a series of booby traps.

To make sure this was fair, and that all cars are equipped with the same menacing array of death traps, the government needs to introduce legislation. But this is where it all gets sinister. The government won't do this, because it wants us to drive fast and dangerously.

They know that if they ban seatbelts, rip down all crash barriers and douse all roads with a mixture of diesel oil and washing-up liquid every morning, people would never dare drive at more than 10 mph.

And this would remove one of the most iniquitous taxes ever dreamed up – the speeding ticket.

It's all so obvious. By forcing car makers to give us safer vehicles, and by making the roads less dangerous, they are encouraging us to drive faster and faster. Couple this with ridiculous vigilant police patrols, and they have a small fortune.

People are dying out there, to pay for the National Health Service.

Speed

When Stephenson launched his Rocket locomotive, sceptics were convinced that passengers would not be able to breathe when it was moving along at top speed.

The strange thing is that even though the great man proved them wrong, the world is still full of people who reckon that speed kills.

Barely a week goes by without a sad-faced policeman coming on the television to tell us how a whole family has been wiped out because someone was going too fast.

On *Top Gear*, we are forever being harangued by tweedy liberals on nonsensical quangos who reckon that speed is the root of all our evils. Kill your speed, not a child, they wail.

Well, if speed really is this dangerous then how come Concorde isn't the most dangerous form of transport ever devised? I mean, here we have a plane which rockets across the Atlantic faster than the speed of sound but which, in all its years, has never killed a soul.

How come Japanese commuters don't dive for cover whenever the 200-mph bullet train hisses to a halt at their station? Worse, they climb on board and drink coffee, while what's left of Japan slides by in a blur.

No astronaut has ever died while circling the earth, something he is doing at speeds in excess of 17,000 miles per hour.

Speed, all on its own, is safer than lying in bed all day. It can only kill when it is mixed up with something else, like inattentiveness. So instead of worrying about speed, we should concern ourselves with what causes people to lose concentration.

It certainly isn't speed. The faster you go, the more you have to think about what you're doing, so I laughed at all those yellow-toothed members of the British Vegetarian Society who leaped about when Vauxhall introduced the 170-mph Lotus Carlton.

They called it a cancerous menace with gangrene and leprosy and said it was the seven-headed beast from Revelations. Women with short hair began to leave Greenham Common and head for Luton.

Never mind that in any other walk of life, speed is considered essential – faxes and modems for instance – the Carlton was a greater threat to man's survival than Trident.

Well, only a handful were ever sold and some straw-poll research has shown that so far, not one of them has been involved in any sort of fatal crash. So stick that in your pipe and smoke it, Mrs Weird Beard.

The Vauxhall, and all the other fast saloons of its ilk, tend to be safer than the average car because they are usually bought by enthusiasts. These guys are not worried by how the car looks or what badge is nailed to the back: they simply want a car that's good to drive.

And when they're out driving it, they're not listening to the radio or talking on the phone or turning round to try to reason with an incontinent four-year-old in the back. When they are driving, they are driving.

Anyone who is not enthusiastic about cars, but needs one to get from A to B, will not buy a Lotus Carlton or a Jaguar XJR or a BMW M5 because they're too fast. He won't feel safe in them. He doesn't like the racy suspension and the sports seats and the gaudy wheels.

He simply consults the Consumers' Association which, like him, is unconcerned with speed or style; only with reliability and value for money. They like Nissans and Volvos and Toyotas.

So he buys one of those which he drives around in. V-e-r-y S-l-o-w-l-y.

Yes, he goes the wrong way round roundabouts and has heated arguments with colleagues while lurching about on the M40.

Yes, he indicates right when he wants to go left. And yes, he occasionally drinks and drives.

He never drives quickly though so as he ambles past those signs saying Speed Kills, he feels fine. He isn't speeding.

It's the same story on the motorway. He's in the middle lane with a truck two inches from his high-intensity rear lights, which come on the instant it's dark, but he's only doing 50 and that's 20 mph below the speed limit, so he's all right, Jack.

And besides, he hasn't noticed the truck because he's listening to a particularly good play on Radio Four.

Even though he is in control of a ton of metal which is storming along at 50 mph, he is absolutely miles away. It doesn't matter what the weather does or how much traffic there is, he's below the speed limit and he's feeling smug. He may even have a little snooze.

He is a menace but how do you legislate for guys like this? You can't force him to buy a decent car because even if he did have a big Bee Em, he'd still be doing 50 and he'd still be sozzled. And he'd still jam his brakes on every time Tony Blair came on the radio to say something even more stupid than usual.

You can't ban phones and radios in cars and even if you could, people would still daydream. You could, I guess, force cars to be a lot noisier by banning exhaust silencers, but this wouldn't go down too well in residential areas, early in the morning.

You can, however, make people drive faster. A lot faster.

I therefore propose a new minimum speed limit of 130 mph on motorways which will scare away the truly hopeless drivers and force those who could be good if they tried to concentrate.

If you had a motorway network where every single driver was concentrating absolutely on the job in hand, you wouldn't have any crashes at all.

Nasty Nissans

Men in suits, be they government ministers, insurance company bosses or police people are convinced that it is young men in fast cars who constitute the biggest hazard on the road.

This hazard is perceived to be so great that the punishment metered out is horrendous. Drive too fast, even for a moment, and they will remove your licence. As a result, your job disappears down the lavatory and you will come home one night to find that your wife has moved in with someone else. Someone who still has wheels.

Steal a car and they'll send you to the Red Sea for some scuba diving. But drive a car too quickly, and they'll wreck your life.

However, I have never been inconvenienced by a young man in a fast car. Blink, and you've lost sight of him in the smoke from his own tyres. Who cares?

By far the most terrifying sight on the roads today is the Nissan Sunny. This is Freddy Kruger on wheels. If I may liken all cars to the City of New York, the Sunny is Harlem, at 2 am on a Saturday night.

Anyone who is not interested in cars tends not to make a very good driver. And there is no better way of demonstrating a complete lack of interest in all things automotive than driving, owning, or having anything whatsoever to do with a Nissan Sunny.

The Sunny is a stupid-looking car that handles like a wheel-barrow and is neither fast, economical nor cheap, but the infernal Consumers' Association says it's unlikely to break down.

So old people buy one and drift around as though it's 1947. They haven't got to grips with roundabouts or motorways or filter lanes or pelican crossings or anything really. So long as they're going roughly in the right direction, that's fine.

Should you come up behind a Sunny, you might imagine that its driver is being deliberately obstructive, veering all over the road, braking for no reason and so on, but usually, this is not the case.

First, the driver's body is so racked with osteoporosis that it has shrunk to a point where he can't actually see where he's going, let alone what's behind.

And second, he assumes there is nothing, simply because there wasn't anything in 1947.

And anyway, if by some miracle he does notice that there is a 30-mile queue of red-faced young men stuck in his 20-mph wake, you must remember that he is a *Which?* magazine reader and will therefore be mean spirited. The passive resistance to your increasingly desperate attempts to overtake will become active.

Last week I followed a Sunny for fifteen miles and never, not once, anywhere in the world, have I seen such a display of truly appalling driving.

And eventually, I could take no more and in perhaps the most idiotic move I've ever made, I slammed my car into first gear and on a blind bend, shot past, flicking Vs and snarling.

Had I crashed, the full force of the law would have been brought to bear as the shrivelled-up has-been explained to anyone who would listen that he was trundling along at 20 mph and that this huge, wailing Jaguar had flashed by and that I deserved everything that was coming.

Since then, I've started to notice Nissan Sunnys more and more, and in 100 per cent of cases, they are being driven not just badly, but in a fashion that leads me to deduce that the driver is blind, mad or dead.

If they indicate at all, it's done on a random basis. I have seen one attempting to turn right at the bottom of London's Park Lane, into Hyde Park Corner. They stall at the lights and if it's an old model, it's likely to stop in the middle of the road, without warning, to let the drunken fare out.

Worst of all though, when attempting to pull out from a side turning into a main road, the driver will wait until the road is clear for eight miles in both directions before initiating the lunge.

The trouble is that 'waiting too long at a junction' is not against the law. You could get them with 'driving without due care and attention', but acquaintances of mine in the traffic police say this is notoriously difficult to prove.

I find myself wondering then whether it is time for some new laws. 'Driving while under the influence of Clement Attlee' might work, but we should stop short of actually making it illegal to drive a Nissan Sunny on the public highway.

Right now, if you see one you can be absolutely guaranteed that it will be doing something strange. You can prepare for that.

If, however, the Sunny was outlawed, all the bad drivers would disperse into other cars like the Proton or the Toyota Corolla or the Rover 200. This would make them hard to spot until, perhaps, it was too late.

So, I think we should keep going with the present system where all the hopeless drivers have Sunnys but that to make them that little bit more obvious at a greater distance, all of them should be painted vivid lime green.

Road Rage

When Tony Blair comes on the television, I usually lose my temper.

So I have no problem with Eric Cantona's kung fu episode. In a highly charged environment, some ghastly man in quite the foulest clothes I've ever seen invited him to go back to France, and was kicked. Eric lost his temper. Big deal.

Same goes with Ian Wright. So he planted a docker's oyster in someone's face. Worse things happen.

There are few people out there who can put their hands on their hearts and say that they have never reached breaking point, that they have never snarled and gritted their teeth and shouted. It's perfectly natural and provided you can keep away from knives and guns, there's nothing really wrong with it.

However, some damnfool feature writer, probably in America, has coined a new phrase for losing your temper in a car – they've called it Road Rage.

So now, when some ninny in a Datsun starts to meander around the road like a twig in a brook, it's not his fault that you blow up. You are suffering from Road Rage.

Yes, now you can drive down the outside lane of a motorway at 40 mph and when the guy behind rips his steering wheel from its mountings and turns puce, you can shrug and put his stupidity down to Road Rage.

I recall reading one story in a newspaper recently about how this poor, unfortunate woman had borrowed a TVR – which was almost certainly the real motivation behind the piece – and how she'd been shouted at by men while driving it.

Well, TVRs are notoriously hard work. The steering is heavy. The clutch is heavy. The brakes are heavy. She was very probably unused to the power and it is therefore not beyond the realms of possibility that she was making a complete Horlicks of everything.

She tried to claim that these men – spit the word out like you've inadvertently eaten a piece of marzipan – these 'men' were cross with her because she was a woman in a flash car. I doubt it somehow. It was very probably because she was a crap driver.

I must confess that I too get irritated by women in cars, mainly because none of them ever, ever let me out of side turnings.

Every morning, I try to turn right onto the slow-moving Fulham Palace Road and every morning it is a man who lets me out. Women have perfected the art of staring straight ahead and pretending they don't know I'm there.

Yesterday, one even went to the trouble of pulling her head-scarf forward a bit so that as she sat, blocking my path, I didn't even trouble her peripheral vision.

Now this made me mad, and if she was a reporter on the *Daily Mail*, I don't doubt that when she arrived at work, she wrote a piece saying that men are beasts, and that women can never reach high office. Except prime minister.

And then she would go into all the complex reasons for Road Rage, trying to intellectualise something that just doesn't need intellectualising.

Doubtless, she would explain that when pushing her trolley round the supermarket, people apologise and smile if they bump into her, or indeed, if she bumps into them.

But in the car park, it's a different story. Out there, if you make a mistake, other drivers engage their fingers in such a way to suggest you are an onanist. They lean on their horns, and shout a lot. Why does this happen?

Well, it's perfectly simple. If you bump into someone's super-market trolley, you won't need to swap addresses. You won't be faced with a £200 bill. You won't need to argue the toss with insurance companies. You won't lose your no-claims discount.

And then there's the open road where you're going much

faster than you are in a car park. If someone makes a mistake on the M1, the result can be a whole lot worse than a cracked indicator lens. You could die, and when you've had a near-death experience, it's only natural that at the very least you shake your fist at the person who caused it.

Now I'm not writing this from some holier-than-thou platform. When I make a mistake on the roads, and it doesn't happen very often because I, like you, am a superb driver, I am the first to hurl abuse at the driver I've carved up.

The reason I feel able to do this is the reason I feel able to yell at Tony Blair when he's on the television. There is a physical barrier, a piece of glass, between me and the enemy, and that makes me feel safe.

Shout at someone face to face and they will probably punch you in the mouth, which would hurt. But do it in the car and not only are you protected but also you have the chance to speed away should the other guy look like he's on for some pugilism.

Now, short of making everyone drive around in convertibles with the hood down, you aren't going to do much about that, and nor will you ever stop people losing their temper.

So what, then, can be done about Road Rage?

It's simple. Eliminate the cause. I would never lose my temper on the road if people didn't do stupid things, and the only way to stop that is to get stupid people off the roads.

They wouldn't let a stupid person drive the space shuttle so why do they let idiots behind the wheel of a car? And they do, you know.

Ford has made a video about Road Rage – it's quite good actually, even though none of the drivers have Fords – and one woman called Emma says, 'Basically, I've just got to be first. I've got to be first off at the traffic lights and I've got to beat that huge Porsche following me and I've got to be in front of that Mercedes, particularly if there's a man behind the wheel.'

She is obviously daft as a brush and she's not alone. I can recall undertaking someone on the M1 who followed me for 80 miles, his face purple with rage. He was a very idiotic person too because he had a small moustache and because he mistook the water pistol I eventually pointed at him for a real gun and backed off.

To start with then, I suggest that the driving test should include some form of intelligence exam. And later, if this works, how about going the whole way and not letting dim people breed?

But in the meantime, would all you women out there who seem to be at war with men on the roads do us the service of actually declaring it. Then we can fight back.

The New Jaguar

The new supercharged Jaguar is better than a good thing. It was bitterly cold out there at seven this morning, and as I watched my postman trudging up the street, past all the cars that I have on test this week, I couldn't help thinking that I have a better job than him.

My desk is piled high with invitations from car firms to join them on exotic trips to faraway lands. And the aforementioned cars outside include a Range Rover, a Porsche 911, a Fiat Cinqecento Sporting, a Mini Cooper, a Volvo T5 and a Jaguar.

But Postman Pat does at least need some modicum of skill and stamina, whereas all you need to be a motoring journalist is a head full of opinions.

Car testing is perhaps the most inexact science ever invented. It's like trying to pick up a bit of mercury while wearing boxing gloves.

It's unfair too. Car firms spend a billion or more on a new car only to have it ripped to shreds by a bunch of hacks who, myself included, rarely know one end of a shock absorber from the other.

It's simply a case of deciding whether I like the car or not, and I'm sad to say, this sometimes has little or nothing to do with the car itself.

Most of the time, I adore the Jaguar XJS, but the last time I drove one, it was raining, I had a headache, a cricked neck and I was trying to reverse it down a narrow mews street, at night. And I absolutely hated the damn thing.

Then there's the Toyota Starlet. This is a dreadful little car but on the two occasions I've been unfortunate enough to find myself in one, the roads have been empty, the sun has been out and I was in seventh heaven. The best drive of my life was in a Starlet, on a deserted mountain road in Portugal.

I try not to let outside influences cloud important verdicts but sometimes, it just can't be helped. All cars feel good on deserted coast roads in the South of France with Tom Petty on the stereo. All cars feel bad in Acock's Green on a wet February night.

Against this sort of background, you can see why it's hard, and sometimes impossible, to be rational. Hell, if motoring journalists were rational, we'd all agree on what is The Best Car In The World. But we don't.

I can't even agree with myself. Within the space of two years, I have had four all-time favourite cars – the Dodge Viper, the Aston Martin Vantage, the Escort Cosworth and the Ferrari 355.

And now, there is a fifth. The Jaguar XJR.

The first time I drove this remarkable new car, I was in Scotland and therefore hungry – food is never recognisable as such up there, so I tend not to eat much.

It was also raining hard and 321 brake horsepower engines go together with streaming-wet country lanes about as well as haggis and chocolate. I knew it was a good car, a very good car, but it wasn't until I had a go in it in England that I realised that good is too small a word. Senbleedingsational is better.

It was getting on for midnight and the darkened and deserted M40 stretched out for a hundred miles. Bob Seger was in the boot and the stars were out.

The exterior temperature gauge showed it was 11 degrees so there was no danger of ice, and the headlines that morning had talked of Home Office cutbacks so the chances of encountering a police patrol were even more remote.

The big cat was impressive enough, thundering down the outside lane – quiet, unruffled and smooth as you would expect, but it was snarling rather than purring and the fat tyres were making pitter-patter noises; unusual in a Jaguar saloon.

So even though it was late, I turned off to see what the monster could do on normal roads. What it can do is unscrew the top of your head and insert a small egg whisk in the resultant cavity. This car is astonishing.

The steering is perfect, weighted so well that you can feel exactly what the front wheels are doing, and you know precisely what the back end is up to, almost as though it's in telepathic contact.

And if you choose to ignore the signals of impending doom, the traction control gently pushes the accelerator pedal upwards, against the pressure of your foot, first as a reminder that it's time to back off, and then more urgently.

It does this rather a lot because that six-cylinder, four-litre, supercharged engine is sublime. It may only do 14 mpg but as the rev counter surges round the dial, in an unending quest for the red zone, and the automatic gearbox blurs the changes, I must confess I'd have been happy with 9 mpg, or less. And yes, I do pay for my own petrol.

Back in London, I recalled its ability to hurtle through tightening bends with almost no body roll at all, as it slithered down the Earls Court Road, ironing out all the bumps and ridges. Here is a car with leather seats, cruise control, beautiful black wood trimmings and matching hide upholstery, which when you're in the mood, can transform itself into a snarling beast with spiky teeth and a penchant for red meat served raw.

Only the BMW M5 can perform this amazing feat even half as well, but it costs £52,000 and the Jaguar is only £45,000.

Within a month, I'm quite sure, I shall have driven another car, on a better road, in finer weather and with faster music on the CD, but for now, the best car in the world is the Jaguar XJR.

Stop Thief; Not Me

So, the police are going to stop answering burglar alarms because nine out of ten times, they find, after a tyre-squealing journey, that the damn thing has gone off by accident.

That, we hear, is a waste of man hours and thus, a waste of money. So, if economics now determines which crimes are investigated and which are not, then I would hope that we'll see an end to radar traps. What's the point of pointing a hairdryer at a stream of motorists all day when nine out of ten are doing nothing wrong?

Actually, the point is simple. A constable is an inexpensive commodity whose time is more than paid for by the resultant fines. Motorists are easily caught, and are subjected to ridiculously heavy fines. Simple economics.

So, the message here is simple. If you're going to break the law, make sure you do something that requires an enormous amount of police time. Indiscriminate murder is good, as is fraud, but the best crime of all, these days, is to be a solicitor.

First, you can sit around all day, fiddling your time sheets instead of actually helping your clients to buy a house. And then in the evenings, you can dream up slogans for your new adverts on the backs of buses.

I saw one the other day and was so shocked, my trousers nearly caught fire. I don't remember the exact wording (though I suspect the word 'hereinuntoafter' had crept in somewhere) but the gist was this: if you've been injured anywhere, give us a call and we'll get you some compensation.

What I should have done is run into the back of the bus and sued the idiotic lawyers who put the ad up there, saying that their stupidity made me lose concentration. And I'd have won.

There have been more ridiculous cases recently. One man has won £300,000 damages after his car skidded on ice and hit a lorry. It seems he managed to convince a court that this was, in fact, the council's fault for not putting enough grit on the roads.

A traffic warden is currently suing her employers for lung damage caused by being on the street, breathing in exhaust fumes.

And best of all, there's a chap who fell asleep at the wheel and, in the ensuing crash, suffered severe facial injuries.

Well, now call me old-fashioned, but I reckon that this is his fault. But no. He's found someone to sue. The producers of the Radio Four play that moved him to the land of nod perhaps? No. In fact, he's suing Ford for not fitting an airbag to his Sierra.

If he wins, and on current form, he may well do just that, it'll open the kind of floodgates not seen since Moses finished his river-bed walk. Common sense will take a back seat to the lure of huge, six-figure settlements. It'll be like a cross between the National Lottery Instants game and *Don't Forget Your Toothbrush*.

'Lose a fingernail in your car's door handle . . . and go to the Caribbean.'

I'll be in there too. If I am caught in a radar trap, I shall sue Jaguar for selling me a car that was capable of breaking the speed limit.

The motor car will become a warning notice on wheels. Do not lean out of the window while the vehicle is in motion. Do not insert a tape in this stereo while driving. Do not speed. Do not attach the battery terminals to your testicles.

I have argued for some time that everyone, at the age of sixteen, should be forced to sign a form which says that they are entirely responsible for their own actions. Trip over a paving stone and it's your own fault. Skid on ice — well, you shouldn't have been going so fast. Got poisoned while serving as a traffic warden — diddums.

But this will never happen. The Americanisation of our legal system is underway and even Paul Condon's fantastic decision to outlaw Freemasonry in the senior ranks of the Met police won't help.

There is a plot but, for once, the Freemasons are not responsible. This time, it's the old boy city network.

For sure, the old lady who sews her fingers together while working at a toy factory may walk out of court with a couple of hundred grand but you need to look behind the headlines to find the real winners.

First, there will be the solicitors and barristers who will help themselves to a slice of everyone's win.

Then there's the insurance companies who'll rack up the premiums to ensure businesses and local authorities are sufficiently covered in case a monster damages claim comes their way.

Life-insurance salesmen and stockbrokers will take up residence outside the High Court to catch the stream of people coming out with fat cheques in their damaged paws.

These pinstriped scavengers can be stopped but it's a brave government who'll take the necessary steps.

At the moment, a great many of the ludicrous actions are being paid for out of the public purse. Well, if legal aid were to be scrapped, completely, they'd never get there in the first place.

And don't worry about innocent men being wrongly convicted in criminal courts. We've already established that the police can't afford to trace or arrest anyone these days, except errant motorists who all plead guilty anyway.

If it is felt that legal aid is vital in a fair and just society then we must add a little twist to the American legal system where lawyers only take payment if they win the case.

What we must do here is agree to hear the cases but insist that if the claimant loses, his entire legal team is shot.

In the meantime, I'm going to bring an action against Volvo. Yesterday, I drove to Brands Hatch with the sunroof open and the resultant wind ruffled up my hair. It made me look foolish.

Go West, Young Man

Yesterday, I drove a car which, under my new system for measuring a car's acceleration, ranks as terrifying.

Under the old system, I would have said it gets from 0 to 60 mph in 3.8 seconds and that as a result, it's the third-fastest-accelerating car in the world behind the McLaren F1 and the Bugatti EB110.

It's called the Westfield S8 and though my drive was brief – just a few minutes – I have to say that never, not once, ever have I experienced anything quite like it.

I have never driven a McLaren and after describing it in this newspaper as somewhat overpriced, I doubt I ever will, but I have had a go in the Bugatti, and the Lamborghini Diablo and all sorts of other supercars which, even by NASA's standards, are fast.

But they all have roofs. You sit there, entirely surrounded by metal, cosseted by creature comforts. They may be loud and proud but compared to that Westfield, they are Austin Maestros, shrinking violets, wallflowers with no dates for the prom.

The Westfield has no roof to speak of, no doors, no windows, no stereo and not much space either. It is tiny and as a result it weighs less than a packet of fags, but under the bonnet is a 4.3-litre V8 engine which develops a massive 350 brake horsepower.

This is 10 per cent more than you get in a Ferrari 348 and things get even more impressive when you talk about horsepower per ton. No road car on earth even gets close.

It isn't even a sophisticated engine either. With carburettors instead of fuel injection, you can see sheets of fuel vapour shooting out of huge grilles in the bonnet. Even on a dry day, you need the wipers to clear it from the windscreen. Smoking is not an option here.

Ear defenders should be, though. Lift your foot from the throttle to change gear and the exhaust pops and bangs like the bowl of rice crispies from hell.

And all this is going on with the top of your head and your right elbow in the slipstream. 40 mph feels like 400. Get above a hundred and you begin to believe you'd out-run the *Enterprise*.

Every fibre in your body is begging the car to slow down but your right foot, down at the bottom of that cramped footwell, just won't obey. I once fired a machine gun and despite the instructor's advice to use short bursts, I became mesmerised and simply couldn't take my finger off the trigger.

Well, it's the same deal in that S8. It gives you everything you could ever want from a wild ride. But you want more. To get a trip like this anywhere else you'd need to sell your house and spend all the money on acid.

The Westfield is cheaper. Fully built, it only costs £25,000 though if you're in any way mechanically competent, you could buy a kit for a lot less and build it yourself. Either way, on the basis of performance per pound (either sort), you simply can't do better.

Happily, it's a neat-handling little car and the rear end does make a half decent fist of transmitting that truly amazing punch to the road. But it's at this point I begin to wonder about the sanity of the thing.

Obviously, you would never drive it on a wet road – you'd be soaked – but even on dry asphalt, if you apply a tiny bit too much power, the rear tyres wail like wounded hares, the back steps out of line and you have to be awake to catch the slide.

Of course, you will be awake because of the noise and the hurricane but let's just say you put on a bit too much opposite lock. Or that you don't wind it off quickly enough. You would crash, and at this point, the Westfield would live up to its reputation as a four-wheeled motorbike. Put simply, I doubt you'd walk away from the accident.

It is therefore absolutely vital that you know how to handle a car like this before you try driving it. It's a well-known fact that most motorists believe they have better-than-average abilities – a statistical impossibility – but in this case 'better than average' simply isn't good enough.

You have to have the reactions of a supercomputer, the strength of some oxen and eyes that can read a number plate at six miles. And more than that, you need to have been trained, properly, not by some dimwit in a cardigan and a Nissan Micra, but by a proper racing driver at a proper racing school.

Now don't get me wrong here: I don't believe there should be government legislation which forces people to take a special test before being allowed to drive a fast car – mainly because this government would probably draw the line at a 2.0-litre Mondeo.

I don't like nanny states. I hate the idea of being told what to do because I am able to make my own decisions. And I have done just that with the Westfield S8.

I would never buy one because I am nowhere near good enough to drive it properly. At best, I'd kill myself but if lady luck was elsewhere that day, I might kill someone else too.

Who Gives a Damn about the Countryside?

Every morning, at exactly eight o'clock, my next-door neighbour starts up his Ducatti and sits there, with the throttle opened up, warming the engine before riding to work.

It is a big motorcycle and its equally large engine causes my windows to rattle, the sparrows to fall out of the trees and our baby to wake up.

Being a good Londoner, I haven't said anything to him because, of course, I try not to speak to anyone.

It is annoying though, mainly because it gives weight to the arguments of friends who visit from the countryside. 'What was that din this morning? I don't know how you can live in London. All that noise. Traffic hum blah blah planes blah marauding gangs blah blah burglar alarms.'

Well, apart from Mr Ducatti, I have news for all you Vyella-shirted, ruddy-cheeked country dwellers. Residential London is a damn sight quieter than Nowhere on the Bloody Wold.

It's eleven o'clock in the morning here and I can hear absolutely nothing. I've just stuck my head outside the front door and it is as silent as snow falling on fur.

Now let's compare this to the countryside, a muddy place full of wasps and murderers.

I film in it regularly and you simply wouldn't believe what a deafening place rural Britain is. There are crow scarers, tractors, church bells, lawnmowers, children playing in the fields, corn dryers and, because there are few houses to act as sound breaks, you can even hear a Hoover four miles away.

In London, we have no low-level RAF jets and because we're richer than you lot, we have fewer diesel-powered cars. Half an hour in the Cotswolds or the Yorkshire Dales and my ears start to bleed.

This has nothing to do with the story but I also want to know why country people always say London is dirty. Listen Mr and Mrs Yokel-Smythe, I can walk up and down Jermyn Street all day long and I won't get any mud on my shoes.

But it's the noise thing that bothers me most and that's why I simply can't understand why so much fuss is being made out of these so-called Green Roads.

At the time of writing, it seems likely that cars will be banned from unmade tracks because various red-socked, brown-beer drinking, walky types say it ruins them.

Well look here weird beard, cars, already, are not allowed on the 250,000 miles of countryside footpaths in Britain and nor can they use the 80,000 miles of bridleways. Surely, that is enough. Why do you want to ban vehicles from the 5000 miles of tracks open to them? That's like having your cake, eating it and then going back for more.

And besides, I have driven down the Ridgeway in Berkshire – on which cars are allowed – and will tell you that tractors cause the biggest problems, not four-wheel-drive cars. It's heavyweight farm machinery that chews up the turf and makes ruts.

And you can't ban this – how else do farmers get their veals from the fields to the airport?

Then there are horses. Four-wheel-drive vehicles have brakes and can stop if your children emerge suddenly from a hedge but a quarter of a ton of muscle, doing 40 mph, cannot. Plus, I'd rather tread in a small rut than a pile of horse excrement.

Now to be honest, I only ever drive on green lanes to test the performance of various four-wheel-drive cars and would never do it for pleasure. I must confess that I don't understand why anyone would want to drive their car into the countryside just for fun.

But if they want to spend all day bumping around in fields, that's fine by me. The numbers are infinitesimal, the damage caused is minute – compared to open-cast mining say – and you certainly can't hear them above the din of the corn dryers and church bells. On top of all this, the only people who mind are a bunch of militant walkers.

Well look, I mind about golf. I don't like the Freemasons who play it, I can't abide the way it dominates television air time and those green splodges completely wreck the countryside. But if a bunch of bank managers want to don a pair of stupid strides on a Sunday morning and have a heart attack, so what?

Everybody's hobby bothers somebody but we must learn tolerance. Fishermen's lines entangle swans, windsurfers hit fish, parachutists land on frogs and yes, four-wheel-drive cars do rearrange mud, but really, we can't ban everything. Except neighbours with Ducattis.

However, it is likely that the historical right of passage over green roads will be eroded in some way. Fresh-air freaks have convinced everyone they're on the moral high ground and it's a brave government who'll tell them to get lost.

It will be a sad day for personal freedom but as with all things, there is a speck of light in the darkness.

If cars are banned from tracks in the woods, rallying will be a casualty. The world's second-dullest sport will be outlawed. There'll be a price on Tony Mason's head. People will throw eggs at Gwyndaf Evans, and not only because he's Welsh.

Oh happy days. Go, beardy, go.

Are Fast Cars a Problem?

When someone asks me to take them out for a spin in a Ferrari, or a Lamborghini, or a Porsche, I don't answer until I've drained a whole bottle of vodka. By which time, they've usually lost interest in the idea.

The trouble is that if you stay sober and say yes, at some point along the way they will ask you to demonstrate what the car can do.

So you weld the pedal to the metal and give them a taste of what 400 horsepower is all about. You let them know what it feels like to do 0 to 60 in four seconds, and how a V12 sounds at 7000 rpm and how you can burn rubber at 80.

And then, you get into trouble. Well, I do anyway, because I am not capable of dealing with a tail slide in what is very probably a mid-engined car. I don't know when to wind the opposite lock off and when to dip the clutch. I am an ordinary driver, like you and your next-door neighbours.

And the simple fact of the matter is this – 150 mph feels perfectly normal when you're going along in a straight line, perfectly in control, but you need to be a Berger or a Coulthard to know what to do when you're out of control at 150 mph.

I've had spins at that speed – in a Ferrari, and a Lotus and a Lexus Coupe – and you simply wouldn't believe how many times they go round. You lose count and you become disorientated so you don't know where, or even who you are.

Only last week, on the runway at Greenham Common, I spun a Honda NSX, at probably 90 mph, and only when the car came to a standstill did I realise that I hadn't touched the clutch or even the brake. I'd just been sitting there, looking like a human goldfish.

That's why I would never, ever agree to take you, your son or even a neighbour who's just complained to the council about your stereo, out for a spin in a seriously fast car. It would end in tears.

Only this morning, I read of an accident where a salesman, out for a spin in a Porsche 911 with a potential client, somehow hit another car, killing himself, the passenger and the driver of the Renault.

Now I don't know who was to blame – the bodies were so badly burned that they can't even tell at this stage who was driving the Porsche – but it did make me think.

Can we really let people who have no natural talent or training drive around in cars that, when out of control, won't stop until they're in the next county?

I mean, the temptation is always going to be there to put your foot down and show your passenger why your car cost £100,000 and his Cortina did not. And in the twinkling of an eye, you'll be doing a hundred or more and you'll turn to your passenger to see how impressed he is and then when you look back, you'll be four inches from a red traffic light.

There are courses which most car companies run, to teach people who've just bought a very fast car how they should be driven.

But here's a tip. In my experience, they're a complete and utter waste of time.

If they're held on a race track, you spend most of the day learning your way around the various corners and then when you're geographically aware, the instructor encourages you to go faster and faster, pointing out that, 'The car will make it, sonny.'

You then drive home with a working knowledge of whatever track you've been on, and a belief that your new car can take any corner at any speed. Certainly, most people with Audi Quattros believe that.

And then there are courses held on the road. I went on one of these once and simply could not believe it when the instructor said I indicated too much when pulling on to a motorway.

Then, on a normal A road, he said that when overtaking, you should pull out first, then change down and accelerate past the slower-moving vehicle.

At this point, I rang the police and asked if any lunatics had escaped recently. None had, so I can only assume that this guy had thought up some new and interesting ways of making his fee seem worthwhile.

Now, I'm not saying all courses are like this but before going on one, make it quite plain that you are not in the least bit interested in silly new techniques or on how Coppice is a double-apex right taken in fourth.

Just explain that you want to experience a tail slide at more than 100 mph.

If you get the car back on line, then you have talent, and there's no reason why you shouldn't have and enjoy a fast car. If you fail to get the car back in shape, the experience will be so terrifying, I promise, you'll go straight down to the auction and buy a Maestro.

And in doing so, you might just save someone's life.

Car Pools won't Work

It's a disaster. I went to Los Angeles once and after one night, decided it should join Spain, Greece and Germany on the Clarkson list of places that are smelly and horrid.

But there's no escape. Work calls, so I've got to go back to the place where Monday morning DJs say it's been a quiet weekend if only 22 people have been shot. It's the phoniest, dirtiest and most dangerous place on earth. When the wobbler comes, I hope it's bloody huge.

Los Angeles was the first place I ever encountered the car-sharing scheme whereby one lane of the motorway is reserved for cars that are full.

Now I don't doubt that this works very well in America where you can learn someone's entire life history as you brush past them in a crowded restaurant.

'Hey sorry buddy, but I've been fat ever since my Daddy left home when I was two. Shacked up with this real lard ass and she kinda abused me 'n' my little sister. So we, you know, kinda became lovers and . . .'

Car sharing in America is perfect because the journey is finite. You get time enough to reveal your innermost secrets, time enough to pull the right faces when your passenger is opening his heart, but not so much time that strays past the average American's attention span. Every morning, you get your own little taste of Oprah on the interstate.

But it wouldn't work in Britain. Here, you can know someone for fifteen years before you get past the weather. The foundations of friendship are deep and strong.

Once, at a party in California, I was invited to stay for a week with someone who I'd only known for five minutes. They needed smelling salts to bring me round. But it would take something a lot stronger than that to get car sharing off the ground here.

Let's assume, for a minute, that you could actually find a near neighbour who works close by, too.

Can both of you guarantee that you will start work at exactly the same time and, more importantly, finish within a few minutes of one another? I mean, these days, when half the population suffers from presenteeism and will sit at their desks long after the day's work is done, what possible chance have you got?

Then there's the other guy's driving to worry about. Everybody sincerely believes that they are better behind the wheel than everyone else which is why so many couples have such spectacular rows in the car.

My wife, for instance, cannot park and I cannot let her get past the third attempt without saying something. But what if I was with a stranger? I'd burst.

And that's just the parking. What if your car sharer thinks it's fun to go the wrong way round roundabouts? What if you climb in on the first morning and he announces that he can never remember whether it's red or green which means stop?

How do you explain, on day two, that you don't want to go with him any more? It's easy in America – you just say, 'Look slimeball, you can't drive and your breath smells worse'n a badger's crotch' – but you can't do that here.

OK, let's say you have found someone who drives well and works close to you, and for the same duration each day: what if he's a berk? What if he is the sort of person who thinks having a sense of humour means having a vast repertoire of jokes?

Every morning. Hey! What do you call the box a satellite dish is attached to? A council house! Ha ha ha.

Every fibre of your body is telling you to punch him right in the mouth but you're British so you have to sit there, smiling and waiting for the next joke, and the next and the next. Your only consolation is that while he's telling funny stories, he is not giving you a blow-by-blow account of home brewing, or how to get brake dust off an MG wire wheel.

The trouble is, of course, that car sharing, despite the problems, does seem like a good idea. It is stupid that one person, driving to work, needs a 15 by 6 foot box all to himself.

But look. If you were to fill all the seats in your car each day, you would be sharing what amounted to a compartment with three people you either didn't know, or didn't like. Or both.

And you'd be cruising down the motorway behind another compartment full of people who didn't know one another.

Indeed, you'd be in a huge long snake full of compartments which would give the jam something of a train-like quality.

Let's face it: the whole point of using your car to go to work is that you can listen to the radio station of your choice while picking your nose. You can sing, rant, chat on the phone and generally revel in being on your own.

If sharing ever becomes compulsory here, I shall buy a bubble car.

The Mondeo V6 is Very Good – Really

I've just spent a month with the Renault Laguna V6 and will not beat about the bush: it was, without any shadow of doubt, the most boring car in the world.

It looks like the humbler four-cylinder versions so there is no way passers-by are able to tell that it cost not far short of £20,000.

If I were to spend that sort of money on a car, I would like my neighbours to be aware of the fact and the only way you could enlighten them with this Laguna is to keep the price tag on the windscreen.

Or offer to take them out for a spin. Inside, to make the outlay seem reasonable, you have a CD player with remote operation, air conditioning and electrical operation for everything. But this, I fear, is like sprinkling a bit of grated parsley on a piece of week-old cod.

The engine is unobtrusive and quiet but I was truly amazed to find that it displaces a massive 3.0 litres. You'd expect the car to be lively, but as it takes 10.3 seconds to get from 0 to 60, you're in for a nasty shock. A Volvo 440 is faster.

I suspect the truly terrible automatic gearbox is to blame. Not only does it sap most of the engine's limited power but it seems to have a mind of its own, changing up and down for no apparent reason, and with the gracefulness of a walrus that's just been taken to a supermarket for the first time.

I haven't finished yet. The seats are awful and the driving position is worse – it feels like you're sitting on the car rather than in it. Indeed, the only redeeming feature I found in the whole car was a neat little storage hole for your sunglasses.

But other than that, it confirmed what I'd always thought – mid-range cars shouldn't be entrusted with large engines and high prices. The Renault Laguna, like the Honda Accord and the Mitsubishi Galant and the Vauxhall Cavalier and all the others, is supposed to cost about twelve grand. It should have a four-cylinder engine and a suit jacket in the back window.

If you want to spend £20,000 on a car, then buy one that was conceived from day one to cost that much – a Saab, or a BMW or a Mercedes Benz – and not something that has had greatness thrust upon it.

Or you could ignore all that and buy a Ford Mondeo V6 LX.

Like the Renault, it looks just like every other Mondeo that you've never noticed but Ford do a nice little body kit and some fat alloy wheels which give it a touch of class.

But unlike Renault, Ford has not thought, Oh my God. We're going to charge twenty grand for this car so break out the parsley. No, they've been realistic, and left the power seats, the CD and all the other wasteful toys in the parts bin.

You still get a sunroof, electric windows, power steering and a stereo but nothing fancy so as a result, this car only costs £16,295. That not only makes it cheaper than all the other tarted-up rep-mobiles but also cheaper than the serious players; the BMW 318i and the Audi A4 to name but two.

As far as value for money goes then, the Ford scores a solid twelve but when it comes to performance, it's off the scale, and then some. This car rockets from 0 to 60 in less than eight seconds and what's more, it feels fast. The engine roars and barks, the power delivery is immediate and the traction control is frequently needed to keep you on the grey bit.

If you are a serious driver who likes to press on a bit, you really can't do much better than this. It is a remarkable and rewarding driving experience, but I fear few will ever find out. I mean, I know a sort of transport café near Newbury which does the best egg and chips in the world – just past Greenham Common on the left, heading towards Basingstoke – but no one is going to take a first date there.

No, people will continue to buy the slower, less well-equipped and smaller BMW 318i because BMWs impress the neighbours and fast Fords don't.

Especially when they don't start. Should you decide to bring a little common sense into your buying equation and actually go for the Ford, I do hope that you have more luck then me.

We have an ordinary 2.0-litre model in the family and it makes a third-world dictatorship look reliable. Barely a week goes by without an unscheduled pit stop and this, I guess, reinforces my original premise.

The Mondeo, like the Laguna and all the other mid range offerings, is a cheap car. And I don't care what engine they shoehorn under the bonnet, it is still a cheap car. Remember that.

Name That Car

A year ago my wife and I spent nearly every moment of free time trying to think what to call our baby.

We knew it would be a girl so that narrowed the list down a bit, and we knew Janet was right out, so that narrowed it down some more. Losing Enid, Barbara, Denise and Brenda helped too.

I wanted to fit knives to the wheels of her pushchair and call her Boadicea, but eventually we went all conventional and settled on Emily Harriet. It was a tough job.

But can you imagine how hard it must be to think of a name for a new car, a name that not only works in any language but which, all over the world, conjures up the right image?

You can, of course, choose any word in any dictionary anywhere in the world, or, if that's too limiting, you can make up your own word like Ford did with the Mondeo.

The trouble is that most of the best words have already been used by the Americans. Surely, the best car name of them all is 'Thunderbird' which says it all. Roll up at a party, announce that you have a Thunderbird and when you go, all the best-looking girls will go too.

Except if you've been beaten to it by Mr Mustang Man. It doesn't matter that the Mustang in question has a feeble 2.3-litre engine and would lose a tug-of-war battle to a bat, the name says otherwise. The name says, 'Hey girls. I'm hung like a donkey.'

Then there's the Pontiac Firebird, the Dodge Charger, the Dodge Viper and the Superbird. These guys really know how to get the pulse racing.

The person who came up with Maestro, on the other hand, does not.

Indeed, choosing the right name for a car is a European blind spot. Maserati were definitely on the right track when they used to name their cars after winds – the Ghibli, the Khamsin and the Bora – and no one is going to say Diablo is all wrong for that piece of rolling thunder made by Lamborghini. Diablo is Italian for Devil.

But don't think all is well. Remember, this is the continent where cars are called things like Cordoba, Montego and Golf. Ford, for heaven's sake, has named all its lesser models after sizzling girly mags: Fiesta, Escort and so on.

Renault have had an even tougher time. They tried to call the 21 estate a Nevada, but the US state said no and then Daihatsu said that 'Chamade' was too close to their 'Charade' and it must go too. Thankfully, it was never sold in Britain, but they became so desperate recently, they called a top spec 21 the 'Manager'.

That will go down in history as the stupidest name of all time even though Fiat have tried for the title more than once. Their seventies hatchback became known in Britain as the 'Strada' (road) because the original name, 'Ritmo', was shared with an American sanitary towel.

Since then, we've had the Fiat One, the Fiat Type and the Fiat Point which are all fantastically wrong.

But for almost unbelievable wrongness, look no further than Japan where I see the new, and completely bland, five-door Mitsubishi is called the 'Carisma'. That's like calling the Rover 400 the 'Power Blaster'.

Mitsubishi have been in trouble before, with the Starion, which was going to be the Stallion until an American importer misunderstood a Japanese person's attempt at pronouncing the 'l's.

Daihatsu take the Japanese honours though for calling one of its new cars the 'Clever Little Fellow'. This is not a bird puller, but is better, I guess, than the Nissan Spam. It hasn't happened yet but there's time. There's time.

I mean we already have the Nissan Silvia, the Nissan Gloria and the spectacular Nissan Cedric.

All of which proves that letters and numbers are always going to be more successful than names, if the car is in any way serious.

BMW, for instance, would never dream of giving one of its Teutonic masterpieces a silly name. No, a 5-series car with a 3.0-litre engine becomes a 530. Very German.

And it's the same story at Mercedes where you have the C class, the E class and the S class. You know where you are.

But even this can lead to problems. I can never help smiling while driving along behind a BMW diesel because the badge says TDS, and that, as anyone who can do speed writing knows, is a short form for tedious.

Citroen came a cropper too with its Visa Diesel which it tried to sell here as the VD. And what about the BX diesel which they called the TRD.

But if you want the best name story of them all, you need to go back 40 years, to Japan, where Toyota was busy designing a new small car which would be sold in America.

And it wasn't until the very last minute that the American importers convinced their Japanese masters that Toyopet would make the car more appealing than the intended name: Toyolet.

Hello. I drive a Toyolet.

You sure do buddy. You sure do.

Bull Bars Should be Banned

To a geo-stationary satellite above Britain, I will have looked like a giant pinball over the past fortnight.

With my wife operating the flippers from our Battersea bunker, I've been despatched to the flatlands of Lincolnshire, the pastoral splendour of Dorset and the rain-lashed horror that is Birmingham. I've been to Bath, Sheffield, Northampton, Worcester and Eastbourne too.

In the course of these travels I've seen many species which were officially human but which didn't look that way. In Sheffield, everyone seemed to slouch. In Eastbourne, half the population was dead or very, very close to it.

People in Bath have had their friendly genes taken out so that if you stop and ask for directions, they act like you've just trumped, and strut off. In a contest to find the rudest town on earth, Bath would walk all over Paris.

I have seen much in the way of countryside too. Lincolnshire was best and the farmers have thoughtfully chopped down all the trees so you can see more of it.

No such far-sightedness in Somerset where each 200-year-old oak, you just know, is shielding Jethro; someone with one eye and a penchant for camouflage trousers. He says his ambition in life is to 'murder someone'.

Blackpool was fascinating. In my experience, every single town in the whole country has been changed out of all recognition in the last fifteen years. Out-of-town superstores have killed off high streets, which are now dominated by building societies and estate agents. But Blackpool is exactly the same as I remember it as a child, which was a pleasant surprise.

There have been different roads too, including the M1 which

I simply cannot believe. Anywhere else in the civilised world, the man responsible for this ramshackle half-built and hopelessly inadequate country lane would have been killed and fed to his family. Who would then have been shot.

But no, the man in charge of the M1 lives in Surrey, as do all his relations and friends. He was born in Godalming, educated in Woking and thinks the north is a barren place where people eat mud, so every penny at his disposal is spent on the Surrey section of the M25.

This makes him something of a hero at local dinner parties where he is seen to be spending wisely. Well, matey, I'll be something of a hero in the north when I come round to your house one night with some copper wire, a brace of crocodile clips and a battery.

I digress. There were other roads too, like the simply glorious A631 from Gainsborough to Bawtry. It's smooth and mostly straight and everyone drives quickly. Obviously, everyone up there has sports cars paid for by EC farm subsidies but really, they do drive well.

They do not drive quite so well in Wiltshire. Here, nearly everyone has a Vauxhall Nova saloon with quite the skinniest tyres it is possible to imagine. From behind, these cars look like an elephant on four bite-sized unicycles.

And they drive so slowly that you really need sensitive measuring equipment to ascertain that any forward progress is being made at all. On the wonderful A350, you will find cars that have been travelling from Warminster to Blandford Forum for the last seventeen years.

I know about the slower pace of life in rural Britain, but surely, they must be hungry by now. And in need of a haircut, I should think. By the time they get there, the people they wanted to see will have moved to Australia.

However, having spent the past fifteen months travelling the world, the last fourteen days have, despite it all, convinced me that Britain is a truly remarkable country, with tiny pockets of individualism around every corner. I know of no country which can offer such a rich tapestry in such a small place. Move twenty miles and everything from the architecture to the accent changes.

But there is one thing that ties this whole country together. There are no kangaroos here.

Which makes me wonder just a little bit why on earth so many people with large four-wheel-drive vehicles feel the need to fit 'roo bars.

It doesn't matter that they've been named bull bars in this country, I'd be willing to bet that, in your entire driving career, you will never, ever round a bend to find the way blocked by either species.

You may, however, find a person, in which case your bull bars turn the probability of his death into a foregone conclusion.

Being hit by a two-ton Range Rover is pretty much guaranteed to make someone's day less enjoyable than might otherwise have been the case, but if the blow is dealt by a small piece of ironwork, he'll be playing the harp by the time you've stopped skidding.

There's talk of legislation being introduced to outlaw frontal automotive ironmongery but it's far better to try a little bit of persuasion first. So here goes.

Bull bars are only really useful should you hit a bull. All the bulls in Britain are in fields, surrounded by electric fences.

Buttons are Not Just for Christmas

In the olden days, children were lucky to get an orange and a piece of string for Christmas.

Small wonder then that they were happy to charge about the woods in their big shorts, making guns out of twigs. These were simple times.

My generation was a deal more sophisticated. For Christmas, I wanted Hot Wheels and in the woods, I needed a Johnny Seven machine gun with detachable pistol.

But now, toys need to have buttons. Kids don't run around in the woods any more; they sit in front of a computer screen, pretending to shoot people. They don't use Meccano or Lego to build anything, because even the simplest PC allows them to create their own space shuttle. 3D is out. 2D is in.

Why build a buggy out of an old pram and some cardboard boxes when you can have Super Mariokart on your Super Nintendo?

Today, the idea of doing anything mechanically is as daft as diphtheria.

And that means the children of today, when they climb into the car of tomorrow, will find the idea of a gear stick faintly idiotic. Which is why the car of tomorrow will not have one.

Already, the automatic gearbox, which was developed as a labour-saving device for the more mature motorist, is beginning to become more complicated than a life-insurance form.

Even in a basic car like the Ford Mondeo, you have the usual PRND21 arrangement but then there's a button which switches the transmission between sport and economy modes. And then there's another button which cuts the overdrive out. And in more expensive models, you get the option of a winter mode too.

It's like my dishwasher. By the time I've figured out what all the knobs do, I could have gone to the sink and out Nanette Newmanned Nanette Newman. And then there's the video, which frankly, is more useful as a dishwasher than as a device for taping television programmes; something it just cannot do.

However, children can work videos, and washing machines, and if the eleven-year-old I ran home the other day is anything to go by, they're pretty bloody impressed with the sport/economy switch on my Jaguar's gearbox too.

But this, by the time he's driving, will be small fry – a DC3 alongside HOTOL. I know this because I've just been driving a BMW B3 Alpina Switchtronic.

Now this, I want to make it quite plain from the outset, is my kind of car. It has a huge 3.0-litre engine shoehorned into a tiny body and it goes like stink. Everything's blueprinted and balanced too. It is a £45,000 honey.

But by far the most impressive feature was that switchtronic box which enables you to alternate between Mr Cardigan and Mr Shoemaker at the touch of, guess what, a button.

You can, if you like, pootle around all day with the automatic gearbox doing all the work but when the road is empty and the red mist descends, you simply take over manual control.

And then you change gear by hitting one of two little buttons on the back of the steering wheel: the one on the left takes you down a cog, the one on the right upshifts.

There is no clutch pedal and there's no need to lift your foot off the throttle when changing gear – when the revs hit the red line, your index finger twitches and whoosh, the engine's back on cam, hurling you at the horizon like you inadvertently hit the hyperspace switch.

The trouble is, you need to concentrate. For me, there is nothing natural in this process and while I can see it improves performance and enables you to keep both hands on the wheel at all times, I kept running up against Big Brother.

First, when you've made two quick changes, you need to wait

a couple of seconds before you can make a third. Second, it won't change down if your speed is too high. Third, if you forget, it will change gear for you automatically. Fourth, it goes into second when you stop and finally, I could never remember what gear I was in.

In a normal, manual car you reach for the gear stick and its mere location reminds you what's what. With switchtronic, I kept trying to change up from fifth and then, in desperation, hitting the other button to see if I could get a reaction from that one.

Which I got from the car behind as, without the benefit of brake lights, I started to slow dramatically.

There is a little light which says what gear you're in but there's the problem. It is little. Very little.

I don't doubt that with practice, I'd get the hang of it and that I'd never want to go back. In the same way as I've now got the hang of this Apple Mac and would not want to revert to a typewriter.

The thing is, though, that today's children will expect a car to be operated by a series of buttons and will therefore find switchtronic completely natural. They will not need a period of adjustment and they will not care that the car's computer won't let them make mistakes.

And there's the pity. Switchtronic, like traction control and anti-lock brakes, does enable you to go that bit faster and that bit more safely. But without the risk, where's the fun?

In the woods, in 1967, if I shot you with my spud gun, you knew about it. In 1995, when a Nintendo dinosaur eats me up, I only have to hit the reset button.

I like gadgets. I like things that make a car go faster. And I especially like devices that keep me away from trees. But I also like driving, and there's the rub.

Fly by wire may work in airbuses but real cars should have levers.

Don't Get Noticed

Don't be fooled into thinking that there is no such thing as a bad car these days.

The Nissan Serena is a bad car. So is the Terrano. The Mini Convertible is a bad car and the same goes for the BMW 316i Compact. Then there's the diesel Golf and the equally diesel Mercedes C class. I could go on. I haven't mentioned the Lada Samara, for instance.

So why then, given the huge choice of cars on offer these days, do people buy cars like them?

Well, you only have to look at what some people wear to see that idiocy is alive and well these days.

I'm usually a bit baffled when I see someone ambling along in a curious pair of strides because he must have walked into a shop – and actually chosen them. He must have gone along the rack, discounting sensible, subtle alternatives. He must have pulled out the nasty pair, ignored the titters of the staff, tried them on and stood around in front of a mirror thinking, YES, these are the ones for me.

But hey, it's only 30 quid. The average price people pay for a new car these days is £10,200 and that is big bucks. So how come people get it so wrong so often?

Well, figures show that most people don't take test drives. Dealers report that nearly 90 per cent of BMW 7- and 8-series customers never set foot inside the model before they take delivery. They're handing over maybe £50,000 for a car which, for all they know, could be absolute rubbish.

So if they aren't taking test drives, how have they made the choice? Car magazines? I think not, as most tend to be read by children and even the biggest seller of the lot – *Top Gear* – only has a circulation of 137,000 which is small beer compared to the 2 million cars sold in Britain every year.

Motoring journalists in general perhaps? Nope. On the *Top Gear* television programme, I praised the Alpine A610 to the hills and Renault sold six. Quentin Willson told 6 million viewers that the top of the range Citroen XM was marvellous – and they sold seventeen.

It works the other way round too. I said the first incarnation of the current Escort was awful and within months, it became Britain's best-selling car. I said the Toyota Corolla was worse and it is the world's best-selling car.

I can only conclude from this that people are making their choice exclusively on advertising. Which explains everything.

People are buying the BMW 316 Compact because they really do believe it is the Ultimate Driving Machine. It is not. Damon Hill's Williams Renault is.

Mothers are choosing that ghastly Nissan Serena because they understand it can seat a boy-scout troop. Yes, well so can a bus stop but you wouldn't buy one of those to use on the school run, would you?

The Car In Front Is A Toyota. Not necessarily. I've just come home from the pub and I followed a Mercedes. Besides, what does that strap line tell me about a Toyota? Nothing.

Same goes for the new Nissan QX commercial. It Exists. So does dog dirt but I don't want any outside my house.

And what the hell is going on with that Honda Civic on the television? For a start, I had to watch the ad four or five times before I knew what sort of car it was, and second, what is so clever about playing a film backwards?

But the absolute prize must go to Volvo. Now, the T5 is a truly terrific car and I was jumping around like a small boy when the 850 beat all comers in the recent Touring Car race at Donington, but why did that funny-looking chap in a big T-shirt drive across the Corinthian Canal on two rails when there's a perfectly good bridge just upstream?

Of course, I do understand that television commercials are only supposed to let us know the car is available and that press ads give us a bit of meat for the bones, but really, you can't go around spending thousands of pounds on something just because someone with blue spectacle frames at Goodyear Stickleback and Bunsen Burner has dreamed up a snappy strap line.

You Can With A Nissan. You can go to bed with Claudia Schiffer if you have a Sunny? You can use water instead of petrol in the 200? Ooh, I'd better have one then.

Nicole. Papa. Oh f *** off.

With advertising, car companies are trying to create an image but I am not inclined to spend ten grand on a Clio just because it is the favoured transport of a doddery old Frenchman and his daughter who spends all day with cucumbers on her eyes and some chocolate sauce on her face. Plus, she wears French knickers and I hate French knickers almost as much as I hate the French.

And then there's the dude in the clever ad for the equally clever Audi A4. He's a prat who likes to win and who thinks badges are important. He doesn't like the A4 because it's too understated.

All this tells us about the A4 is that it's not a BMW which is a dangerous game to play in a country where people would sell their children to Moroccan drug dealers if it meant they could have a 316.

There are good advertisements though. I enjoy the aborigine and the Vauxhall Calibra much more than I enjoy that Tigra running into some big space hoppers on the beach.

The space hoppers tell us that the chaps at Lowe Howard and Spink were desperate whereas with the aborigine, we understand the Calibra is a quiet car. The trouble is that while it may well be the most aerodynamic production coupe in the world, it is not especially quiet.

If you want a quiet car, you should come round and buy my

neighbour's Volkswagen which this morning was utterly silent on account of the fact it would not start.

If only everything in life was as ridiculous as a car commercial.

Gadgets

I remember the first time I experienced the sheer magic of electric windows. I stood, eyes wide and bladder bursting with excitement as the Peugeot salesmen tried desperately to talk my dad into buying a 604.

It was an ugly car, and probably slow and thirsty too, but it had powered windows and I wanted my dad to buy it so much, I ached. There have been other disappointments in my life since – a divorce springs to mind – but no memory is quite so painful as the day when my father rejected the Peugeot and bought an Audi, which did not have electric anything.

But here we are, 23 years down the line, and electric windows are even fitted to absolute bottom-of-the-line hatchbacks.

The trouble is, of course, as base-level cars have begun to feature a long list of standard equipment, the makers of more expensive models have been forced to trawl the very outer reaches of what is sensible to make their cars look like value for money.

I sort of knew things were going wrong when Nissan brought out its Bluebird. Here we had a car with two trip counters. Sometimes, even now, late at night, I can't sleep as I try to work out what was going on in the mind of the man who reckoned that two trip switches was a good idea.

There must have been a reason, or his bosses would have said no, but for the life of me, I can't work out what it might be.

Gimmicks have long been a Japanese thing. While every other car maker in the world was offering four wheels and a seat, they came along with four wheels, a seat . . . and a radio.

When everyone else began to fit a radio, they did a trip switch. And then two.

And now, it's all gone silly. The Mitsubishi 3000GT, for instance, features a number of television screens which tell you what sort of air is coming from which sort of vent. If you have a hot face and cold feet, you glance down to see a red arrow pointing at your head and a blue one at your toes.

Clever stuff, but it goes further, because another TV screen tells you how much of what sort of frequency your stereo is pushing out. An LED graphic equaliser read-out. Of course. How ever did I get by without one?

Now I want to make it quite plain here and now that I love toys. I have an aluminium can crusher. I lust after everything on GQ magazine's 'Objects' page. I bought my stereo only because it came with a power amp that hums and has a huge red light on the front.

This, I'm sure a hi-fi expert would tell me, is only a big empty box with a light on the front but I don't care because it looks good. As do all those screens in a 3000GT.

Two trip switches don't on the other hand, and nor do the fold-away head restraints in a Mercedes. These are the people who brought you a double-glazed car and illuminated vanity mirrors in the back. These are the people who devised an arm which delivers your seatbelt when you shut the door and now they've gone further. Hit a button on the dash and the rear headrests drop down to make reversing easier, but short of getting into the back and pulling them up again, they stay down, flat and flaccid.

And talking of things that move, what about the spoiler on the back of a VW Corrado. At 40 mph, it raises to provide questionable extra downforce – fair enough, at a pinch, but why is there a manual-override button?

Apart from trying to fool the guy in the car behind into thinking that you are bigger in the trouser department than you really are, there is no benefit at all in driving around town with your spoiler up.

Talking trip computers, happily, have gone to that great

gimmick scrapyard in the sky but when they were in vogue, my colleague on *Top Gear*, Chris Goffey, turned a speaking Maestro on its roof. And as he dangled there, upside down, the silicon back-seat driver announced: 'Oil pressure low.'

Today, we have multi-faceted automatic gearboxes. Now call me an old hasbeen but I thought the whole point of automatic transmission was to save effort. You put the stick in D and off you go.

Not any more. The gear lever in the Vauxhall Omega I drove last week was festooned with more buttons than a nineteenth-century bodice.

There was one for economy driving, one for sporty moments and one for when it snows. Then there was the overdrive facility.

But there are more stupid things. Audi fits stereos which have buttons that can only be operated by micro-physicists. If you use a finger to adjust the volume, you'll inadvertently nudge nine other controls which, if you're very unlucky, means you could finish up with Terry Wogan shouting at you.

For a true button frenzy, you just can't beat Saab. The top-flight 9000 model comes as standard with no fewer than 104 switches at a driver's disposal.

And none of them operates what I consider to be the most significant gimmick yet invented.

Both the Ford Escort Cosworth and the Jaguar XJ6 that I have run in the past two years had a heated front windscreen and I can't tell you how much I miss it on the new Jaguar, which does not.

Cars do steam up and being impatient, most people will set off before the fan has strutted its stuff. Well, with a heated screen, you just touch a button and before you've put your seatbelt on, the glass is pine fresh and as clear as morning dew.

Nissan, I hear, are working on a car with two heated wind-screens.

Formula One Racing – as Dull as Ever

They don't televise inter-county basket weaving. They don't charge spectators £70 for the privilege of watching sheep-dog trials. And when someone wins a beetle drive, the results aren't disputed by laboratory technicians.

But in Formula One, they do all of these things even though it has become, with the exception of cricket and golf, by far and away the most tedious spectacle in the world.

I've made half-hearted declarations before, about not watching F1 any more, but Brazil was the final straw.

Damon Hill promised, just before the start, that we were in for one of the most exciting championships in years. Then, a couple of hours later, Murray Walker admitted that the only thing keeping the race alive was the fuel stops.

Well, now look Murray, you are the best sports commentator I've ever heard, but you must admit that there are more exciting things to do on a Sunday than watching cars being filled up with petrol, some of which wasn't really petrol at all, we later discovered.

If I want to watch people refuelling, I can pop down to the local Texaco station. Hell, I can even do it myself, but as I screech up to the pump and stand there watching the numbers click round, there are no crowds, and BBC Sport doesn't pay my agent billions for the exclusive rights. This is because filling up with petrol falls into the category of things labelled 'Not Interesting'.

Indeed, it's hard to think of anything that is less interesting. Ironing springs to mind but even duller than that is what happens in a Formula One race between the fuel stops.

Nothing happens, that's what. In the televised highlights from

Brazil, there wasn't a single overtaking manoeuvre, except when the car in front broke down. And mechanical failure isn't interesting either. I ran out of petrol the other day and for damn sure, no one gave a toss.

The tabloid newspapers have realised that the only interest in Formula One is the Damon Hill versus Michael Shoemaker battle, which is a thinly disguised rerun of World War Two. Only we won that.

And anyway, if I want to watch Britain giving the Germans a good pasting, I'll go down to the video shop and rent *The Dambusters*.

So look; if you want to see good car racing, forget F1. Switch off in droves and turn your attention instead to the British Touring Car Championship where the lead will change more times in one lap than it does in a whole year of Grand Prix.

You can bang door handles in the BTCC and push the car in front round a corner, in the fairly certain knowledge that the result won't be a black flag, a spin, or death and manglement.

In Brazil, Mr Shoemaker was so much faster than everyone else, he very nearly lapped himself. In the BTCC, you win by inches, not light years.

And another thing. I've been going to Grand Prix for years and I never, ever see a driver. They hang around in their motorhomes nibbling a little light pasta and sipping an isotonic drink until just before the off.

And then at the end, they're on a helicopter halfway back to Monaco before you're out of the car park.

BTCC drivers are forced by the rules to mingle with the paying punters in the paddock on race day. They must sign autographs and they must do a parade lap, and if they refuse, they're fined.

This means everyone has a chance to meet the stars and form opinions. If Patrick Watts or Paul Radisch says something nice to your wide-eyed son, you can cheer the guy on in the race.

Or you can form opinions based solely on the cars they drive.

My wife has a Volvo and desperately wants them to win this year. I'm not that bothered just so long as the BMWs lose.

All around Europe, other countries are copying the BTCC and all around the world, television companies are buying the rights to broadcast it. And that gives the car companies, who've only paid a paltry 5 million to be on the grid, a nice warm feeling in their underpants.

And on top of all this, the major tittle-tattle dominating the run up to the F1 season was the size of Nigel Mansell's arse. In the BTCC, people have had a weightier problem – like who's going to win.

Can You Really Own a Lotus?

In Britain, Lotus is a bit of a joke.

To those who have actually owned one, it stands for Lots Of Trouble, Usually Serious, while to those who pay little attention, it's a Formula One racing team that doesn't win very often.

And then there's the corporate side of things. Founded by Colin Chapman in 1948 with a tarted-up Austin Seven, it struggled along for 40 years, becoming embroiled in the De Lorean fiasco and emerging as a corporate plaything for General Motors.

But last month, faced with a need to do something about its huge losses, GM paid off Lotus's debts and sold the whole shooting match, except the race team, which is now independent, to Bugatti.

This, in itself, is odd because though Bugatti has a huge and ultra-modern factory, along with grand and ambitious plans, it has, so far, not made very many cars: perfume, head scarves and models, yes, but cars? No.

Geographically, Lotus has always been disadvantaged too. We can understand that cars are made in Detroit because this is Motown and we know about Essex and Coventry and Birmingham but it is hard to equate Norfolk with motor-car manufacturing.

Lotus has become world famous for its technology, its work on anti-sound and active ride suspension is well documented and state of the art, yet this seems at odds with Norfolk, just about the only county in England with no motorways in it.

You expect to see a lot of agriculture in Norfolk, a lot of turkeys too, but for heaven's sake, the garages don't even take credit cards. No, in Britain, Lotus is a bit of a joke.

And, in recent years, the cars haven't helped either. There was the Elan, lovely to drive but blessed with the reliability of British Rail. Then there was the Elite, lovely to drive but odd-looking. The Excel was lovely to drive too but it was unreliable and over bumps, it had a habit of banging the driver's head into the roof.

Then there was the best Lotus of them all, the Seven, as driven by Patrick McGoohan in *The Prisoner*. But Lotus sold this design to Caterham Cars who last year sold 550 of them, earned a Queen's Award and can now boast that they make more cars than the company to which they owe their existence.

In 1990, it looked like Lotus would make a decent car in the new Elan, but it proved too expensive and unreliable, so GM pulled the plug on it. There's talk now that Bugatti wants to start making it again, but don't hold your breath.

Small wonder then that Lotus has never quite managed to shake off its image as a kit car manufacturer, a place to go for plastic cars that break down a lot.

So why then did James Bond use a Lotus, twice? In *The Spy Who Loved Me*, he tooled around under water – where the plastic wouldn't rust, of course – and in *For Your Eyes Only*, he went to Cortina in one for some skiing and spying.

And why is Lotus such an obvious hit in America? Richard Gere wooed Julia Roberts with one in *Pretty Woman* and then both Sharon Stone and her girlfriend used Lotuses in *Basic Instinct*. A new soap, set in the Caribbean and due for launch next year, also sees the hero behind the wheel of a Lotus every week.

Well, here's the deal. All these people have used the Esprit, a mid-engined two-seater which was designed by the master of Italian style, Guigaro.

He was responsible for the first Golf and the mark one Scirocco. He did the Alfasud and the Maserati Merak. He is a genius but his finest hour came when he finished his coffee, sharpened his pencil, and did the Esprit.

And even the seventeen years which have elapsed since then, and the countless design changes by Lotus themselves, have failed to remove the sheen. Indeed, today's Esprit, the S4, is the best looking of the lot and must rank as one of the most beautiful cars in the world.

Perhaps that's why it is now the only car Lotus make, at the rate of one a week.

But that's more because, though it is a pretty car, and a fast one, and a car chosen by the stars, it is not desperately expensive. £46,995 is not much for a car that should, given enough road, be capable of 165 mph.

In a straight race away from the lights, up to say 100 mph, it will hang on, gallantly, to the tails of far more expensive machinery, like the £80,449 Porsche Turbo and the £144,000 Lamborghini Diablo. It is actually faster than the £78,000 Ferrari 348GTB.

And this is quite an achievement for a car whose engine looks like something out of a Moulinex Magimix. It is a mere 2.2-litre, four-cylinder unit, making it about the same as the engine in your Ford Mondeo, but because it has a sophisticated turbocharger, it develops 264 bhp which is enough to make the plastic, and thus light, car very, very fast indeed.

And because it is so small, there's room behind it for that rarest of rare things in a supercar; a boot.

Now that's the on-paper stuff, the kind of material you can find in a brochure; but two questions will be at the forefront of any potential customer's mind. What is it really like to drive, and how far will it go before I need to telephone the RAC?

Well, I managed 1500 miles in a week before I needed to call someone out. But it was Autoglass, and not the RAC, and it was because a mutant had broken in and not because the engine had gone bang. In fact, nothing went bang and nothing dropped off. Nothing looked like it was going to drop off either.

I have telephoned Norris McWhirter to see if 1500 miles is some kind of record for a Lotus, and he's checking.

It must be said that I hadn't really looked forward to my stint with this car because the last model, the S3, was a dog. The brakes were useless, the steering was unassisted and furiously heavy as a result, and it wasn't big enough inside for anyone other than Colin Moynihan.

But as the miles rolled by in the S4, my mind changed. New seats, in black leather with yellow piping, mean the interior is big enough for big people, and a new instrument panel means you can see all the dials except the clock but this is no problem because you WILL get there on time.

It really is every bit as fast as it looks and more, it feels every bit as fast as the figures say it is. The noise isn't desperately exciting – it sounds like a Cortina – but it goes from 0 to 60 in less than five seconds and that can, and does, hurt your neck.

It corners beautifully but on a private test track, it proved the point that mid-engined cars can be tricky if you have only average driving ability. When you step over the mark, they bite.

So, they pulled me out of the field and I was off again, enjoying the decent ride, the positive power steering, the chunky gear change, the prodigious power, the stares of other road users and a cockpit that's every bit as user friendly as a telephone, only more stylish.

But the Lotus didn't play its trump card until its last evening in my tenure. There were a whole load of cars at home that night – the Escort Cosworth, a big Mercedes, a Honda Prelude VTEC and a Porsche 968. My wife, staring at this metallic playground, said, 'Let's take the Lotus.'

Soft Tops

Sports cars are coming back. Strangely.

Amidst all the brouhaha which accompanied the launch of the new MG last week, it was easy to miss a startling new trend.

For the last twenty years, car firms have been run by bean counters in suits whose only concern has been the figure at the bottom of the profit and loss accounts.

The designers and engineers have been as clever as ever but the suits in charge have systematically erased all free thinking. Any daring new idea was presented to a bunch of ordinary people in so-called 'customer clinics' and if the invited guests, in their anoraks and cardigans, raised so much as an eyebrow, the car was scrapped and the designer beaten.

The result has been plain to see. Cars have been getting duller and duller to the point where the only reason why you would buy a Ford Mondeo rather than a Renault Laguna was the proximity of your nearest dealer or the advertising. Did you want a car with inner strength or a car you can believe in? Me? I wanted neither.

What made the whole scenario even more depressing was the public apathy to cars that were in any way radical. Take the Mazda MX5. Here was a simple sports car that blended old-fashioned, rear-wheel drive, roof-down motoring with sixties style and modern-day, Japanese reliability.

To begin with, it sold well enough but once the fashion victims had bought one, sales began to slump. The trendies moved on to something else after a year and there was no one to take their place. In 1994 only 1000 MX5s were sold in Britain.

BMW had the same problem with the Z1 – the best car they ever made just didn't sell. And we all know how long the Lotus

Elan lasted. Things were so bad last year that the best-selling convertible in Europe was the hugely expensive Mercedes SL.

Now, bearing this in mind, you might imagine that the suits at the top of all the car companies would be even more adamant than usual that they wanted aeroblob styling, chintzy seats and five doors.

But no. Quite apart from the MG which is radical enough from Auntie Rover, there's a new Renault Speeder which has to be seen to be believed. Not even Gerry Anderson could have conceived of this car! If the producers of *Space 1999* had suggested this design for Martin Landau's personal wheels, they'd have been sacked.

For Christ's sake, it doesn't have a roof of any description and one version of it doesn't even have a windscreen.

But despite the truly wild styling, which can only have been done after a heavy, heavy night on LSD, it is hurried along by the 150 bhp engine from the Renault Clio Williams. That keeps the price down to 'less than £20,000'.

Then there's the Fiat Barchetta. Renault's people had used up Europe's entire supply of drugs while doing the wonderful Speeder so the Fiat is a little more normal, but then so is the price – just fourteen grand.

Nevertheless, here is a little two-seater sports car which sounds and looks wonderful. And who cares that the steering wheel is on the wrong side? This is a car with a 'must have' factor. I simply adored it.

And the list doesn't stop there. BMW might have felt that the sports-car market could be left to the MG division of its Rover arm, but no. Next year, there'll be a Z3 which, guess what, is a little two-seater sports car which should sell for less than £20,000.

And the story doesn't end there either. Mazda, who can claim that they started this particular ball rolling, are said to be close to a replacement for the MX5, and we can therefore be assured that Toyota and Nissan are on the case too.

Had enough? Good, because there's more. For some time,

Porsche has been touting a little, mid-engined sports car around the world's motor shows, and now, we hear, it too is destined to become a production reality.

Called the Boxer, it is going to be a little more expensive than the MG, the Speeder and the Z3 but the figure of £25,000 has been mentioned. And that, for what is a startling car with a Porsche badge, is cheap.

But if we're talking value for money, then you are well advised to reach for your Yellow Pages right now. Ring your Mercedes dealership and tell him that you want an SLK.

This a scaled-down version of the SL which is likely to arrive in Britain next year wearing a price tag of around £25,000. For that you'll get a supercharged engine, Batmobile humps on the boot lid and what is said to be serious sports handling. Mercedes never get things wrong, and I very much doubt if the SLK will break that tradition. It, among all the sports cars about to come out, is the one I find most tempting.

But before I went as far as signing on the dotted line, I'd need to be assured that this global warming business is for real. If it really is true that the planet is heating up, then I shall buy a convertible.

Odd, isn't it? The car industry created global warming and now it's delivering a wave of soft tops so that we can all enjoy it.

Ugly Cars Got No Reason

Until last week, any discussion about what is an ugly car and what is not would have provoked a lively and interesting debate.

Until last week, if you'd asked a thousand people to name the most hideous car of all time, you'd have got a thousand different answers.

Until last week, it would have been entirely possible to argue that beauty is in the eye of the beholder and that one man's meat is another man's diarrhoea. I, for instance, would label Princess Diana as one of the world's great-looking women, whereas others I know think she is a big-nosed twit with a predilection for using twice as much peroxide as is really necessary.

And the same goes with cars. Until last week, I'd have argued that the Ferrari Berlinetta Boxer was the best-looking car ever made and that the most recently departed Toyota Celica was the ugliest.

Other people, with some justification, may say the boundaries are drawn by the E-Type Jaguar and the Reliant Robin, or the Lotus Esprit and the Lancia Dedra. One chap I know says he feels sick whenever he sees a Nissan Micra, which means he doesn't get out much.

But, now, Ford has ended all the debate. We can still bicker about superlatives at the top end of the scale, but at the bottom, we can draw a line. The new Granada is, without a question or shadow of doubt, the ugliest car ever made.

If it was a film it would be *Top Gun*. If it was a woman, it would be Ena Sharples. If it was an office block, it would be that chunk of concrete which now sits in the middle of the roundabout at Hammersmith.

A Ford spokesman said, 'We wanted a bold look and are happy

that we have something which gives the car a real identity.'
Quite.

I have spoken with a number of designers about it, and while
all wish to remain anonymous, each agrees that Ford has gone
mad. One said he saw the writing on the wall at this year's
Geneva motor show when their new concept car – the Ka –
looked like a piece of 'pink vomit'.

Another said that a car is often likened by members of the
public to a human or an animal's face. Some cars look startled,
some like they're smiling. Some look cross, or evil or like the
proudest lion in the jungle. 'But,' said our man, 'the new Granada
looks like someone's just rammed a banana up its bottom.'

The question that bugs me is that hundreds of senior Ford
people must have been agonising over the shape for years and
that none of them has had the wit to stick up his hand and say
no. This, according to a senior British designer, is called the
Emperor's New Clothes theory.

He explains that at Jaguar recently, various Ford designers
were bamboozling executives with all sorts of weird and not-so-
wonderful designs which were progressing along nicely until a
kid on the production line stood up and said they were nasty.
Then another hand went up, and another and another until the
top brass were forced to agree that they too thought they were
wrong.

Nevertheless, if anyone ever dreams up a Right Stuff bravery
award, it must go to the man at Ford who walked into a board
meeting with those drawings and said, 'This is it boys. This is the
new Granada.'

And they bought it, which means that now, Ford's stunningly
effective marketing team has what might fairly be termed a right
old problem on its hands. And in order to take our minds off the
shape, they're telling us that this may very well be the last large
Ford ever to be designed and built in Europe.

Good. Even the Americans with their golfing trousers and
their fondness for Formica could not make such a hash of it.

Even they would not fit that oval nose and think it looked anything other than daft. Even they would not have chosen those headlights.

And round at the back, even Ray Charles would have had something to say about the way the boot lid curls down, like it has melted. I have yet to see the interior but fear it will be no better.

Ford has become a favourite uncle to the British, as ingrained in society as the BBC and fish and chips. Its cars are a more common sight out there than acne at a youth club dance.

None are dynamically perfect but they're all quite good at everything. There's no reason NOT to buy a Ford and for that reason alone, I always advise people who don't really care what they drive to buy whichever model they can afford. You can't go wrong with a Fiesta, or an Escort, or a Probe, or a Mondeo or even, though this is stretching it a bit, a Maverick.

But with the new Granada, it rather looks like the favourite uncle has gone a bit loopy. It's like going round for tea one day and finding him engrossed in a spanking magazine.

The new car will be launched at the Motorshow this autumn but if Ford has any sense at all, it will have had a face lift by then. Either that, or it will be the first new car ever to be supplied in a plain brown wrapper.

Why are Van Drivers Mad?

It was sad to see that Northern Foods is to sack a couple of thousand people and even worse to note that the whole future of doorstep milk deliveries now hangs in the balance.

There's something very British about a rosy-cheeked milkman whistling his way up your drive in the morning. He may have been up since four but he's always smiling, bringing good cheer to the elderly and dispensing bonhomie to lonely housewives in their negligees.

However, while it may be sad to see an end to this very British tradition, I shall be rejoicing. And so will every other commuter.

Because milkmen adopt an entirely different persona as soon as they are behind the wheel of their floats.

In recent months, this column has produced a stream of bile for motorists of one type or another but I'm the first to admit that, broadly speaking, most people are pretty good drivers . . . so long as they are in an ordinary, anonymous saloon.

In his Sierra, a milkman is polite and charming but in his float, he begins to cackle the cackle of someone who is terminally deranged.

As the round wears on and the punch from his battery pack begins to fade, the top speed of his float falls to a crawl. By 8.30, with the morning rush hour in full flood, only the most sophisticated global postioning satellite can tell he's moving at all. On any sort of incline he isn't.

But he doesn't care. And if he has a delivery to make at number 23, he will pull up directly outside number 23, and never mind that by doing so, he completely blocks the road.

Impeded drivers blow their horns and swear but Milkie doesn't seem to notice. He's now in full whistle mode so there's no way the people at number 23 can guess their milk has been brought to them by one of Lucifer's disciples.

And milkmen are not the worst offenders. That accolade goes to the Dustbinerie, a sinister bunch of men who, when back at base, slaughter goats and drink their blood.

What I want to know is this – why do our dustbins have to be emptied first thing in the morning when half the population is asleep and the other half is trying to get to work?

Why can't they come and collect my rubbish in the middle of the day when their banging and crashing is not even slightly bothersome? And at midday, they can park their truck in the middle of the road for an hour, and no one will mind.

Then there's van drivers. What is it that makes all of these people believe their vehicle is three inches narrower than it really is? Or do they get a £5 bonus for every wing mirror they can break?

There is no sight quite so terrifying as being on a narrow street with cars parked on either side and a van with three men in it coming the other way.

You know he won't slow down, which is bad enough, and you know that in a few seconds you won't have a driver's side door mirror, which is expensive, but worst of all, the van will be doing at least a hundred miles an hour. More, if it's an Astramax.

It's hard to say which company breeds the biggest maniacs. *Evening Standard* delivery drivers are pretty suicidal but the title of biggest kamikaze murderers goes to those who pilot Royal Mail Sherpas.

I've never seen an advertisement for post-office van drivers but I suspect that they insist on some Grand Prix experience. Either that or they trawl the schizophrenic wards of psychiatric hospitals.

You see, like milkmen, and dustbinmen and, for that matter, plumbers and carpenters and other people with Take That haircuts and white socks, postmen are ordinary people when they're not at work. They live amongst us, drive standard cars carefully and are courteous and charming.

It's when they climb into a van that things begin to go awry. And this is worrying when you start to think a little bit about school minibuses.

As vans can obviously affect anyone who climbs inside, why should teachers be any different?

Citroen has recognised this and has launched a safety initiative with RoSPA whereby teachers are taken on a one-day advanced driving course. They'll be taught how to use safety equipment, how to check vehicle roadworthiness and how to drive defensively.

On top of all this, the new fifteen-seater Citroen minibus designed for use on school runs is supplied with full three-point belts for every passenger and proper, individual, high back seats.

Obviously, it will still be driven in a fashion that will lead passers-by to suspect the driver's trousers are on fire but now, when it crashes and the teacher climbs out of the wreckage – and becomes a normal human being again – he will find that the children are well. And even if they're not, that he is capable of tending to their injuries.

A Christmas Tale

Yet again, the Christmas lights were up round these parts back at the end of August. And Santa was to be found collecting catkins for the harvest festival.

And once again, with the actual date almost upon us, church leaders up and down the land are trying to remind an audience that won't listen that Christmas is more than getting hog-whimperingly drunk. It's more even than having to think of something appropriate to say about your new socks.

And it is certainly more than sitting in front of *The Great Escape*, after lunch, wondering why your tummy button, which for 30 years has been an 'inny', is now an 'outy'.

For those who think Christmas is all of these things, I should remind you that in fact it's a religious festival which takes its name from the birth of someone called Jesus Christ who went on to do many good deeds: bringing people back from the dead, walking on water, turning water into wine; that sort of thing.

While mulling this over the other day, I found myself wondering how things might have been if there had been cars kicking around back in the year dot. What would the key players have driven?

Well Joseph, of course, was a carpenter, and so it's a fairly safe bet that he'd have had a Vauxhall Astramax van.

The Bishop of Durham would have us believe he was a bit gullible, which is why, I daresay, his van would have been propelled by a diesel engine. But that's OK because the Astramax is the only vehicle made where your choice of engine has no effect at all on performance.

Whether you have petrol, diesel or fuel made out of donkey droppings, the Astramax is faster than anything on the road. No matter what car I happen to be driving, I have learned that it's best to pull over and let the guys in the Vauxhall van go by. I have seen these vehicles on the M1 doing 170 mph, which would make Joseph and Son very much the people to call on if your TV cabinet broke just before *The Great Escape*.

The question is: would he have been using the van when Mary was obviously close to the big moment? Would he have had a car as well? I think he probably would. And I think it may have been a Nissan Bluebird.

I don't see Joseph as a very successful carpenter and have him clocked as the sort of bloke who, to make ends meet, might do a bit of mini-cabbing on the side. That's why he'd have gone for the Bluebird which may well have been one of the nastiest cars in the world but which, when all was said and done, was reliable.

Plus, I don't see Joseph as the sort of man who would be all that bothered by a need for a flash set of wheels. If he was prepared to rest up for the night in a stable, we're not talking about someone with a Golf GTi, are we?

The shepherds, on the other hand, were almost certainly members of the local rally club. I know this because here we have a group of guys on a hillside, seeing angels in the night sky.

That makes them drunk, and that makes them young farmers and all young farmers are in a rally club of one sort or another.

At home, all these boogaloo dudes would have Escort RS2000s and XR2s but as they were out and about, I figure they'd have been on quad bikes. This would also explain how they managed to reach the stable without being stopped and breathalysed by the police.

The police, of course, in those days were Romans so they would have had Fiat Puntos, with police written in Latin on the doors.

There is, as far as I know, no record of any police involvement at all during the nativity, but there were some wise men from the East. And the East, as we all know, means Arab land.

Now these, we must presume, were rich people because they

brought gold, and frankincense and myrrh – which I bet was bloody expensive. You can't get it at all these days. Even in Boots.

So, if they were Arabs and rich, we can assume there were some pretty tasty wheels on the streets of Bethlehem that night.

I wonder what the innkeeper thought when he noticed that the people who he'd just despatched to the stable block had friends turning up in a Lamborghini Diablo, a Mercedes 600SEC and a Ferrari Testarossa.

Serves the vindictive little twerp right. If only he hadn't been so snobby – as all people with Granada Ghias are – he would have found Joseph and Mary a room, then all their rich, and drunk, mates would have filled his tills in his bar.

I mean, if someone follows a star for thousands of miles, thinking it's talking to him, you can bet he's going to be in the mood for a party when it turns out he was right.

And there's nothing the Arabs like more than a good party. Except their cars, which is why I see them in the Ferrari, the Lambo and the S Class, all finished I suspect in white, with white leather, white carpets and white trimmings, except perhaps for the centre of the steering wheel which I see as gold. Don't know why. Just do.

So that then completes the scene at the birth itself. But what about various other biblical figures? Well, with the same certainty that Galileo would have had a car with a sunroof, I just know that Moses had an amphi-car.

Herod would almost certainly have had a Porsche with a car phone. I can see him now, in a stripy shirt barking half-formed thoughts and orders into his Motorola. 'I want everyone under the age of two killed.' Only a Porsche driver could come up with that one.

Caesar would have had a Lancia Thema, bullet-proofed I suppose. Well spear-proofed anyway – they didn't have guns back then, did they?

And what of the disciples? Well, call me old Mr Cynical

Trousers but I've always had Peter clocked as a bit of a drip. He was always doing the moaning about there not being enough fishes, and how it was dangerous to try to walk on water. And let's not forget about his behaviour, three times, before the cock crowed. No, he was a wetty and I can see him now, in a pair of pressed trousers and an apple-green, bri-nylon shirt, behind the wheel of a Mini.

Darren was altogether more gutsy, and without any doubt at all had an Escort Cosworth. Thomas, I feel equally confident, had a Volvo of some type. We know he couldn't make up his mind about things, and the sort of guy who dithers about at road junctions almost always has something large and Swedish.

And Judas? Well Judas is the easiest of the lot. Judas had a BMW. Fact.

Greenslade – Music and Cars

It is a commonly held belief that the average speed of traffic in London is 9 miles per hour.

That makes for some great stories in the newspapers because 9 mph means we are now moving around more slowly than the Victorians. 'Why not walk?' scream those in open-toed sandals.

Well, I can give you one very good reason. The average speed of traffic in London is not 9 mph. It is, according to my on-board trip computer, nearly 18 mph and I just can't walk that fast.

Yesterday, however, I rather wished it was 9 mph because then I would not have arrived in the West End twenty minutes before my appointment. I would not have been able to browse through the racks in Tower Records. And then I would not have wasted twenty quid.

But because I averaged 18 mph, I did have time to do some browsing and now I have an album, recorded in 1973, by a band called Greenslade.

It has a cover by Roger Dean, which should have been a warning, but it wasn't enough. I recalled seeing Greenslade live and worse than that, I remembered enjoying the performance.

So, when the subsequent meeting ended, I slipped the CD into my autochanger and sat back to let Dave Greenslade's melodic synthesiser fill the leather and wood cockpit of the Jag.

At first I thought something had gone terribly wrong with the stereo, but this proved not to be the case. In fact, something had gone terribly wrong with my memory. Greenslade's first album may have been wild and different in 1973, but in the intervening 22 years we've had the Pistols and the Police and Madonna, so that now it sounds somewhere between awful and odd.

The message, then, to all you ex-public-schoolboys out there is clear. Do not, when you have time to kill, wander into a record shop and fill your basket with albums that you used to enjoy, late at night, in study eight. Snow Goose sounds daft. Yessongs is idiotic. Focus are now a bunch of hasbeens and Golden Earring only had one hit for a reason. But Greenslade are the worst of the lot.

And it's the same story with cars. Just because you remember your Alfasud so fondly, do not imagine that you'll get the same thrill from it now, after you've been exposed to the delights of a Golf GTi and a BMW 325.

Your first car may well have been an MG but drive one today and you won't rekindle a lost youth. You'll simply get a headache and wet. And then it will break down.

However, there are some albums which, through punk, disco, grunge, rap, Wet Wet Wet, techno and heavy metal, continue to sound fresh and pertinent. I'm listening to *Crime of the Century* right now, and *Dark Side of the Moon* is another case in point. And that's without dipping into early Stones, Who and Led Zep. Or even James Brown and Beethoven for that matter.

Some bands and individuals, for whatever reason, just don't date.

So what about cars? Are there any which, if you could buy them new today, would not feel disgraced by modern-day techno marvels?

Assuming that we could do the automotive equivalent of digital remastering, by which I mean building them properly and incorporating air conditioning and electric windows, is there a single car out there which wouldn't feel as dead as something dead?

I'm struggling here. I recently drove an Aston Martin DB5 and can only liken it to Barclay James Harvest's live double album from 1974.

My first car was a Fort Cortina 1600E which, though I haven't driven one for seventeen years, I'm sure would feel like Rick Wakeman on wheels.

However, I have ended up with a list of four cars which have managed to bulldoze their way through fashion and the sea of technological change. Sure, they've been digitally remastered along the way and are now bought on DAT rather than scratched vinyl, but they've made it.

All are still in production even though each has remained basically the same. And they are the Porsche 911, the Mini, the Range Rover and the Jaguar XJS.

They are the motorised supergroups. Here we have Jagger and Richards in metal. By keeping fit, staying alive and adapting, they feel every bit as good today as they did when Labour were in power.

And that makes me wonder some more: what if they'd persevered with, say, the Volkswagen K70? What if it was now available with a catalytic converter and fuel injection? What if they'd changed the dashboard a little bit every now and again and added height-adjustable seatbelts? If they'd done all this, would the K70 feel good today?

No, I don't think so. Here we have Dave Greenslade with an engine; a car that would only be available on import to sad, sad old hippies who liken modern cars to modern music and dismiss both groups as characterless rubbish.

It was while I was sitting watching the Doobie Brothers at Wembley last week that the answer came. Old cars are fine . . . so long as they were made yesterday.

20 Things You Always Wanted to Know about Jeremy Clarkson

What is your everyday car?
Ford Escort
How many miles a year do you drive?
20–30,000
What's the most fun you've ever had in a car?
Doing the Rubicon Trail in a Jeep Wrangler
Do you prefer front/rear/four-wheel drive and why?
Couldn't care less – handling is unimportant
What one car, cost no object, would you most like to drive every day for the next 12 months?
Aston Martin Vantage
What car should never have got past the prototype stage?
Nearly all cars in current production
You've got a CD stacker in the boot of your car and a drive across Europe planned – which six CDs do you take?
Bob Seger – *Night Moves*
Bob Seger – *Nine Tonight*
Bob Seger – *Live Bullet*
Bob Seger – *Fire Inside*
Bob Seger – *Smokin' OPs*
Doobie Brothers – *Captain and Me*
If someone borrowed your car, which tape – or radio station – would they find playing?
Radio Four, I suppose, 'cos my wife likes it
Who is your hero?
Auberon Waugh
If you were a car, what car would you be?
1979 Ford Granada Ghia

What is your favourite quote, or line from a song?
Then ten years have got behind you,
No one told you when to run,
You missed the starting gun
(Pink Floyd, 'Dark Side of the Moon')
What did you want to be when you grew up?
King
What was the worst job you ever had?
Road-testing the Toyota Corolla
What is the bravest thing you have ever done?
I never do brave things
What is your greatest achievement?
Going five years through public school and never once playing cricket
Who would you most like to see gunged?
Lynn Faulds-Wood
What was/is your favourite 'children's' TV programme?
Paddington Bear
Who or what always makes you laugh?
Auberon Waugh
You're in a rapidly descending hot-air balloon with Jeremy Beadle, Jeremy Clarkson and Jeremy Paxman and you have to throw one out to stop it crashing – who goes first?
This is not fair